New Testament Commentary

Galatians
to
Philemon

F B Hole

Scripture Truth Publications

First published as articles in the magazine "Edification" 1928-29-33.

Hardback edition first published in February 1981 as "Paul's Epistles (Volume Two)" by Central Bible Hammond Trust Limited, Wooler.

Reprinted in April 1995 as "Paul's Epistles (Volume 2): Galatians - Philemon" with ISBN-10: 0-901860-13-1 by Scripture Truth Publications, Wooler.

Transferred to Digital Printing 2007

ISBN: 978-0-901860-44-6 (paperback)

ISBN: 978-0-901860-48-4 (hardback)

Published by Scripture Truth Publications
Coopies Way, Coopies Lane,
Morpeth, Northumberland, NE61 6JN

Scripture Truth is an imprint of Central Bible Hammond Trust, a charitable trust

Printed and bound by Lightning Source

CONTENTS

GALATIANS

INTRODUCTION

IN HIS EPISTLE to the Galatians the Apostle Paul is not so much concerned with expounding his Gospel as with defending it. The mischief-makers were evidently certain Jews who professed conversion to Christianity, and yet were more zealous of the law than they were of Christ; men of the same stamp as those we have mentioned in Acts xv. 1 and 5.

We find allusions to their mischievous activities in some of the other epistles. They had gained a certain measure of success amongst the Corinthians, for instance. There are faint allusions to them in the first epistle, but in the second, chapter xi., the Apostle denounces them in no uncertain terms. They were Jews right enough, as verse 22, of that chapter shows, but he does not admit their being truly Christian, as we may see by reading verses 13 and 14. The Colossian Christians were warned against their beguilings in the epistle addressed to them, (ii. 14-23), and even the faithful Philippians had a word thrown in about them in, "Beware of evil workers, beware of the concision" (iii. 2).

Evidently however their greatest success was with the Galatians, who were a people of fickle temperament. The "churches of Galatia" had very largely embraced the ideas they pressed, hardly realizing how they cut at the root of that Gospel which they had first heard from the lips of Paul himself. This the Apostle shows them in the epistle. Consequently he stresses just those features of the Gospel which exposed the falsity of these newer ideas. He shows them moreover what a fall from grace, as regards their own thoughts and spiritual state, it had involved them in. The seriousness of this fall accounts for the restraint and even severity of language which characterizes this epistle.

CHAPTER 1

IN OPENING HIS letter Paul not only announced his apostleship but emphasized the fact that he held this place directly from God. It had reached him from no man, not even the twelve who were chosen before him. Men were not the source of it, nor had he received it by means of them as channels. God was the source of it, and it had reached him by Jesus Christ. Hence he had a fulness of authority not possessed by the Judaising teachers who were troubling them, for they at best could only pretend to be the emissaries of brethren in Jerusalem. Moreover, as he points out, all the brethren in his company at the moment of his writing associated themselves with what he said in the epistle. There was ample weight behind his utterances!

He writes, you notice, not to one assembly of Christians only, but to the assemblies of the province of Galatia, who all had evidently been affected in the same way. Now the Gospel had reached them through Paul's

GALATIANS

labours, as is intimated in chapter iv. verses 11-15. They had given him a wonderful reception and had seemed to be most devoted to him. Miracles were wrought amongst them (iii. 5), and it was a most enthusiastic time. There is no record of any opposition. Nobody appears to have hurled stones at Paul's head! Yet in the Acts all this is ignored. We are only told that they went "through . . . the region of Galatia" (xvi. 6), preaching the Gospel, and that later they "went over all the country of Galatia . . . strengthening all the disciples" (xviii. 23).

This is significant! Evidently it was one of those times when there was too much surface work—too much of the stony ground element. We must not disparage the Apostle's work because of this, for the Lord assumed that this shallow work would be found even when He Himself was the sower. It all looked so wonderful and yet the Holy Spirit knew from the outset what lay beneath the surface, and when Luke was inspired to write his second treatise this apparently wonderful time in Galatia is dismissed with the barest mention.

In the opening salutations (verses 3-5) the Lord Jesus is presented in a very significant way. He truly gave Himself for our sins, but the purpose in view was our being delivered from "this present evil world." As we proceed with the epistle we shall see how the law, the flesh and the world go together; inasmuch as the law was given to put a curb on the flesh and thus to make the world what it should be. In effect it did neither, though it revealed both in their true character. We shall find on the other hand, that the grace of the Gospel brings in faith and the Spirit, and delivers from the world, which is treated as under condemnation.

The "world" here has the sense of "age" or "course of this world." It is the *world system* rather than the people in the world. It is a *very present* system today, and it is a *judged and condemned* system; hence it is the will of God that we be delivered from it, and to this end the Lord Jesus died for us.

With verse 6, Paul plunges straight into the main burden of his letter. The Gospel which he had preached to them had called them into the grace of Christ, and now they had turned aside to a different message which was no true gospel at all. He was filled with wonder at their folly, indeed as we read these solemn words we can feel the hot indignation which lay behind them. They were following "a *different* gospel, which is not *another*,"—as it should read. They may have imagined that they were receiving a new and improved version of the old message. They were not. It was a radically different message, and a false one at that.

In verse 8, Paul contemplates himself perverting God's Gospel in this way, or even an angel from heaven doing so; not a fallen angel, but an angel hitherto unfallen and coming from the presence of God. Upon either or both he solemnly pronounces the curse of God. Having done so it seems as though he anticipates that some will regard him as extreme in

2

his denunciation and wish to remonstrate with him. He anticipates this by repeating the curse, only this time making its force even plainer. As a matter of fact neither he nor an angel from heaven would so pervert the Gospel, but certain men had been doing so amongst the Galatians, so now he says, "*If any man* . . ."

If any are inclined to think that this was just a petulant outburst against a set of rival preachers, let them consider what was involved in the matter, and they will soon see that the curse was the curse of God, with all the weight of His might behind it.

What then was involved? Let us answer by asking a question by way of illustration. Do you think that a person who surreptitiously tips a dose of poison into somebody's teapot is worthy of condemnation? You most certainly do. What then do you think he is worthy of, who should in the dead of night shoot a whole cartload of virulent poison into the water-works supplying a town? You have no language in which to express your abhorrence of such an awful deed. But here were men who were perverting the message which is the only river of salvation and spiritual life for a fallen world. In what language can the Spirit of God express His abhorrence of a deed like that? Only in pronouncing upon them the solemn curse of God.

You will notice that these men did not contradict the Gospel, but *perverted* it. For one who utterly denies the Gospel you will find many who pervert it. They dexterously give it just that subtle twist which completely falsifies its true character. Let us be on our guard against them.

The real motive which underlay the teachings of these men was the desire of pleasing man. This is exposed for us in verse 10. Later on in the epistle we shall see that they desired to glory in the flesh, and to capture the Galatians as followers of themselves. They wished to please men in order that, being pleased, the men might run after them and become their followers. Thus at the back of everything lay the desire for self-exaltation.

In contrast to this the Apostle Paul was the true servant of Christ. It was Christ he aimed at pleasing and not men. Men might censure or they might praise, it was no great matter to him. This was specially true if he thought of men at large, yet it was true even when it was a question of the judgment of his fellow-apostles, as we see in the next chapter. The Gospel that he preached he had received directly from the Lord Himself, and this lifted him far above all human opinion.

As to this matter no preacher of today can possibly be in Paul's position. It would therefore ill become us to adopt his tone of authority. We have all been taught the Gospel through men. The Word of God has not come out from us, but unto us only (see 1 Cor. xiv. 36): and hence we do well if we listen with deference to what our brethren have to say, should they feel it right to take us to task as to any matter. Even so the final court of appeal is of course the Word of God.

3

Still we do well when we do not set before us as an object the pleasing of men. The very Gospel which we have believed, and which perhaps we preach, should preserve us from that; inasmuch as it is "not after man," as stated in verse 11. If the Gospel has reached us in a defective or mutilated form, then doubtless we may not have realized this, but it was the case with the Gospel that Paul preached. Man was not the source of it, nor had he received it through man, as a channel of communication. He received it by direct revelation from the Lord Jesus. It came to him first-hand from God, as did his apostleship, as we saw in considering verse 1. Consequently it had upon it the stamp of God, and not the stamp of man.

The characteristic feature of the Gospel therefore is *"after God"* and *"not after man."* What is after man honours man, flatters man, glorifies man. The Gospel tells man the humbling truth about himself, but glorifies God and accomplishes His ends.

This fact alone provides us with a very pertinent test as whether what we hear as gospel is really Gospel. "I like hearing Mr. So-and-so," is the cry, "He speaks so reasonably. There is such common sense. He has such faith in humanity, and makes you feel so much more hopeful and content in this rather discontented world." Quite so! The fact is it is all so thoroughly *after man.* Consequently it is all so pleasing to the natural man. Yet it is false. It is not the Gospel of God.

At first sight it might appear as though what Paul says, in the last verse of 1 Corinthians x, is a contradiction of this. If however the whole of the chapter be read, and the previous chapter also, it will be seen that his point there is that the Christians should have the greatest possible consideration and care for their weaker brethren, and indeed for all men. Hence they should avoid all occasions of offence and seek the profit of all. Here, on the other hand, it is a question of the truth of the Gospel. The tendency to alter it, or whittle it down in order to please men, must be resisted at all costs. There cannot be a moment's compromise here.

From verse 13 to the end of the chapter the Apostle recounts a little of his history; evidently in order to support what he had just stated in verse 12.

First he recalls what marked him while unconverted. In his life he united great zeal for Jewish tradition, and a progress in Judaism which outstripped his contemporaries, with great persecution of the church of God. Twice in verses 13 and 14 he speaks of "the Jews' religion." This is significant, for the Galatians had fallen into the snare of trying to bring the very essence of that religion into the Gospel. He would have them realize—and us also—that far from being supplementary to the Gospel it is antagonistic to it. He had been brought clean out of it by his conversion.

Three steps in Paul's history are plainly marked for us. First he was set apart by God even before his birth. Then he was called by the grace of the Gospel. Thirdly God revealed His Son in him that HE might be the theme of his testimony among the nations. Though Paul was born of the purest Hebrew stock he needed to be set apart as much as if he had been a heathen, and was set apart from his Judaism—a point of much moment to the Galatians. Moreover he was set apart for God's service, the character of which was determined for him by the nature of the revelation which reached him.

It was the revelation of the Son of God, and not merely of Israel's Messiah. The Lord Jesus was both of course, but it was in the former character that He appeared to Paul and, as we know from other Scriptures, He appeared to him thus from glory. From that great moment on the road to Damascus Paul knew that the Jesus of Nazareth, whom he had despised, was the Son of God. And this was revealed not only *to* him but *in* him.

The use of the preposition, "in" would indicate that the revelation was made thoroughly effective in Paul. If you went to an observatory you might be permitted to view the moon through a large telescope. You would perceive the wonders of its surface, its mountains, its craters. Yet though revealed to your eye they would not be in your eye, for the moment you remove your eye from the telescope everything vanishes. But let the astronomer attach a camera to the eyepiece of the telescope and expose therein a sensitized plate for the necessary time. Now under suitable chemical treatment something appears in the plate. That which was only revealed *to* your eye has now been revealed *in* the plate, and permanently so. It was like this with Paul. The Son of God who was in glory had produced a permanent impression in Paul, and so he was able to preach Him as One whom he *knew* and not merely knew *about*.

It was this that characterized the Apostle's unique ministry and service, and from the outset lifted him above reliance upon other men, even the best of them. Consequently he did not need to make his way to Jerusalem immediately after his conversion. Three years elapsed before he saw any of those who had been apostles before him, and then he only saw Peter and James for a short period.

There is no mention of this visit to Arabia in Acts ix. and hence one can only surmise where it comes in. Very possibly it comes in between verses 22 and 23 of that chapter, and the episode of his escape from Damascus, by being let down over the wall in a basket, occurred when he had returned there from Arabia. If so, it was just after that happening that his visit to Peter took place. At all events the Apostle is very emphatic as to the correctness of that which he writes to the Galatians, and that the churches of Judæa only knew of his conversion by report; while glorifying God for the grace and power, which had transformed the raging persecutor, under whom they had suffered, into a servant of Christ.

And all these historical details, be it remembered, are given in order to impress us with the fact that the Gospel of which he was the herald, had reached him direct from the Lord Himself.

GALATIANS

CHAPTER 2

OUR CHAPTER FALLS quite simply into two parts. First, verses 1 to 10, in which the Apostle recounts what happened on the occasion of his second visit to Jerusalem after his conversion. Second, verses 11 to 21, in which he tells of an incident that happened at Antioch not long after his second visit to Jerusalem, and which had a very definite bearing upon the point at issue with the Galatians.

The first visit was about three years after his conversion (i. 18), so the second, being fourteen years later, was about seventeen years after that time, and is evidently the occasion as to which we have much information in Acts xv. That passage therefore, may profitably be read before proceeding further. From a careful reading several interesting details appear.

Acts xv. begins with mentioning "certain *men* who came down from Judæa," who taught circumcision as essential to salvation. They are not termed "brethren," we notice. In our chapter Paul unhesitatingly labels them "false brethren unawares brought in." Thus early do we find unconverted men getting amongst the saints of God, in spite of apostolic vigilance and care! It is sad when they are brought in *unawares* in spite of care. Sadder still when such principles are professed and practised as leave the door *open for them to enter.*

In Acts we read that "they determined" that a visit to Jerusalem was needful. But here Paul gives us a view behind the scenes of activity and travel, and shows us that it was "by revelation" that he went up. The temptation might have been strong upon him to meet these false brethren and vanquish them at Antioch, but it was revealed to him by the Lord that he should stop disputation and carry the discussion up to Jerusalem, where the views his opponents pressed were most strongly held. It was a bold move; but it was one which in the wisdom of God preserved unity in the church. As a result of his obedience to the revelation the question was settled against the contentions of these false brethren in the very place where most of their sympathizers were. To have so settled it amongst the Gentiles at Antioch might easily have provoked a rupture.

Further, in Acts xv. it is just stated that "certain other of them" went up with Paul and Barnabas to Jerusalem. Our chapter reveals that amongst these "certain other" was Titus, a Greek. This of course raised the point at issue in its acutest form. The apostle gave no quarter to his opponents. He did not submit to them for an hour, and in result Titus was not compelled to be circumcised.

This being so, Paul's action in regard to Timothy, related in Acts xvi. 1-3, is the more remarkable. It is an illustration of how that which has to be strenuously resisted under certain circumstances may be conceded under other circumstances. In the case of Titus circumcision was demanded in order to establish a principle which cut at the very root of the Gospel.

6

In the case of Timothy no such principle was at stake, the whole question having been authoritatively settled, and Paul did it that Timothy might have liberty of service amongst Jews as well as Gentiles. By birth Timothy was half a Jew and the Apostle made him completely a Jew, as it were, that he might "gain the Jews" (1 Cor. ix. 20). To Paul himself and to the Corinthians, and so to us, both circumcision and uncircumcision are "nothing" (1 Cor. vii. 19).

It is possible that you might observe some servant of Christ acting after this fashion today. Pause a moment before you roundly accuse him of gross inconsistency. It may after all be that he is acting with divinely-given discernment in cases where you have as yet perceived no difference. The apostle speaks of "Our liberty which we have in Christ Jesus." It was liberty to refuse circumcision where legal bondage was involved, and yet a year or so later to practise it when nothing of principle was involved.

Then again during this visit to Jerusalem Paul took opportunity to convey formally to the other apostles the Gospel which he had preached among the Gentiles. Though he had received it directly from the Lord he was not above conceiving that possibly error might have crept into his understanding of the revelation. This is indicated in the latter part of verse 2. In effect however it was far otherwise. The most instructed amongst the apostles and elders at Jerusalem had nothing to add to Paul's gospel when they conferred upon the point. The rather they recognized that Paul was clearly called of God to carry the Gospel into the Gentile world, while Peter had a similar commission in regard to the Jew. Hence the three apostolic leaders, perceiving the grace given to Paul, expressed the fullest fellowship and sympathy with him in his work.

This fact had a very definite bearing on the point at issue with the Galatians. If the men who had been at work in Galatia attacked Paul as being an unauthorized upstart, he was able to counter this by showing that he had received his message from the Lord by first-hand revelation. This established his authority. If on the other hand they attacked him as a man proceeding thus on his own authority and so being in opposition to those who were apostles before him, he countered this lie by the fact that James, Peter and John had shown fullest confidence in him and fellowship with him after thorough conference had taken place.

It remained for him to show that there had been a time when even Peter had yielded somewhat to the influence of men similar to those now opposing Paul, and to relate how he had opposed him then, and the grounds on which he had done so.

There is no mention in the Acts of this visit of Peter to Antioch, but it evidently happened after the decision of the council in Jerusalem as narrated in Acts xv. In that council Peter had argued in favour of the acceptance of Gentile converts without the law of Moses being imposed upon them. He had then spoken of the law as "a yoke . . . which neither our fathers nor we were able to bear." At Antioch however when certain came down from James holding strict views as to the value of circumcision he no longer would eat with the Gentile believers but withdrew himself. His example had great weight and others followed it—even Barnabas who had formerly stood with Paul, as recorded in Acts xv. 2, and 12.

To many doubtless such action would have seemed a very small matter— just a little prejudice to be condoned, a fad to be smiled at. To Paul it was far otherwise. He perceived that under this apparently small question of how Peter took his food, grave principles were at stake, and that Peter's action was not upright "according to the truth of the Gospel."

Oh, that we may all seize the point so strongly enforced here! Departure from the truth, even of the gravest kind, is generally presented to us under cover of seemingly trifling and innocent circumstances. Most of us would have been tempted to exclaim, "Oh, Paul, what an exacting man you are! How difficult to please! Why make such a fuss over a small detail? If Peter wants now to eat only with Jews, why not let him? Why disturb our peace at Antioch and make things unhappy?" We are so often ignorant of Satan's devices. He sees to it that we shall be diverted from truth over something of an apparently harmless nature. The railway engine runs from the main line into a siding *over very fine points*.

Incidentally let us at this point take note that the idea that church in the apostolic age was the abode of peace and free of all contention has no support from Scripture. From the outset the truth had to be won and maintained through conflict—a great deal of it *internal*, and not merely with the world without. We have no right to expect absence of conflict and trouble today. Occasions are sure to arise when peace can only be purchased by compromise, and he who sees most, and hence is constrained to raise his voice in protest, must be prepared to be accused of uncharitableness. Failing such protest peace is maintained, but it is the peace of stagnation and spiritual death. The quietest spot in the throbbing heart of London is the city mortuary! So beware!

If we find ourselves in a position where we feel morally bound to raise our voices, let us pray earnestly that we may be able to do it in a way similar to Paul. "When I saw . . . *I said unto Peter* . . ." Our tendency always is to launch our complaints into the ear of someone other than the culprit himself. Notice, for instance, in Mark ii., that when the Pharisees object to the action of Jesus they complain to His disciples (ver. 16), and when to the action of His disciples, they complain to the Lord (vers. 23, 24). We shall do well to make it a rule, when remonstrance is needed, to make our remonstrance directly to the person concerned, rather than behind his back.

Paul however did this *"before them all."* The reason for this is that Peter's defection had already affected many others and so become a public matter. It would be a mistake in a multitude of cases to make *public* remonstrance. Many a defection or difficulty has not become public, and if met faithfully and graciously in a private way with the person concerned it may never become public at all, and thus much trouble and possible scandal be avoided. Public defection however must be met publicly.

Paul began his protest by asking Peter a question based upon his earlier mode of life, before the sudden alteration. Peter had abandoned the strict Jewish customs in favour of the freer life of the Gentiles, as he himself had stated in Acts x. 28. How then could he now consistently retreat from this position in a way that was tantamount to saying that after all Gentiles should live after the customs of the Jews? This question we have recorded in verse 14.

In verses 15 and 16 we have the apostle's assertion which succeeded his question. In this assertion Paul could link Peter with himself and Peter could not deny it. "WE," he says. "We, who are Jews by nature" have recognized that justification is not reached by "the works of the law, but by the faith of Jesus Christ," and hence have turned from law to Christ and been justified by Him. Thank God, that was so!

Now comes a second question. If it were true, as Peter's action seemed to suggest, that even when standing in all the virtue of Christ's work we still need something, in the way of law-keeping or the observance of Jewish customs, to complete our justification, is not Christ then discredited? He puts the proposition with extreme vigour of language,—is He not even "the Minister of sin" instead of the Minister of justification? To ask such a question is to answer it. It is impossible! Hence he adds, "Away with the thought," or "God forbid."

This was followed by a second assertion in verse 18, a statement which must have fallen as a sledge-hammer on Peter's conscience. Peter's action had inferred that Christ might be the Minister of sin; but it also was without a doubt of the nature of building up again the wall of partition, between Jew and Gentile who are in Christ, that the Gospel had thrown down, and which Peter himself had destroyed by his former action in the house of Cornelius. Whichever was right, Peter was wrong somewhere. If he was right now, he was wrong formerly. If right formerly, he was wrong now. He stood convicted as a transgressor.

As a matter of fact he was wrong now. Formerly he had acted as instructed of God in a vision. Now he was acting impulsively under the influence of the fear of man.

In these few words from the lips of Paul the Spirit of God had revealed the true inwardness of Peter's action, however innocent it may have appeared to most. Only two questions and two statements, but how effective they were! They quite destroyed Peter's *false* position.

Not content with this however the Spirit of God led Paul to forthwith proclaim the *true* position. He had perceived at the outset that Peter and his followers "walked not uprightly according to the truth of the Gospel," so now he very plainly, yet in fewest possible words, states *the truth of the Gospel.* He states it moreover not as a matter of doctrine but as a matter of experience—his own experience. He does not now say "we," but "I," which occurs no less than seven times in verses 19 and 20.

In the Acts we have striking examples of *the preaching of the Gospel* through the lips of Paul. In Romans i.-viii. we have the *exposition of the Gospel* from his pen. In Galatians i. we have *the defence of the Gospel*— by setting forth its characteristic features, which hall-mark it, as it were. Now we are to consider *the truth of the Gospel.*

In the closing verses of this second chapter, Paul speaks for himself alone. Previously (verses 15 to 17) he had said, "we," since he spoke of truth generally acknowledged by Christians, Peter included. But now he comes to truth which Peter's action had challenged, and so he could not assume that Peter acknowledged it. However *truth* it was, and Paul stand-ing in the enjoyment and power of it could set it forth in this personal and experimental way.

At that moment Peter had the law before his soul: he was living to the law. "For myself," says Paul, in effect, "I have God, and not law before my soul, and am living to Him." How much greater is God, who gave the law—God, now revealed in Christ—than the law He gave. But what set Paul free from the law, under which once he had been, as well as Peter? Death had set him free. He had died to the law, and that by the law's own act! This is stated in verse 19.

Nevertheless, here he was very much alive, and boldly confronting Peter! *How* then had he died to the law? And in what sense was it true that he had died *through* the law? Both these questions are answered in that great statement, "I am crucified with Christ."

In those words we have Paul seizing upon the truth of the Gospel, and giving it an intensely personal application to himself. The Lord Jesus, in His death, not only was the believer's Substitute, bearing his sins, but also thoroughly identified Himself with us in our sinful state, being made sin for us, though knowing no sin Himself. So really and truly did this take place that one of the things we are to know, as a matter of Christian doctrine, is that "our old man is crucified with Him" (Rom. vi. 6). The crucifixion of Christ is therefore the crucifixion of all that we were as fallen children of Adam. But here we have Paul's personal appropriation of this. As crucified with Christ he had died *to* the law.

Then again the crucifixion of Christ was not merely the act of evil men. Viewed from the divine standpoint, the very essence of it is seen to be that act of God whereby He was made sin for us, and wherein was borne for us the curse of the law (see, iii. 13). As dying under the curse of the law, Christ died *through* the law, and as crucified with Christ Paul was able to say that he had died to the law *through* the law, in order that he might live unto God.

The force of this great passage may perhaps become clearer to us if we consider the five prepositions used.

1. *Unto*, which indicates the *end in view*. To live unto God is to live with God as the End of one's existence.

2. *With*, indicates *identification*, or *association*. We are crucified with Christ by reason of that complete identification which He effected in His death for us. Consequently His death was our death. We died with Him.

3. *In*, which here signifies *character*. Though crucified we live. We are still living people on earth, yet we no longer live the old character of life. We live a life of a new order, a life, the character of which, summed up in one word, is CHRIST. Saul of Tarsus had been crucified with Christ. Yet the individual known as Saul of Tarsus was still living. Still living, yet in another character entirely. As you observed him you saw not the Saul-of-Tarsus character coming into expression, but Christ. In keeping with this he did not retain his old name, but soon after his conversion he became known as Paul, which means, "Little one." He must be little if Christ is to live in him.

4. *By*, which introduces us to the *Object* that controlled Paul's soul, and made this new character of life possible. Presently, when the life we now live in the flesh—that is, in our present mortal bodies—is over, we shall live by the *sight* of the Son of God. Meanwhile we live by the *faith* of Him. If faith is in activity with us He is made a living bright reality before our souls. The more He is thus before us objectively, that is, as

> ". . . the object bright and fair,
> To fill and satisfy the heart."

the more will He be seen in us subjectively.

The Lord Chancellor's "Great seal" is a remarkable *object*. If you wished to see it however, you would probably find it impossible to get access to it. Possibly they would say, "No, we cannot let you see the seal itself, but look at this large spot of wax affixed to this state document. Here you virtually see the seal, for it has been impressed into it." The wax has been *subject* to the pressure of the seal. You see the seal *subjectively* expressed, though you could not see it *objectively*. This may illustrate our point, and show how others may see Christ living in us, if as Object He is before our souls.

5. *For*, which here is the preposition of *substitution*. It introduces us to that which was the constraining power and motive of Paul's wonderful life. The love of the Son of God constrained him, and that love had expressed itself in His sacrificial and substitutionary death.

We may sum up the matter thus:—Paul's heart was filled with the love of the Son of God who had died for him. He not only understood his identification with Christ in His death, but he heartily accepted it, in all that it implied, and he found his satisfying Object in the Son of God in glory. Consequently the sentence of death lay upon all that he was by nature, and Christ lived in him and characterized his life, and thus God Himself, as revealed in Christ, had become the full End of his existence.

Thus it was with Paul, but is it thus with us? That our old man has been crucified is as true for us as for Paul. We have died with Christ even as he had, if indeed we are really and truly believers. But have we taken it up in our experience as Paul did, so that it is to us not only a matter of Christian doctrine (highly important as that is in its place) but also a matter of rich spiritual experience, which transforms and ennobles our lives? The plain truth is that most of us have only done so in a measure which is pitifully small. And the secret of this? The secret clearly is that we have been so little captivated by the sense of His great love. Our realization of the wonder of His sacrifice for us is so feeble. Our convictions as to the horror of our sinfulness were not very deep, and hence our conversions were comparatively of a shallow nature. If we track things back to their source, the explanation lies just here, we believe. Let us all sing with far more earnestness,

"Revive Thy work, O Lord!
Exalt Thy precious Name;
And may Thy love in every heart,
Be kindled to a flame!"

If in each of our hearts love is kindled to a flame, we shall make progress in the right direction.

The Apostle's closing words, in the last verse of our chapter, plainly implied that the position Peter had taken was of such a nature as to lead to the "frustration" or "setting aside" of the grace of God. It would imply that after all righteousness could come by the law, and lead to the supposition that Christ had died "in vain," or, "for nothing." What a calamitous conclusion!

Yet it was the *logical* conclusion. And, having reached it, the moment had arrived for a very pointed appeal to the Galatians. This appeal we have in the opening verses of chapter iii.

CHAPTER 3

THE APOSTLE CALLS them "foolish" or "senseless," for they had not themselves had the spiritual sense to see whither these false teachers had been leading them. They had been like men bewitched, and under a spell of evil, and they had been led to the brink of the awful conclusion that Christ had died for nothing—that His death had been in fact a huge mistake! On the edge of this precipice they were standing, and the Apostle's pungent reasoning had come as a flash of light amidst their darkness, revealing their danger!

What made their folly so pronounced was the fact that formerly there had been such a faithful preaching among them of Christ crucified. Paul himself had evangelized them, and as with the Corinthians so with the Galatians, the cross had been his great theme. It was as though Christ had been crucified before their very eyes.

Moreover, as a result of receiving the word of the cross, which Paul brought, they had received the Holy Spirit, as verse 2 implies. Well, in what way and on what principle had they received the Spirit? By the works of the law, or by the hearing of faith? There was but one answer to this question. For the Galatians to reply, "We received the Spirit by the works of the law," was an absolute impossibility, as Paul knew right well.

Hence he does not pause to answer his own question, but at once passes, in verse 3, to further questions based upon it. Having received the Spirit by the hearing of faith were they going to be made perfect by the flesh? Does God begin with us on one principle and then carry things to completion on another and opposing principle? Men are erratic enough. They change about in this fashion when their earlier plans miscarry. But is God erratic? Do His plans ever miscarry so that He needs to change? The Galatians were senseless, but were they SO senseless as to imagine that? And were they themselves prepared to change, and to throw away as worthless all they had previously held and done; so that their earlier sufferings for Christ had all to be treated as in vain, as null and void? What questions these were! As we read them are we not conscious of their crushing force?

But why did the Apostle speak of our being made perfect *by the flesh*? Firstly, because it is that which is particularly opposed to the Spirit; and secondly, because it is closely related to the law. It completes the quartette contained in verses 3 and 4. Faith and the Spirit are linked together. The Spirit is received as the result of the hearing of faith, and He is the power of that new life which we have in Christ. The law and the flesh are linked together. The law was given that the flesh might fulfil it, *if* it could do so. In result it could *not*. Nor could the law put an effectual curb on the propensities of the flesh; for the flesh "is not subject to the law of God, neither indeed can be" (Rom. viii. 7). Yet here were the Galatians inclined to turn from the all-powerful Spirit to the flesh, which though powerful for evil was wholly impotent for good. It was folly indeed!

In verse 5 the Apostle repeats his question of verse 2, only in another form. In verse 2 it concerned the Galatians. How did they receive the

Spirit? Here it concerns himself. In what way and on what principle did he labour when he came amongst them with the Gospel message? Miracles were wrought amongst them and when the Gospel was believed the Spirit of God was received. Was it all on the ground of works, or of faith? Once more he does not pause for a reply, knowing right well that only one answer could be given by the Galatians. Instead he at once appeals to the case of Abraham, that they might realize that before ever the law was instituted God had established faith as the way of blessing for man.

From the very outset faith was the way of man's blessing, as Hebrews xi. reveals so clearly. With Abraham, however, the fact came clearly to light even in Old Testament times. Genesis xv. 6 plainly declared it, and that verse is quoted here, as also in Romans iv. 3 and James ii. 23. Abraham was the father of the Jewish race, who had circumcision as their outward sign, but he was also, in a deeper and spiritual sense, "the father of all them that believe" (Rom. iv. 11).

The Judaising teachers had been trying to persuade the Galatians to adopt circumcision, that thereby they might put themselves into a kind of Jewish position, becoming children of Abraham in an outward way. It would have been a poor imitation thing, if compared only with the true-born Israelite. And all the while, if they were "of faith," that is, believers, they *were* children of Abraham, and that in the deepest possible sense, as verse 7 makes manifest.

Every believer is a child of Abraham in a spiritual sense; and not only so, but as verse 9 shows us, every believer enters into the blessing of Abraham. Verse 8 indicates what it is that is referred to as the blessing of Abraham. It was not merely his own personal blessing, but that in him all nations should be blessed. Not only was he to be accounted righteous before God and to stand in the blessings connected with righteousness, but myriads from all nations were to enjoy similar favour, which was to reach them in him.

But why in Abraham? How could this be? It will be worth while reading the passages in Genesis which refer to this matter. The promise of the blessing was first given when God's call first reached him. This is in chapter xii. 3. Then in xviii. 18 it is confirmed to him. Again, in xxii. 16-18 the promise is amplified, and we discover that the accomplishment is to be through "the Seed" who is Christ, as verse 16 of our chapter in Galatians tells us. Then further, the promise is confirmed to Isaac and Jacob respectively, in xxvi. 4, and xxviii. 14; and in both these cases "the Seed" is mentioned. Once introduced, the Seed is never omitted, for in truth everything in the way of fulfilment is dependent upon Him.

The blessing then was only in Abraham inasmuch as, according to the flesh, Christ sprang out of Abraham. The Jews boasted themselves in Abraham as though he were of all-importance in himself. The Galatians had been tempted to ally themselves with Abraham by adopting his covenant of circumcision. But the real virtue lay not in Abraham, but in Christ. And the very circumcision which would outwardly ally them with Abraham, would virtually cut them off from Christ (see, v. 2) in whom everything was found, not outwardly, but inwardly and vitally.

From the outset God intended to bless the heathen (or, the nations) through faith. It was no after-thought with Him. How gracious was His design! And how comforting it is to us to know it! He called Abraham out from the nations that had fallen into corruption, that He might, in spite of all the defection that marked His people, preserve a godly seed out of whom might spring in due season, *the Seed*, in whom all the nations should be blessed, and Abraham as well. Hence the nations are to be blessed by faith, as Abraham was, and not by the works of the law.

God is omniscient. He can foresee what He will do, in spite of all eventualities. But here this omniscience is attributed to the Scripture! A remarkable fact surely! God's Word is of Himself, and from Himself, and is therefore to be very closely identified with Him. Let men beware how they handle it. There are those who utterly deny and deride the Scripture; and there are those who honour it in theory, and yet corrupt it. Both will ultimately have to reckon in judgment with the God whose Word it is. And, woe betide them!

The Scripture itself foresees, and it foretells their doom!

From beginning to end this third chapter is filled with contrasts. On the one side we have the law and the works that it demanded, the flesh, upon which the law's demands were made, and the curse which fell when the law's demands were broken. On the other side we find the faith of the Gospel, the Spirit given, and blessing bestowed. We have spoken of contrasts, but after all the contrast is really one, only worked out in a variety of different ways.

The Spirit and the flesh are brought into contrast in verse 3. Now in verse 10 we get the curse of the law in contrast with the blessing of believing Abraham. The curse was pronounced against *every one* that did not *continue* doing *all things* that the law demanded. No one did so continue, and hence all who were placed under the law came under the curse. It was enough to be "of the works of the law"—that is, to have to stand or fall in one's relations Godward by the response one gave to the law's demands —to be under the curse. Man being what he is, the moment any one has to stand before God on that ground he is lost.

The Jews, who had the law, hardly seem to have realized this. On the contrary they looked upon the law as being the means of their justification. Contented with a very superficial obedience to some of its demands, they were "going about to establish their own righteousness," as Paul puts it in

Romans x. 3. In this of course they utterly failed, for in their own Scriptures it had been put on record that, "the just shall live by *faith*." And faith is not the principle upon which the law is based, but rather that of works. The whole matter briefly summed up stands thus:—By law men come under the curse and die. By faith men are justified and live.

The curse which the law pronounced was a perfectly just sentence. The Jew having been placed under the law, its curse rested upon him, and it had to be righteously borne ere it could be lifted off him. In the death of Christ the curse was borne, and hence the believing Jew is redeemed from beneath it. In the days of Moses, the curse had been specially connected with the one who died as a transgressor by hanging on a tree. Many a one in ancient days, reading Deuteronomy xxi. 23, may have wondered why the curse was thus linked with death on a tree, as distinguished from death by any other means, such as stoning, or the sword. Now we know. In due season the Redeemer was to bear the curse for others, thus honouring the law, *by hanging on a tree*. It is another case of how the Scripture foresees!

The bearing of the curse was in view of the bestowal of the blessing. Verse 14 speaks to us of this, presenting the blessing in a twofold way. First, there is "the blessing of Abraham," which is righteousness. Second, there is the gift of the Spirit, a blessing beyond anything bestowed upon Abraham. The wonder of the work of Christ is this, that righteousness now rests upon Gentiles who believe, as well as upon believers who are Abraham's children according to the flesh. All who believe are in a spiritual sense the children of Abraham, as verse 7 informed us.

In Old Testament days the Spirit was promised, as for instance in Joel ii. 28, 29. We who believe, whether Jews or Gentiles, receive the Spirit today. Thus by faith we anticipate the blessing so fully to be enjoyed in the millennial day.

For the moment however the Apostle does not pursue the subject of the Holy Spirit. When we enter chapter iv. we learn something as to the meaning of His indwelling, and in chapter v, we have an unfolding of his operations. In our chapter is pursued the subject of the law, and the place it had in the ways of God, and this in order to lead up to the unfolding of the proper Christian position—as stated in the early verses of chapter iv.,—which is the central theme of the epistle. And first of all certain difficulties are cleared out of the way; misconceptions and objections flowing from a false view of the functions of the law, held by the Judaising teachers and doubtless instilled by them into the minds of the Galatians.

The first of these is taken up in verses 15 to 18. In so many minds the covenant of law had completely overshadowed the covenant of promise made with Abraham. But as we have just seen the covenant of law inevitably brings nothing but its curse. Blessing can only be reached by way of the covenant of promise which culminates in Christ. It cannot arrive partly by law and partly by promise. Verse 18 states this. The inheritance of blessing if by the law is not by promise, and this of course is true *vice versa*. The fact is, it is by promise. Thanks be unto God!

But was not the law intended as a kind of revision of the original testament, a kind of codicil, so to speak? Not at all, for as verse 15 says, it can be neither disannulled nor added thereto. It is an old trick of dishonest men to procure the rejection of a disliked document by foisting into it an addition so contradictory of its main provisions as to stultify the whole. This is not allowed amongst men, and we must not conceive of God's covenant of promise as being less sacred than human documents. The law, which was not given until 430 years after, has not disannulled it. Nor has it been added to it in order to modify its blessed simplicity. It was never intended to do either of these things.

Verse 16 is worthy of special note, not only because it declares in such an unmistakable way that from the outset the covenant was in view of Christ and His redeeming work, but also because of the remarkable way in which the Apostle argues as to the Old Testament prediction. The Holy Spirit inspired him to hinge the whole point upon the word, "Seed," being in the singular and not in the plural. Thereby He indicated how fully inspired was His earlier utterance. Not merely was the word inspired, but the exact form of the word. The inspiration was not merely *verbal*, i.e. having to do with *words*, but even *literal*, i.e. having to do with *letters*.

Accepting Paul's argument, stated in the verses we have just considered, a further difficulty might well present itself to any mind. If then the law, given over 400 years after Abraham, had no effect upon the earlier covenant, neither annulling it nor modifying it, does it not seem to have lacked any definite purpose? An objector might declare that such doctrine as this leaves the law shorn of all point and meaning, and feel that he was propounding a regular poser in simply asking, Why then the law?

This is exactly the question with which verse 19 opens. The answer to this is very brief, and it appears to be twofold. In the first place, it was given in order that men's sins might become, in the breaking of it, definite transgressions. This point is more fully stated in Romans v. 13. In the second place, it served a useful purpose in connection with Israel, filling up the time until the advent of Christ, by proving their need of Him. It was ordained through angels, and through a human mediator, in the person of Moses. But then the very fact of a mediator supposes two parties. God is one; who is the other? Man is the other. And since the whole arrangement was made to hinge upon the doings of man, the other party, it promptly failed.

In definitely convicting men of transgressions the law has done a work of extreme importance. What is right, and what is wrong? What does God require of men? Before the law was given there was some knowledge, and conscience was at work, as is indicated in Romans ii. 14, 15. But when the law came, all vagueness disappeared; for all, who were under it, the plea of ignorance totally disappeared and, when brought into judgment for their transgressions, not a shred of an excuse remained. We Gentiles were never formally placed under it, but as a matter of fact we know about it, and our very knowledge of it will make us amenable to the judgment of God in a way and degree unknown to the savage and unenlightened tribes of the earth. So let us take care.

In verse 21 another question is raised, which springs out of the foregoing. Some might jump to the conclusion that if, as shown, the law was not supplementary to the covenant of promise it must necessarily be in opposition to it. This is not so for one moment. Had the law been intended by God to provide righteousness for man, He would have endowed it with power to give life. The law instructed, demanded, urged, threatened and, when it had been broken, it condemned the transgressor to death. Yet none of these things availed. The one thing needful was to bestow upon man a new life, in which it would be as natural to him to fulfil the law, as now it is natural to him to break it. *That* the law could not do; instead it has proved us all to be under sin, thus revealing our need of that which has been introduced through Christ.

Thus the law, instead of being in any way in opposition, fits in harmoniously with all the rest of God's great scheme. Until Christ came it has played the part of "the schoolmaster," acting as our guardian and maintaining some measure of control. In verse 24 the words, "to bring us," are in italics, there being no corresponding words in the original. They should not be there. The point is not that the law leads us to Christ, but that it exercised its control as tutor until Christ came. When Christ appeared, a new order of things was instituted, and there was justification for us on the principle of faith, and not by works.

This new order of things is spoken of in verse 23 as the coming of faith. Again in verse 25 we have the words, "after that faith is come." Faith was found of course in all the saints of Old Testament days, as is shown by Hebrews xi., and by the passage from Habakkuk, quoted in verse 11 of our chapter. When Christ came, the faith of Christ stood revealed, and faith was publicly acknowledged as being the way, and the only way, by which man can have to do with God in blessing. In that sense "faith came," and its coming marked the inauguration of an entirely new epoch.

By faith in Christ Jesus we have been introduced into the favoured place of "sons of God." The word in verse 26 is "sons," and not "children." The saints under the law were like children in a state of infancy; under age, and hence under the schoolmaster. The believer of the present age is like a child who has reached his majority, and hence, leaving the state of tutelage behind, he takes his place as a son in his father's house. This great

GALATIANS

thought, which is the controlling thought of the epistle, is more largely developed in the early verses of chapter iv. Before reaching them however, we have three important facts stated in the three closing verses of chapter iii.

By our baptism we have, as a matter of profession, put on Christ. Had we submitted to circumcision we should have put on Judaism, and thereby committed ourselves to the fulfilling of the law for justification. Had we been baptised to John's baptism we should have put on the robe of professed repentance and committed ourselves to believe on the One that should come after him. As it is we have, if baptised to Christ, put on Christ and committed ourselves to that practical expression of the life of Christ which in the next chapter is spoken of as "the fruit of the Spirit." As sons of God, having now the liberty of the house, we put on Christ as our fitness to be there.

Further, we are "in Christ Jesus," and consequently we are "all one," with all distinctions obliterated, whether national, social, or natural. When we get to the last chapter we shall find that in Christ Jesus there is new creation, which accounts for the removal of all the distinctions belonging to the old creation. This new creation work has reached us as to our souls already, though not yet as to our bodies. Hence we cannot as yet take up these things in an absolute way. For that we must wait until we are clothed upon with our bodies of glory at the coming of the Lord. Still even now we are in Christ Jesus, and hence can learn to view each other apart from and as lifted above these distinctions.

Let us take note that what is taught here is the abolition of these distinctions *in Christ Jesus*, and not *in the assembly*. We say this to safeguard the point and preserve from misconceptions. In the assembly, for instance, the distinction between male and female is very definitely maintained, as is shown in 1 Corinthians xiv. 34, 35.

We have already had three things which mark the believer of today in contradistinction from believers before Christ came. We are "sons of God;" we have "put on Christ;" we are "in Christ Jesus." The last verse of our chapter gives us a fourth thing: we are "Christ's," and belonging to Him we are in a spiritual sense Abraham's seed, and consequently heirs, not according to law, but to promise.

CHAPTER 4

THE OPENING VERSES of chapter iv. gather up the thoughts that have occupied the latter part of chapter iii., and summarize them in very crisp fashion. The custom that prevailed in the houses of the nobility—and that still in measure prevail is such circles—are used as an illustration. The heir to the estate, so long as he is in infancy, is placed under restraint, just as the servants are. Tutors and governors hold him in what appears to him

19

to be bondage. He just has to do as he is told, and as yet he knows not the reason why. He cannot yet be given the full liberty of his father's house and estate, for his character and intelligence is not yet sufficiently formed. However his father knows when the time will arrive, and the day is fixed when he will come of age and enter into the privileges and responsibilities of life.

It was thus with God's people in the former day under the law, which was as a schoolmaster to them. Children they might be, but they were treated as servants, and rightly so. It was no question of their individual eminence as saints of God, but simply of the dispensation in which they lived. No greater man than John the Baptist was ever born, yet as the Lord has told us, "he that is least in the kingdom of heaven is greater than he" (Matt. xi. 11). In their days God had not yet been fully revealed, redemption had not been accomplished, the Spirit had not been given. Until these three great events had come to pass, the conditions were not established which permitted the "coming of age" of the people of God. All three did come to pass when on the scenes there arrived the Son of God.

When He came God's people passed from under the schoolmaster of the law, whose control was exercised according to the "elements," or "principles," of the world, and they came under the control of the Spirit of God, exercised according to the principles of grace and of God.

The trouble today with a good many of us is that we have been brought up on loose and easy-going lines, and consequently we know very little of the stern dealings of the righteous old schoolmaster! If only our consciences had been brought more fully under the righteous admonition and condemnation of the law, we should possess a far keener sense of the mighty emancipation which has reached us through the advent of the Son of God.

The coming forth of God's Son was the event which marked the commencement of a new epoch in God's dealings with men. The steps, by which that new epoch was inaugurated, are given to us in verses 4 to 6.

First, the Son of God was sent, "made of a woman," or, more literally, "come of woman." Thus His incarnation is expressed, the guarantee to us that He was *a Man*, in the full and proper sense of the word.

Second, it could be said of Him, "come under law." When He came God's attention was focused upon the Jew, as upon a people who were in outward relationship with Him and responsible as under His law. Amongst that people He came, *assuming all the responsibilities*, under which they had wholly failed.

Third, He wrought *redemption* for those under the law, thus delivering them from its claims, in order that a new position might be theirs.

Fourth, as thus delivered we receive "*the adoption of sons,*" or, "*sonship.*" This wondrous position in regard to God is ours as a free gift, according to His eternal purpose.

Fifth, being made sons, God has given to us *the Spirit of His Son*, in order that we may be enabled to enter into the consciousness and enjoyment of this new relationship, and respond to God as our Father. By the Spirit given we cry, "Abba, Father!"

The above is a brief summary of these remarkable verses, but now let us notice in them a few points of importance.

The redemption spoken of in verse 5 goes further than the truth which we met with in verse 13 of chapter iii. We might have been redeemed from the curse of the law and yet left under the law, and consequently left still in the place of servants. The glorious fact is that the believer is not only redeemed from the curse, but also from the law that righteously inflicted the curse; so that now we stand in the liberty of sonship and the days of bondage under the "schoolmaster" are over.

Notice also the change from the "we" of verse 5 to the "ye" of verse 6. Only the Jew had been in the bondage of the law, hence redemption from law applied to Jewish believers of whom Paul was one. Consequently he says, "we." But, on the other hand, the place of sonship, in which Christians are set, is the portion equally of all, whether Jew or Gentile by nature. Hence the change to "ye." The wonder is that those, who once were degraded Gentiles far from God, should now be sons and happily responding to God the Father's love by the Spirit given to them.

The Spirit of God's Son does not give us the place of sons. That is ours as the fruit of God's purpose and gift on the basis of redemption. The Spirit gives the consciousness of the relationship and the power to respond to it.

In verse 7 the Apostle brings home the fact of this wonderful relationship to us each individually. And not only is sonship an individual blessing, so that he can say, "thou art . . . a son," but heirship is individual also. Each of us is, "an heir of God through Christ." This shows us that when the Apostle used "the heir" in verse 1 as an illustration of his theme, he was using an illustration which applied in a very exact and literal way. Such is the amazing grace of God to us as believers, whether we were Jews or Gentiles. How little we have taken it in!

We call upon our readers to pause at this point and to meditate upon this truth. It is an established fact, and so stated without any qualification. The Galatians were not in the enjoyment of the fact. They were actually behaving themselves as though they were servants and not sons, yet the Apostle does not say, "Wherefore thou *oughtest to be* no more a servant but a son," but, "Thou *art* no more a servant but a son." Our relationship does not flow from our understanding of, or our response to, the place we have, nor from behaviour suitable to it; but rather our behaviour flows from the relationship, once it is understood and responded to. Let us each say to ourselves again and yet again, "I am a son and heir of God through Christ." Let us take time that this wonderful truth may sink into each heart.

When once the fact has really laid hold of us we shall be able to appreciate how Paul felt as he penned verses 8 and 9. The Galatians were formerly in bondage, not to the law indeed, but to false gods; and now having been brought to know God, as the fruit of God having taken them up and brought them into this wealthy place, what possessed them to turn again to the old principle of standing before God in their own merits—or rather demerits? What indeed?

The principle of the law of Moses was that each should stand before God according to his own doings. This too is a root principle with every false religion, and thus the Galatians had proceeded in their former days of paganism. In now turning aside to Judaism they were slipping back into the old principles which are weak and beggarly. What expressive adjectives! *Weak*, since by them man accomplished nothing that counted for good. *Beggarly*, because they left him stripped of all merit and of all excuse. But if we wish to realize *how* weak and *how* beggarly we must view them in contrast with the principles of the Gospel, and its results in making us sons and heirs.

In verse 10 the Apostle gives an instance of what he alluded to, when he spoke of their turning back to legal principles. They were taking up Jewish feasts and customs. That might seem a small matter, but it was a straw which showed the way the wind was blowing, and it made him afraid lest there should be with them a lack of reality—lest their professed acceptance of the Gospel were not sincere after all; and consequently the labour he had expended upon them should be in vain.

This was a sad thought, and it leads directly to the touching appeal which follows in verses 12 to 20. He beseeches them in the first place to be as he was as to their experience and practice, inasmuch as both he and they were just on the same footing as to their place before God. Alike they had been brought into sonship, and therefore alike they should all be walking in the liberty of sons. It was not a personal matter at all. He nursed no sense of personal injury against them.

This leads him to recall the great reception that they gave him when first he came amongst them with the Gospel message. He was at that time in much infirmity of a physical sort, and it would seem that his eyesight was particularly affected. On turning to Acts xvi. 6 we note that his first visit to Galatia was during the early part of his second missionary journey. The stoning of Paul even to the point of death took place at nearly the end of his first journey, as recorded in Acts xiv. 19. It is more than likely that there is a connection between the two events, and that this "temptation . . . in my flesh" resulted from the ill-treatment that he received, and is the same as the "thorn in the flesh," of which he writes in 2 Corinthians xii. 7. Be that as it may, he arrived amongst them in fullness of power and they received him with great gladness. Now it would appear that in speaking the truth to them he had become their enemy!

The fact was of course that the Judaising teachers, who had got amongst them, were aiming at producing alienation between the Galatians and Paul, their spiritual father, in order to capture them as followers for themselves. In verse 17 the Apostle in few words unmasks this, their real objective. "They are very zealous after you" he says, "but not in the right way. They are simply anxious to shut you away from us, in order that you become zealous adherents, following them." What Paul wanted was to see them always zealous after the things that are really good, and that as much when he was absent as when he was with them.

As things were however he could but stand in doubt of them. When first he visited them it was with great exercise and travail of soul. He did not preach himself but Christ Jesus as Lord, and their spiritual birth only came to pass when Christ was formed in them. The photographic artist takes care to have a good lens in his camera, that will throw on the screen a very accurate picture of the features of the sitter. But the photograph only comes to the birth when the sitter's features are formed in the sensitized plate as the result of the joint action of light and certain chemicals. This may serve as an illustration of the point. Paul travailed that as the fruit of Gospel light Christ might be formed in them. Then his birth pangs on their behalf were over.

But along come these Judaising teachers, and lo! instead of Christ these men, their sabbaths, their new moons, their circumcision, seem to be forming themselves in them. No wonder that Paul, in his ardent affection for them as his children, felt as though he must go through birth pangs *again* on their behalf, and was perplexed about them. Under these circumstances he wished that, instead of being at a distance and having to communicate by writing, he were in their midst, able to judge of their exact state and to change his voice, speaking to them in instruction, in rebuke, or even in severity, as the occasion demanded.

However as they seemed to be so anxious to place themselves under the law, they would at least be prepared to listen to what the law had indicated! Hence from verse 22 to the end of the chapter he refers them to the allegorical significance of an occurrence in Abraham's life.

Abraham was the great example of faith and promise, as we saw when reading chapter iii. Yet before ever he received by faith the child of promise, there was the episode in which by works he obtained a child through Hagar. Ishmael was born after the flesh, whereas Isaac was by promise.

We can now see that there was an allegory in this, and that Hagar and her son picture for us Sinai, whence was proclaimed the law system which results in bondage, and also "Jerusalem which now is," *i.e.*, the Jewish people, who though under law are still in virtual unbelief. The Christian, on the other hand, is in the position of the child of promise, and connected with "Jerusalem which is above", which is free.

The proud orthodox Jew might rightly boast that according to the flesh he was a true-born son of Isaac. Yet in a spiritual sense he was only a son of Ishmael and in bondage under the schoolmaster. True the schoolmaster regime came first, and later came the promise, which materialized in the advent of the Son of God. But that only confirmed the type, for Ishmael came before Isaac. The type was further confirmed by the fact that it was the proud Jews who persecuted the humble Christians, as verse 29 points out.

Again, the truth of the allegory finds a corroboration in the words of Isaiah liv. 1. That verse indicates that Israel in the time of her desolation would be more fruitful than she had ever been when she was acknowledged as in relationship with Jehovah. But then that verse is the immediate consequence of the glorious truth predicted in chapter liii. It was to be as the fruit of the advent of the suffering Messiah, and not as the result of law keeping.

When the law was imposed from Sinai no one broke forth into song. Very soon there were cries to the effect that such words should not be spoken any more into the ears of the people. Yet when Isaiah unfolds before us the marvellous story of the Christ who suffers and rises again for sins not His own, the first word that follows is, "SING." Bondage is over, liberty is come!

Of old there was the inevitable clash between Ishmael and Isaac, just as now there is between the Judaiser and the believer who stands in the liberty of the grace of God. And yet it is not the clash that decides the question, nor even the persecution of the one "born after the Spirit" by the one "born after the flesh." What decides the matter is the voice of God. And that voice reaches us in the Scriptures.

"What saith the Scripture?" That is the decisive question. And the answer is that, "the son of the bondwoman shall not be heir with the son of the freewoman." The servant is displaced in favour of the son. He, who would stand before God on the basis of the law, falls. He, who stands in the fullness of grace, stands indeed.

Happy indeed it is for us if we can truly say, "We are not children of the bondwoman, but of the free." Then indeed we stand in Christ, and Christ Himself is formed in us. We are in the liberty of sonship, and that is liberty indeed.

GALATIANS

Chapter 5

IN THE FIRST verse of chapter v. we have the main point of the epistle compressed into a few words. Christ has set us free in a wonderful liberty, and in that we are to stand fast, refusing to be again entangled in bondage.

Let us refresh our memories as to the extent and character of the liberty into which we have been brought.

In the first place we have been set free from the law as *the ground of our justification before God*. This was previously stated in verse 16 of chapter ii. We are "justified by the faith of Christ."

Further, we have been set free from the law as *the basis of our relationship with God*. The "adoption of sons" is ours as having been redeemed from under the law. This is stated in verse 5 of chapter iv.

Consequently, in the third place, we are set free from the law as *the rule or standard of our life*. This came out in the whole passage, iii. 23 to iv. 7. For as long as God's children were in the place of servants, the rule of life for them was the law. Now, as full-grown sons in the house of their father, possessing the Spirit of God's Son, we have a higher rule or standard than the law of Moses—even the "law of Christ," of which verse 2 of chapter vi. speaks.

The liberty into which we are brought, then, is the complete emancipation which has reached us as being made the sons of God. It is the freedom of which the Lord Jesus spoke when He said, "If the Son therefore shall make you free, ye shall be free indeed" (John viii. 36). We are no longer like servants of the household, who rightly have their conduct regulated by the rules suitable to the servants' hall; and to put ourselves in our thoughts and behaviour back into that position is to sadly entangle ourselves. It is indeed to *fall from grace*, as verse 4 has it.

The words "fallen from grace" are often taken to mean that such have fallen out of the gracious hand of God—that such are no longer saved. The phrase however, refers to what was produced *in their consciousness*, not to what is true *as before God*. The verse begins, "Christ is become of no effect *unto you*." Is Christ of no effect REALLY?—that is, IN THE SIGHT OF GOD? Far be the thought—an impossible supposition! But *to them— in their experience and consciousness?* Yes. If they considered themselves as justified on the principle of law, Christ was most evidently disallowed in their minds, and they had descended from the divine and lofty principle of grace to the far lower level of law. And the descent between the two is so pronounced and precipitous that it can only be described as a *fall!*

To fall from grace is not a difficult thing. How many a professed believer there is today that is guilty of it! Are we all clear on the point? Do we stand in the liberty of grace in all our dealings with God?

25

In verses 2 and 3 Paul again alludes to the matter of circumcision as this was being used as a test question. It was the spearhead of the adversaries' attack on their liberty. It doubtless appeared to many to be a small and unimportant point, but it was quite sufficient to establish the principle. The law is one whole. If taken up in *one* detail it must be maintained in *all* details. This is quite in keeping with what James writes—"whosoever shall keep the whole law, and yet offend in *one* point, he is guilty *of all*." (ii. 10). This enforces the fact that if the law be broken in *one* detail, it is broken *altogether*. Both statements correspond and show us that the law cannot be taken up piecemeal. It is one whole and must be considered as such. If but a very small stone be thrown through a large pane of glass it is a broken pane, as really as if it were shivered to atoms by a large chunk of rock. Or, to change the figure, the law is like a chain of many links. It is as really a broken chain if one link be fractured as if a dozen were snapped. Conversely, let a boat be connected with but *one* link of a chain and that boat is attached to *all*, and may be controlled by the hand that pulls *any* link in the chain. And this is the particular point that Paul is enforcing here.

Now note the contrast between the "ye" of verse 4 and the "we" of verse 5. "Ye"—such among the Galatians as were abandoning in their thoughts the place in which grace had set them. "We"—the mass of believers, standing in the grace of the gospel. It is the Christian "we"— if we may so speak; and verse 5 describes what the proper position of the believer is: not now his position of privilege before God as a son, but his position of liberty as left in the world, which is in sharp contrast with all that the Jew had ever known.

Our position is one of expectancy. We wait, but not for righteousness as was the case with the Jew, who under the law was always "going about to establish his own righteousness," and yet never arriving at it. We have righteousness as an established fact in the Gospel, and are only waiting for the hope that is connected with it. The hope of righteousness is glory, as Romans v. 2 makes manifest. Now we are waiting for glory—by the Spirit given to us; and on the principle of faith—not the principle of the works of the law.

Is not this a position of wonderful liberty? The more we have experienced the drudgery and despair of seeking righteousness by diligent efforts at law keeping, the more we shall appreciate it; and see that faith working by love is the only thing that counts in Christ Jesus.

Once the Galatians had been like earnest runners in the race, now they were hindered and no longer obeying the truth. Take note that "the truth" is not something merely to be discussed and analysed and understood, but to be *obeyed*. Are we sons of God? Then as sons we are to behave ourselves. Are we no longer under the schoolmaster? Then we no longer order our lives on a legal basis. Are we crucified with Christ? Then we do not aim at living unto ourselves but that Christ may live in us. Every bit of truth that we learn is to have a practical expression in us. We are to obey it.

The Galatians however were turning aside not only from obedience to the truth, but from the truth itself. They had been persuaded to embrace these new ideas, which did not come from the God who had called them; and further, they had to remember that ideas and doctrines can work like leaven. They might be flattering themselves that they had only embraced a few minor items of Judaism, yet thereby they might become wholly Judaized.

The saying which we have here in verse 9 is also found in 1 Corinthians v. 6. It states the essential nature of leaven. In Corinthians it is applied to a matter of conduct and morals. Here it is applied to a matter of doctrine; for it was virtually "the leaven of the Pharisees" which was threatening the Galatians, just as that threatening the Corinthians was in its nature near to the leaven of the Sadducees and the Herodians. Still when the Apostle thought of the Lord and His gracious working in souls, he felt confident that his letter of remonstrance and correction would have its effect on the Galatians, and that the workers of mischief, who had troubled them and perverted their thoughts, would eventually come under God's dealings in judgment.

In verses 11 to 15, Paul reinforces his appeal by one or two further considerations. He was no preacher of circumcision. Had he been he would have escaped persecution. The "offence" or "scandal" of the cross consists in the fact that it puts no honour upon man; in fact, it totally condemns him. Circumcision on the other hand, assumes that there is some possibility of merit in him, that his flesh in this way can be made profitable to God. And what is true of circumcision would also be true of any other rite which is performed with the idea that there is virtue in it. This explains why men so dearly love rites and ordinances. They induce in men a comfortable feeling of complacency with themselves. The cross makes nothing of them. Hence its *scandal*.

The Apostle longed for the true liberty of the Galatians and could have desired that those who were so zealous for the cuttings of circumcision would cut themselves off. Liberty, he points out, is not licence to sin but rather freedom to love and to serve. And this love was what the law of Moses had been aiming at all the time. Yet, as a matter of fact, while boasting in the law they had been biting and devouring one another, instead of loving and serving one another. It is ever thus. Legality leads to the very opposite of love in action, and the Galatians had to beware lest their pursuit of holiness by law only led them to the unholy end of consuming one another in their contentions and criticisms. They would avoid the scandal of the cross only to come utterly to grief in the scandal produced by their own unholy conduct. We have sorrowfully to remark that this just sums up the history of Christendom. In proportion as the scandal

27

of the cross has been refused and avoided, the scandal of its divisions and misbehaviour has increased.

The Galatians, however, might turn round to Paul and say, "you have pretty definitely and effectively shown us that our thoughts as to pursuing holiness by law-keeping are wrong, but what is right? You have demolished what we have been saying, but what do you say?" His answer to this begins in verse 16. *"This I say then, walk in the Spirit."*

Walking is man's earliest and most primitive activity. It has consequently become the figure or symbol of man's activities. To "walk in the Spirit" is to have one's activities, whether of thought or speech or action, in the energy of the Spirit, who has been given to us. The Spirit of God's Son, conferred upon us as God's sons, is to govern all our activities. This is the way of liberty, a liberty which is the very opposite of licence, for walking in the Spirit it is impossible for us to fulfil the desires of the flesh. The coming in of the higher power completely lifts us above the pull of the lower.

The flesh is not thereby altered, as verse 17 makes plain. Its nature, its desires, its action remain the same, and always contrary to the Spirit of God. But the Spirit prevails—if we walk in the Spirit—against the flesh, so that we "cannot" (or, more accurately, "should not") do the things that otherwise we would. And then if we are "led" of the Spirit we cannot be at the same time under the leadership of "the schoolmaster"—the law.

In verse 16, then, the Spirit is regarded as the new Power in the believer, energizing him. In verse 18, as the new Leader, taking him by the hand and directing him in God's will. In Romans viii. 14, the Spirit is also presented in this capacity. The sons are led by the Spirit. The servants are led by the schoolmaster.

The fact that there exists a total and absolute contrast and contradiction between the flesh and the Spirit is very manifest when we consider the outcome of each. Verses 19 to 21 give us the dreadful catalogue of the works of the flesh. Verses 22 and 23 present the beautiful cluster of the fruit of the Spirit. The former wholly under the condemnation of God and to be excluded from His kingdom. The latter wholly approved of God and hence no law existing against them. In the one list we discover the hideous features which characterize fallen Adam: in the other the character of Christ.

Notice the contrast between the "works" and the "fruit." It is easy to understand the "works." The earth is filled with the noise of them. Their confusion and disruption are visible on every side. "Fruit," on the other hand, is of silent growth, even in nature. In summer time, amidst the orchards no one is driven to distraction by the noise of maturing fruit. The wonder of its growth takes place without a sound. So it is with the fruit of the Spirit. It is "fruit" you notice, not "fruits;" and this, because these lovely moral features are conceived of as a bunch; nine in number but all proceeding from one stem—the Spirit of God.

These lovely traits of character are going to fill the kingdom of God, whilst the blatant works of the flesh are totally excluded. No *true* Christian is characterized by these works of the flesh, though alas, a true Christian may fall into one or other of them, and only be extricated by the advocacy of Christ and at the cost of much suffering to himself both spiritual and physical. To belong to Christ means that we have come to a definite judgment as to the evil of the flesh, and have crucified it by heartily ratifying in our own conscience and judgment the sentence against it pronounced by God at the cross.

We do well to enquire if we have really arrived at this, which is the proper attitude of the Christian. Have we definitely put the sentence of death on the flesh? Have we crucified it with the affections and lusts? Is it what we profess to have done as being Christians: but are we up to our profession? A very serious question which we must each answer for ourselves. Let us give ourselves time for conscience to answer!

Certain it is that we live by the Spirit and not by the flesh. Well, then, let us walk by the Spirit. Our walk must certainly be according to our life. A bird cannot have its life in the air and yet all its activities under the water. A fish cannot have its life in water and yet its activities on land. Christians cannot have their life in the Spirit and yet their activities in the flesh.

The last verse of our chapter is another pretty plain hint to the Galatians that the Apostle well knew what their false pursuit of holiness was coming to. Depend upon it, if we fall into their snare the same sad effects will be displayed in ourselves.

Only in the Spirit of God can we reproduce, even in small measure, the beautiful character of Christ.

CHAPTER 6

A CONTRAST SEEMS to be implied between verse 21 of chapter v. and the first verse of chapter vi. The former contemplates those who are characterized by doing certain evil things. The latter speaks of a man being overtaken in an offence. Those who are characterized by evil will never enter the kingdom of God, whereas the man overtaken in evil is to be restored. It is taken for granted that he is a true believer.

The appeal to restore such an one is addressed to "ye which are spiritual." There were not many such amongst the Galatians, as the last verse of chapter v. infers. To approach a fallen brother in the spirit of vain glory would necessarily be provocative of all that was worst in him. To approach him in the spirit of meekness would help him. Let us take note that the spirit of meekness is a necessary accompaniment of spirituality, for there is a spurious spirituality, all too often to be met with, which is allied with a self-conscious assertiveness which is the very opposite of meekness. A truly spiritual man is one who is dominated and controlled by the indwelling Spirit of God and hence is characterized by "the meekness and gentleness of Christ" (2 Cor. x. 1). But even such an one as that is not beyond falling in the presence of temptation. Hence while restoring another he has to take good heed to himself.

Verse 2 is an exhortation of a more general character. It applies to all of us. We are to fulfil the law of Christ—which in one word is LOVE—and bear one another's burdens. Very frequently the brother who falls has been bearing burdens to which we are strangers, and had we been walking in obedience to the new commandment of John xiii. 34, we should have been helping to lighten them.

And why do we not thus fulfil the law of Christ? What is it that so frequently hinders us? Why, we think ourselves to be something or somebody, and when we do we feel ourselves too great and important to lift other people's burdens. And all the time we are deceiving ourselves. We are nothing, as verse 3 so pointedly tells us. A man is never nearer to zero than when he fancies himself to be somebody—even a "spiritual" somebody!

The fact is we need sobriety of thought. We need preparedness to face facts; testing our own work. If we do so we shall be brought down from the high thoughts we had entertained. And if indeed we do find that which stands the test we may rejoice in what is really our own, and not in that which we are in other people's estimation. For we must each bear the burden of our own individual responsibility before God. There is no contradiction between verses 2 and 5 save an apparent one as to the words employed. In verse 2 "burden" refers to that which presses upon us each in the way of trial and testing. In verse 5 "burden" refers to the responsibility Godward which lies upon us each and which none can bear for another.

With verse 6 the apostle passes to a specific responsibility which lies upon all who receive instruction in the things of God. They are to be prepared to give help to those who teach them, and that in all good things.

Naturally we are selfish creatures. The great majority of us are glad enough to receive, but very parsimonious when it is a question of giving. Verses 7 and 8, with their solemn warning, are written in view of this. We are plainly told that our own spiritual prosperity hinges upon this matter, and since we are very apt to invent in our own minds ample reasons for not giving, but rather hugging to our own bosoms as much as possible, the apostle prefaces his warning with, "Be not deceived." It is so easy to deceive oneself.

The principle that he lays down is doubtless true in any and every connection. Still here it stands in connection with this matter of *giving*, and we are brought face to face with the fact that our reaping must inevitably be according to our sowing. This is true of course as to *quantity* and that fact is stated in 2 Corinthians ix. 6. The point here is rather that of *quality*, or perhaps we had better say of *kind* or *nature;* that just what we sow *that* we reap.

To sow to the flesh is to cater for it and its desires. To sow to the Spirit is to yield to Him His place, and lay oneself out for His things. If the former, we reap corruption. If the latter, eternal life. The corruption comes from the flesh. Eternal life, from the Spirit. In both cases it is just the proper outcome of what is sown; as normal as it is to obtain a field of thistles from the sowing of thistledown, or wheat from the sowing of wheat.

In the light of this fact how differently our lives would appear. How many things which may seem strange and arbitrary to us should we discover to be perfectly natural, just what we might have expected having regard to our previous course of action. We wonder why such and such an experience was ours, whereas the wonder would have been had it not been ours. Happy for us it is when our sowing has been such that an abundant crop of "everlasting life" begins to appear.

No one can sow to the Spirit save he who has the Spirit; that is, is a true believer. Having the Spirit, and indeed having eternal life in the sense of John v. 24, we reap eternal life as the proper consequence of cultivating the things of the Spirit of God. This verse plainly sets "eternal life" before us not as the life *by* which we live, but as *the life we live.* As we cultivate the things of the Spirit we lay hold of and enjoy all those blessings, those relationships, that communion with the Father and the Son, in which life consists from the practical and experimental side of things.

Here, then, we are supplied with the reason why we so often have to bemoan our spiritual weakness, or the lack of vitality and joy and power in the things of God. We make but little advance, and we enquire why it is. How many scores of times have we heard this question asked and often in a kind of plaintive way that infers that God deals out His favours capriciously, or that the whole question is wrapped in mystery! There is really no mystery about it.

The matter is simply settled by asking oneself the question, "What am I cultivating?" I shall never get figs from thistles nor reap eternal life save by sowing to the Spirit. The trouble with most of us in these days is dissipation of energy. Not exactly the cultivating of harmful things, but rather of useless and needless things. We are not like the Apostle himself who could say, "One thing I do" as he concentrated steadily on the one great thing that mattered.

Does some young believer ask us to be severely practical, and to come very close home to the point? Then we say, "Cut out of your life those 'harmless' amusements, those unprofitable frivolities, those little time-wasting engagements that accomplish nothing and lead you nowhere. Fill your heart and mind and time with the Word of God and prayer, give yourself whole-heartedly to the glad service of the Lord Jesus, and ere long your profiting will appear unto all."

You notice of course that we are back again at the point we reached in verse 16 of chapter v., only here we are carried a step further. There the point was mainly negative—*not* fulfilling the desires of the flesh. Here it is positive—*reaping* everlasting life.

The reaping does not come directly the seed is sown. Hence the need for patience as stated in verse 9. But reap we shall—*in due season;* and God, not we, is Judge as to when the fit season arrives. Still *arrive* it certainly shall. Genesis viii. 22, stands true even in this connection—"seed time and *harvest* . . . shall not cease."

Now, as we previously noticed, all this important truth is brought in to stir up the Galatians and ourselves to generosity in our giving, and to this point the Apostle recurs in verse 10. We are to be givers and doers of good unto all men; whilst the household of faith have upon us the first call. By creation we are connected with all men. By redemption and its results we are found in the household of faith. The former natural, the latter spiritual, and the spiritual has precedence over the natural.

The apostle Paul set great importance upon this letter of his to the Galatians, hence verse 11. Some render it "how long a letter" in keeping with our authorized version; others "in what large letters." If the former be correct it indicates that instead of employing one of his helpers to write the letter he had written it all with his own hand. If the latter, it signifies that he now took up the pen to add the last few lines with his own hand and wrote in extra large letters. In either case it was to give added emphasis to his words as he commences his closing summary.

In verse 12 he has a final word as to those who had been pressing circumcision on the Galatians. He unmasks once more their real object; namely, to make a fair shew in the flesh and to escape the persecution entailed by the cross of Christ. This was not a random accusation brought against them, for in verse 13 he proves it by the simple fact that while pressing circumcision on the Gentile Galatians as the sign of subjection to the law, they did not keep the law themselves! In that way they really unmasked themselves. They just wanted to be able to boast in some fleshly sign and so conform to the spirit of the world.

In contrast thereto Paul states his own position in the matter. He gloried not in the flesh but in the cross of our Lord Jesus Christ which had put the sentence of God's judgment both on the flesh and on the world. The apostle speaks of the cross in its application to himself as regards the world. Crucifixion was not merely death, but *a death of shame*. It was as though he said, "In the death of Christ the world-system has been gibbetted in my eyes, and I have been gibbetted in the world's eyes. I discard the world as a thing of shame, and it discards me as a thing of shame." And the remarkable thing is that in all *that* Paul gloried. He was not in the least depressed or lugubrious about it.

How was this? Well, he knew the value of the cross and he now had before his eyes the new creation of which the cross is the basis. In virtue of the cross he could be found "in Christ Jesus" and there new creation is, and circumcision and uncircumcision are alike of no account.

Paul walked according to *this* rule; that is, the rule of the cross and new creation. Such is the walk proper to every Christian. The cross is that which has put away all that is evil and offensive, whether sin or Satan, the flesh or the world. New creation introduces all that is of God and in Christ Jesus. To the new creation we, Christians, belong, so according to that rule we are to walk. Peace and mercy are on all such and on the true Israel—at present of course found incorporated in the church of God. The apostle so puts it here, we believe, to pour contempt on the Judaizing teachers who were advocating a spurious thing.

In this sixteenth verse we read of the believer's "walk" for the last time in this epistle. We have read of walking "according to the truth of the gospel" and of walking "in the Spirit." Now we learn we are to walk according to the rule of the new creation. A lofty standard this! But not too lofty seeing we already are brought into new creation in Christ Jesus, in spite of our still being in the body and the flesh still in us. Again we see how all that is true of us is to exert its influence on our lives today.

The epistle closes somewhat peremptorily, even as it opened. There is a feeling of restraint about the two closing verses. Paul had his critics, as he knew right well. They surrounded him in crowds, making all kinds of hostile insinuations, even challenging his apostleship. He brushes them and their objections aside. The Romans had a custom of branding their slaves and thus placing the question of their ownership beyond dispute. He was just like that. He was Christ's servant beyond all dispute. The floggings and stonings endured in His service had left His brand-marks on Paul's body. That was more than could be said of the sleek advocates of circumcision as they sat in their easy chairs. They had suffered nothing. They only knew how to instigate others to inflict suffering on such as Paul.

As for the Galatians, they were not the instigators of the wrong but only the victims of it, and Paul sought their deliverance in the grace of the Lord Jesus. If His grace was with their spirit all would be well.

For us too, the conclusion of the whole matter is this:—"It is a good thing that the heart be established with GRACE." (Heb. xiii. 9).

EPHESIANS 1

INTRODUCTION

AT THE CLOSE of the Epistle to the Romans we noticed that the Apostle Paul earnestly desired the establishment of the saints in a two-fold way; first, "according to my Gospel," and second, "according to the revelation of the mystery." Romans gives us a full unfolding of the former, while Ephesians more fully than any other epistle reveals to us the latter.

Romans moreover, while instructing us in the fulness of the grace of God, presents it to us as meeting in all particulars our need which has been created by sin. Ephesians, on the other hand, unfolds to us that grace of God which is according to His purpose. The words, "according as," or "according to," occur no less than six times in chapter i., and always in connection with His will, His pleasure, His purpose, His power, rather than our need.

A benevolent man of wealth might show great kindness to a poor lad of the streets charged with some petty offence. He might for instance, not only deliver him from the clutch of the law by paying a fine but deliver him from ignorance by having him educated, and from poverty by paying for his keep. That would be kindness in reference to his need. But if he formed designs to place him in a position of great nearness to himself and of great wealth and influence, that would be not according to his actual need but according to the pleasure and purpose of his own benevolent mind. This may serve as an illustration.

CHAPTER 1

AFTER THE OPENING words of salutation the Apostle goes straight to the heart of his theme in the spirit of a worshipper. We have been blessed in such rich fashion by the God and Father of our Lord Jesus Christ that He blesses God in return and carries our hearts with him in doing so. The blessings that are ours are characterized by three things. They are spiritual, not material as were Israel's blessings under the old covenant, in such matters as ample food and health and peace under divine rule. They are heavenly and not earthly, since the sphere where they are to be fully realized and consummated is heaven, and their present administration to us is from heaven. They are in Christ. He, as the risen One, and not Adam, the fallen one, is the Fountain-head of them all. If we are in Christ they all are ours.

But in blessing us after this wonderful fashion God has wrought in keeping with an act of His mind in a bygone eternity. Before the foundation of the world He chose us in Christ. Let those two words, "in Him," be noted, for again and again they, or their equivalents, occur in this chapter. As a matter of history we each were in Adam before we were in Christ, but before Adam was created, God saw us as in Christ, and on that basis we were chosen. What was in view in His choice was that we might be holy and blameless before Himself in love.

Such is the efficacy of the work of Christ that each believer today stands before God as holy and without blame, and is in the embrace of that divine love from which nothing can separate him. This we have seen in Romans viii. The full and ultimate application of these words in verse 4 must however, be carried on into a future eternity. It has been remarked that very little is said in the Bible in the way of a description of heaven; yet these words are practically just that. When the Spirit's work in us has reached its completion, including the quickening of our mortal bodies at the first resurrection, we shall be landed in heaven. We shall then be marked by perfect holiness of nature, and perfect freedom from all blame as to conduct. We shall be for ever in the presence of the God and Father of our Lord Jesus Christ in an atmosphere of perfect love. That will be heaven indeed. Thus verse 4 begins in a past eternity and ends in a future eternity.

Verse 5 carries matters a step further. God had in His mind a certain relationship for us and He destined us to that relationship when He chose us, even the state and place of sons. Now this was not a need or necessity on our side. We should still have been very happy if, rescued from our sin, we had been appointed to a place amongst His servants. The relationship is not according to our need but "according to the good pleasure of His will." How thankful we should be that the pleasure of His will is as good as this! We are sons of God now but we are going to stand forth in the full dignity and glory of sonship when heaven is reached. Then indeed the real glory of His grace will be manifested, and result in eternal praise.

In working out this glorious purpose, certain steps have been taken and these are now detailed for us—acceptance, redemption, forgiveness. We are working downwards to that which is simplest and most fundamental. In our understanding of things we usually begin with the forgiveness of sins. Then perhaps we apprehend the meaning of the redemption which we have in the blood of Christ, and begin to experience the freedom which that redemption has bought. Then on top of this comes the discovery of the fact that not only are we set free from slavery but that we stand in a positive acceptance before God, even in the acceptance of Christ, who is the Beloved One. His acceptance gives character to, and is the measure of, ours. In Colossians iii. 12 the saints are spoken of as beloved of God, and that of course flows out of the fact that they are accepted in the Beloved.

All this, whether it be redemption or forgiveness, is ours "according to the riches of His grace." We were in the poverty of our sin, and this has become the occasion for the display of the wealth of His grace. If we read 1 Kings x. we may see how Solomon gave to the Queen of Sheba all she desired, and then capped it by that which he gave her "of his royal bounty." He satisfied her large desires and then went beyond them in the superlative greatness of his kingly munificence. In this he acts as a type. God has acted according to His exceeding riches of grace. The very forgiveness of sins which He has accorded us has been granted in a style and with a fulness worthy of the great and gracious God He is.

But there is more. Not only has He thus abounded to us in connection with His grace, but also in connection with His wisdom. Verse 8 speaks of "wisdom and prudence [or, intelligence]." The secrets of His wisdom He has made known in order that we may intelligently enter into and enjoy them. God has always acted according to His own will, though in the presence of sin and its ravages He chose for long ages to keep the main purpose of His will as a secret or mystery; and the pleasure of His will and purpose has always been good, for He is good. This is a great fact that we do well to lay hold of firmly. The "pleasure of His will" is good (ver. 5). The "pleasure which He hath purposed in Himself" is good (ver. 9). God's pleasure and purpose is not connected with judgment, though that work, which He calls His "strange work," is necessary, and to be fulfilled in due season.

Verse 10 tells us what the real secret of His will and purpose is. In the coming age, spoken of here as "the fulness of times," He is going to gather together in one all things in Christ, both things earthly and things heavenly. No mention is made here of things infernal, for this predicted gathering together is in connection with a world of blessing, and consequently things infernal lie outside it. By establishing Christ as the exalted and glorified Head of all things there will be established on earth as well as in heaven a divine system of unity and blessing. Sin is lawlessness: it makes of every man in effect a little unit on his own, finding his only centre in himself. Hence during all these ages in which sin has been reigning, no matter how skilfully men try to engineer their unities, disintegration has been the order of the day. God has His unity. He is working towards it. When Christ is publicly established in glory as Head, God's purpose as to unity will be reached, as far as His government of heavenly and earthly things is concerned.

The coming age is going to witness at last the fullest possible harmony between the heavens and the earth, and Christ Head in both spheres, producing the unity. All is in Him. But then through grace we are already in Him, and thus have obtained an inheritance in all this wealth of blessing. That to which we are destined has been settled beforehand, not according to our need, nor even according to our thoughts or wishes, but according to the purpose of God, who effects all things as He pleases. We may be sure, as a consequence of this, that no possible slip can come between us and the inheritance to which we are destined.

The Apostle does not stop at this point to instruct us as to the particular character of this inheritance, but he does tell us that when all is consummated we shall be to the praise of God's glory. Angels and men will gaze at that which God has accomplished in regard to us, and they will see in it some fresh display of His glory and utter to Him their praise. We need not wait until that day. These things are made known to us so that instructed in them we may gain fresh glimpses of His glory and be filled with His praises now. We may enjoy communion with God about these purposes of His grace, and realizing that all centres in Christ and is for His glory, we find subject matter and material for our praise and worship.

As we pass from verse 12 to verse 13 we notice a change in the pronouns, from "we" to "ye." In writing, "we . . . who first trusted in Christ," the Apostle's mind was dwelling on saints gathered out of Israel including himself, whereas the "ye" referred to saints gathered out from the Gentiles. The Jewish believers were a kind of firstfruits of their nation. By and by a redeemed and restored Israel will be for Jehovah's praise on earth. But those who trusted in Christ beforehand during this gospel age will have part in the heavenly calling and be to His praise in the heavenly places.

In all this however, the Gentile believers fully shared. They too, had heard the Gospel which brought them salvation, and having believed it they had been sealed with the Spirit, who is the earnest of the inheritance. In His character as the seal, the Spirit marked them out as belonging to God. As the earnest He is the pledge of the inheritance which lies before us, and also He gives the foretaste of the blessings attached to it.

Let us carefully note the order set before us in this verse. First, the hearing of the Gospel. Second, the believing of it. Third, the receiving of the Spirit. This order is quite invariable. We never believe before we hear. We never receive before we believe. If any enquire, Have I received the Spirit? we have to propound to them the previous question, Have you heard and believed the Gospel of your salvation? The one proceeds out of and flows from the other.

Again we shall do well to notice the fact that not only did we trust in Christ but we were sealed with the holy Spirit of promise in Christ. "*In whom* . . . ye were sealed." All is found to be in Christ. The Holy Spirit is a divine Person in the Godhead and to be distinguished from Christ, yet we must not totally separate Him from Christ in our minds. This is the case with all the three sacred Persons. They are to be distinguished but not separated. The Spirit has been sent by Christ from the Father, and in Christ He has sealed us—sealed us, you see until the whole possession purchased by the death of the cross is redeemed from the last adverse power that tends to hold it in bondage; that is, until the coming of the Lord. The Spirit is given to abide with us for ever. We may grieve Him but we cannot grieve Him away.

Having thus given an unfolding of the characteristic blessings of the individual Christian, Paul proceeds to tell the Ephesians of his thanksgivings and prayers on their behalf. He gave thanks for them as he thought of the wealth of spiritual blessing into which they had been introduced, and his prayer was that they might have an intelligent and spiritual understanding of all connected with the calling and inheritance which was theirs. We may be very certain that what he desired for the Ephesians is just what is highly desirable for us today.

In these prayers the Apostle addressed himself to "the God of our Lord Jesus Christ, the Father of glory." God is indeed the Originator and Source of all glory, and to Him our Lord Jesus, when here as the subject Man, looked up as His God, as we see prophetically expressed in Psalm xvi. Our thoughts are thus fittingly directed to the place which the Lord Jesus took as Man, inasmuch as it is as Man that He takes His place as the exalted Head in the wide creation of blessing. Further it is in Him as Man that we see the Pattern and Fulness of all that which is ours in Him. Everything is expressed in Christ, and we have nothing apart from Christ. The thing so greatly to be desired is that we may have the full knowledge of all that is purposed in connection with Him.

We come to know the wonders of God's purposes and work in connection with the knowledge of Himself. As we know Him we know that which springs forth from Him. Hence the first request of the Apostle concerns "the spirit of wisdom and revelation in the knowledge of Him." We can only know Him by revelation, since by no amount of searching can we discover Him; and again on our side wisdom is needed, that spirit of wisdom which comes from the Spirit of God.

The word, "understanding," in verse 18 should really be, "heart." It is not a matter of cold intellectual understanding but rather the understanding of warm affection. Can anything be cold which centres in Christ? And it does centre in Christ; for though the "Him" which closes verse 17 grammatically refers to God the Father, it cannot but also point to Christ, for He alone is the Revealer of the Father. To have the full knowledge of the Father we must know Christ, the Son.

In the first place, the prayer of the Apostle concerned itself with the spiritual state of his readers. The things of God can only be discerned by those who have the eyes of their heart enlightened. Many things there are, both in the world around us and the flesh within, which if permitted by us, inevitably form a kind of cataract film upon our spiritual eyes and hinder our understanding. This helps us to understand why in writing to Timothy Paul said, "Take heed unto thyself and unto the doctrine." Except he began by taking heed to himself he was not likely to obtain much good from the doctrine. Nor are we.

After that, the prayer divides itself into three parts, concerning respectively the calling, the inheritance and the power by which God brings to pass His purposes concerning us. The calling has been indicated in verses 3 to 7, and the inheritance in verses 10 to 14, whereas the power had not previously been mentioned, but is opened up to us in the closing verses of our chapter and in chapter ii.

We might perhaps sum up "His calling," as expounded to us in those earlier verses, in the one word, *sonship.* The prayer however is not merely that we may know the calling, but rather what is the *hope* of His calling. Well, what is this hope? If He who calls is GOD; if the place to which we are called is that of SONS; if that place is ours "by Jesus Christ," and as— "IN CHRIST;" what are we to expect? What but *heavenly glory?*

This indeed was no small prayer. Are we disposed to regard it lightly— and say, Oh, but we all know that: we all expect to go to heaven when we die—we only thereby show that we do not really know as yet what the hope involves and signifies. Were the eyes of our hearts so enlightened that we really knew it, we should be thoroughly delivered from the ensnaring attractions of the world-system that surrounds us. We should be wholly lifted above its unhallowed influences, and thus fitted to go through it in a way that glorifies God.

Nor are we only to know what is the inheritance. That knowledge might easily be arrived at in an intellectual way by reading the few verses that speak of it. But what are the riches of the glory of that inheritance? It is His inheritance, you notice, not ours: and it is "in the saints," which means, we understand, not so much that the saints form the inheritance— though they form part of it, no doubt—as that it is by and in the saints that He will take up His inheritance.

When God took Israel across the Jordan to conquer the land of Canaan, He took the initiative Himself by means of the ark. It was said, "The ark of the covenant of the Lord of all the earth passeth over before you into Jordan" (Joshua iii. 11). The position was that God took possession of the land *in* His people Israel; that is, by putting them into possession. Presently He will make good His claim to the whole earth *in Israel*, and the glory of the millennial age will commence. It will be very great glory on earth. Now what will be the riches of that heavenly glory when Satan and his hosts are cast out of heaven, and the saints established in the heavens, and, as verse 10 has told us, Christ is the supreme and unifying centre in those realms of blessedness? It will be riches beyond all our conceptions. Only the Father of glory can give us the spiritual eyesight to take it in.

Thirdly, we are to know the greatness of the power of God, which acts on behalf of us who have believed. That power has fully expressed itself in the raising of Christ from the dead and in His exaltation, and is now actively working towards us. We have only to think of the resurrection and exaltation of Christ to realize how appropriate is the adjective, "exceeding," or, "surpassing." His power is characterized not merely by greatness but by *surpassing* greatness.

We do well to bear in mind that when the Lord Jesus went into death He put Himself, if we may so say, beneath all the weight of antagonistic human power, and also all the power of darkness wielded by Satan, and further beneath all the weight of the divine judgment due to sin. Out of all this and into resurrection He was lifted by the power of God. This emphasizes very clearly the greatness of the power of God.

But further, we have to consider all that into which He has been lifted, as detailed in the closing verses of chapter i. Here we see a greatness which is surpassing indeed. He is gone into the heavenly places and is seated at the right hand of God; that is, in the place of supreme administration. In that position He is above every other name and every other power, whether in this age or the age to come. And not merely above, but "far above." No comparison can be instituted between any other and Him. All things are put beneath His feet, and He is given to be Head over all things. All these things are facts, though as yet we do not see all things subjected to Him.

There is in all this something which very intimately concerns ourselves. In that place of extreme exaltation where He is Head *over* all things, He is Head *to* the church which is His body. To that church every true believer belongs. There is a great difference between the significance of these two prepositions, which may be illustrated by the case of Adam, who is "the figure of Him that was to come." Adam was created to be head *over* all other created things that filled the garden, but he was head *to* Eve, who was his body as well as his wife. The second headship is far more intimate and wonderful than the first.

Christ is not only Head over all things but He is to fill all things, so that all things are ultimately to take their character from Him. The church is His body and consequently His fulness—the body in which He is adequately expressed. This passage evidently contemplates the church in its largest and widest aspect, as the sum total of the saints of this dispensation; that is, the saints called out between the coming of the Spirit on the day of Pentecost and the coming again of the Lord Jesus.

CHAPTER 2

THE CHURCH IS not yet completed, and the saints are here in weakness, but our Head is exalted far above all by the surpassing greatness of divine power, and this exhibits how great is the power that works toward us in life-giving energy. Hence chapter ii. simply opens with, "And you, who were dead in trespasses and sins." God's power has wrought, "in Christ . . . and you." It wrought in Christ when He was dead *on account of* our trespasses and sins. It wrought in us when we were dead *in* our own trespasses and sins. His quickening power in us is according to that supreme display which took place in regard to Christ.

In verses 2 and 3 we again meet with the distinction between the Gentile "ye" and the Jewish "we." Yet both had their activities in that which was wholly evil. The walk of the Gentile is declared to have been particularly characterized by the world and the devil, inasmuch as they followed false gods, behind which lay the power of demons. The walk of the Jew was more particularly characterized by the lusts of the flesh, as verse 3 indicates. They were not worshipping demons, but they were by nature the children of wrath, just as others. Just the same indictments may be brought today against those who are openly irreligious and profane, and those who profess a form of piety, yet simply follow "the desires of the flesh and of the mind." The desires of the mind may have often a very attractive and even intellectual appearance, and yet be wholly astray from God.

Such were we, whether Jew or Gentile. At one and the same moment we were dead in trespasses and sins and yet active in all kinds of evil. Very much alive to everything wrong, yet wholly dead to God. Being dead towards God we were without any point of recovery in ourselves: our only hope lay in Him. Hence the great words with which verse 4 opens, "But God —"

What has God done? We were full of sins and were subject to the wrath that sins deserve. God is rich in mercy and toward such as ourselves He had great love. Accordingly He has made us to live together with Christ. And not only have we been made to live but we have been raised up and made to sit in the heavenly places in Christ Jesus. Let us note three things in connection with this striking passage.

First, observe that since it is wholly a question of God, His purpose and His actings, we are carried clean outside all question of time. That which is not to us exists for Him. Hence our sitting in heavenly places is an accomplished thing to Him, and is so spoken of here.

Second, observe how the word "together," occurs. In our unconverted state, as Jews or Gentiles, as the case may have been, we were very different and very antagonistic. Now all that has been done has been done in regard to us together; all differences having been abolished.

Third, all that God has done He has wrought in connection with Christ. If we have been quickened, it has been together with Christ. If raised up and seated in heavenly places, it has been in Christ. Two prepositions are used, *with* and *in*. We have already been actually quickened in the sense of John v. 25, though we wait for the quickening of our mortal bodies. As quickened we live in association *with* Christ, because living of His life. We have not yet been actually raised up and seated in the heavens, but Christ has and He is our exalted Head. We are in Him, and consequently raised up and seated *in* Him. Presently we shall actually be raised up and seated with Him.

We have only to meditate a moment on these wonderful things to be assured that none of them has been accomplished according to our need, but according to the mind and heart and purpose of God. Hence, when all is brought to final fruition in the coming ages, the marvellous kindness shown in Christ Jesus towards us will display the surpassing riches of the grace of God. God is indeed the God of all grace. His dealings with Israel, blessing them ultimately in spite of all their unfaithfulness, will redound to the praise of His grace. But when we think of what and where we were, according to verses 1-3, and then contemplate the heights to which we are lifted, according to verses 4-6, we can see that His dealings with us set forth a richness of grace that surpasses anything seen in Israel or anywhere else.

The contemplation of it leads the Apostle to again emphasize the fact that our salvation is all of grace. He had stated this previously, in verse 5, in a parenthetical way. In verse 8 he enlarges upon this important fact, and adds that it is also through faith. The grace is God's: the faith is ours. Yet even our faith is not *of* ourselves. Faith is not a natural product of the human heart. The weeds that grow by nature in the heart of man are detailed for us in Romans iii. 9-19. Faith is no weed at all, but rather a choice flower which once planted by the heavenly Father can never be rooted up. It is the gift of God.

Now this necessarily excludes works; that is, works done in order to obtain life and blessing. The only works of which we were capable were those detailed in verses 2 and 3, and in those works we were spritually dead. God Himself is the Worker and we are His workmanship; a very different thing. Further, the work necessary was nothing short of *creation*. How obvious then that human works must be excluded.

God has created us, you observe, in Christ Jesus. This is new creation. We were in Adam according to the old creation, but the Adamic life has been wholly corrupted. We have now been created in Christ Jesus with a view to our walking in good works in the midst of this world of sin.

This brings us back to the point with which we started. The surpassing greatness of the power of God, which wrought in the resurrection of the Lord Jesus, was needed to accomplish so mighty a work in us.

We have been newly created in Christ Jesus, as stated in verse 10. This is the work of God *in* us, but it is not to be dissociated from the work of God wrought *for* us by the blood and cross of Christ. From verse 11 to the end of the chapter we are bidden to remember three things: the depths from which we Gentiles have been brought; the heights to which we have been introduced; the basis upon which the mighty transference has been accomplished—the death of Christ.

The picture of the natural condition of Gentiles, drawn by the Apostle in verses 11 and 12, is a very dark one. Nor is it made any brighter for us today by reason of our living in the midst of a civilization which has been slightly christianized. It matters little that we should be called Uncircumcision by the Jew: but the other six items in the count against us matter very much indeed.

Being "in the flesh," means that the fallen Adamic nature characterized our state, and consequently controlled us. This alone would account for all the gross evil which fills the Gentile world.

But then we were "without Christ." Without, that is, the only One who could bring in any way of salvation from our lost estate.

Again, God had at an earlier date brought in certain very definite privileges. He established the commonwealth of Israel, making them the depositories of the covenants of promise, though putting them for the moment under the covenant of law. And further, inasmuch as they did have the covenants of promise they were the only people with definite hopes securely founded upon the Word of God. As regards all this the Gentiles were "aliens" and "strangers" and "without hope." Not a streak of light appeared upon their dark horizon.

Lastly they were "without God in the world." Idols they had without number, and the modern world has them too, though in a different form. God was, and is, unknown.

To sum it all up: they had the flesh and the world, but they had no Christ, no privilege, no hope and no God. We too were in exactly the same plight.

Now let us turn to survey that into which we have been brought, as detailed in verses 13 to 22. First of all we have been "made nigh" in Christ Jesus. Being made nigh means that we now have God. The blood of Christ has given us a righteous place in His presence, and the wonderful thing is that we are brought near as introduced into a wholly new relationship. This is indicated in verse 18. Our access to Him is not merely as God, but as Father.

In what way are we made nigh? Israel had a certain nearness under the old covenant. Are we to be a kind of duplicate of them? No, for according to verse 14 both have been made one. The word, "both" indicates believing Jews on the one hand, and believing Gentiles on the other. This oneness has been brought to pass by Christ. He has broken down the dividing wall and made peace between the warring factions. He has abolished the enmity in His flesh: that is, by the offering up of His body in death.

The enmity was connected with "the law of commandments contained in ordinances." The law of Moses contained great moral enactments, which are never abrogated, but there were also many ordinances of a ceremonial nature connected with it. These ceremonial rules separated

Israel from the nations by making them a peculiar people in their habits; indeed, they were intended so to do. Such ordinances were annulled for believers in the death of Christ, and at once this great cause of hostility was removed. Acts xxi. 20-26, shows how little this was realized by the early believers in Jerusalem, and how even Paul himself seems to have been for the moment deflected from what he here lays down. We see in that passage also how great the hostility was on the part of Jews; an hostility which was fully reciprocated by the Gentiles.

Having thus abolished the enmity, the Christ has made the two into one *in Himself*. It is not that the Gentile is now one with the Jew, but that the Jew in Christ is now absolutely one with the Gentile in Christ. Both are found in a position and condition before God which is wholly fresh and original. They are no longer two men but *one* man, and that man is altogether *new*. This is a complete solution of the enmity difficulty—"so making peace." Two men might quarrel. One man cannot very well do so. And he has no inclination to do so, for he is a new kind of man. In all this we are of course looking at what God has accomplished in an abstract way: that is, according to its essential character, and without introducing those modifications found in our practice, owing to the flesh still being found in us.

Verse 16 brings in an additional thought. Not only are believing Jews and Gentiles one new man—that expresses their new *character*—but they are formed into one *body*, and as such reconciled to God. Reconciliation was needed because they both were in a state of enmity Godward, as well as being in a state of enmity between themselves. Again, you notice, the death of Christ is introduced; this time as, "the cross." By it He slew the enmity—that enmity Godward, which was in the hearts of both, and not only the enmity they had cherished between each other.

Having done it, and thus effected the great basis of reconciliation, He has Himself acted as the Messenger of peace to both Gentile and Jew. The former were "afar off" in the old dispensation, and the latter were "nigh." This is a remarkable sentence. Christ is presented as a Preacher to Gentiles and to Jews *after the cross;* that is, *in resurrection*. Yet, as far as we are told in Scripture, He has never been seen or heard by any unconverted person since He was hanging dead upon the cross. He did appear in resurrection to His disciples and speak peace to them, but when did He preach peace to either Jews or Gentiles? The only answer we can give is—Never at all in Person. He only did it by means of the apostolic preaching, or in other words, by proxy.

This mode of speaking may seem to us somewhat strange, but it is found elsewhere in the Bible. I Peter iii. 19, is a striking example, and verse 11 of chapter i. in the same epistle furnishes us with something very similar. If the verse in 1 Peter iii. had been read in the light of Ephesians ii. 17, we should have been spared many mistaken explanations of the

EPHESIANS

former passage, for there can be no doubt that the preaching alluded to here was that of the apostles and other servants of Christ, who in the earliest years of Christianity carried the tidings of peace far and wide.

The word, *one*, occurs for the fourth time in verse 18. It is evident that special emphasis is laid upon the word. Verse 14 states the fact that we are one. Verse 15 adds the fact that it is as one new man. Verse 16 shows that we are one body. Verse 18 completes the story by showing that we both are given to possess one Spirit, whereby we have access to the Father. How evident it is then that in the Christian circle all distinction between Jew and Gentile is completely gone.

These glorious facts being established, Paul introduces these Gentile believers to the height of their spiritual privilege. They were no longer strangers and foreigners, nor are we: rather we are fellow-citizens with the saints and of the Divine household, and built into the structure that God is rearing. Three figures are laid under contribution in these closing four verses—the city, the household, the building. It would seem as if we are introduced step by step to that which is more intimate.

We are fellow-citizens with the saints. This is rather a general thought. God has prepared a heavenly city for believers of Old Testament days, who are to enjoy a heavenly portion. This is stated in Hebrews xi. 16. In all that heavenly portion believers of this day are to share. Its privileges are ours, for our names have been written in heaven (see, Luke x. 20); inscribed upon its rolls we can say that our citizenship is there.

An household is a place of greater intimacy than a city. The Lord Mayor of London, for instance, appears in greater splendour when he acts in that capacity as the head of the City, but he is known more intimately when he has laid aside the proud trappings of his high office and acts simply as the head of his own household. Now we are not merely citizens but are also of God's household. Thus it is that we are brought near and have such liberty of access; but thus also it is that we are responsible to wear the character of that One to whose household we belong.

When we come to the thought of the building we have to consider ourselves as stones—as suitable material for the structure—and God Himself as the Builder on the one hand, and as the One who dwells within the shrine when constructed, on the other. The house of the Lord is where one may behold "the beauty of the Lord" (Psa. xxvii. 4). In the temple of God, "doth every one speak of His glory" (Psa. xxix. 9), or as the margin has it, "every whit of it uttereth, glory." That we should be thus "fitted together" on the foundation of the apostles and prophets, Jesus Christ Himself being the chief corner stone, and all speaking forth the glory of God is a matter of extraordinary intimacy indeed. The wonder of it is increased when we remember that we were nothing but Gentiles by nature.

The third figure, that of the building, sub-divides itself under two heads. There is first the building viewed as a progressive work all through the

45

present age and only reaching its completion in glory, though each stone that is added is fitly framed together. Completed, it will indeed speak forth the glory of God.

Secondly there is the building viewed as an habitation of God all through the present age—a complete thing at any given moment, though those who constitute it change. All along from the Day of Pentecost God has dwelt in the church through the Spirit—that church which is composed of every Spirit-indwelt believer on earth at any given moment. He does not dwell in temples made with hands, but in this house He does dwell by His Spirit.

Let us not overlook the two words with which both verses 21 and 22 open—"in whom." When we were considering the blessing into which we are brought as individuals we saw all was ours in Christ. It is just the same when we consider the blessing in which we stand in a collective or corporate way. All is in Christ. The church is builded together *in Christ*, and God dwells in it *in Spirit*.

All these things are not just ideas, but rather great realities. If perchance they sound strange in our ears, is it not because we are more familiar with what men have made of the church, largely perverting it according to their own ideas, than with what the church really is according to God? And remember, all men's perversions and adaptations will pass, and God's handiwork will remain. So we had better make haste to acquaint ourselves with what God has made the church to be, otherwise all too much of our service may be lost, and we ourselves be sadly unprepared for what will be revealed when the Lord comes, and in the twinkling of an eye the church comes forth *altogether* according to divine workmanship and *not at all* according to man's organization.

CHAPTER 3

HAVING PRESENTED US with this great unfolding of truth, Paul commences to exhort us to walk in a way that shall be worthy of such an exalted vocation. This may be seen if the first verses of chapters iii. and iv. are read together. The whole of chapter iii. excepting verse 1, is a parenthesis, in which he points out how definitely the Lord had entrusted to him the ministry of all this truth—which he calls, "the mystery"—and in which he again puts on record that which he prayed for the Ephesian believers.

He evidently felt that his exhortation to walk worthy would come with greater force if we realised how fully the authority of the Lord was behind it. A "dispensation" or "administration," of the grace of God towards such as ourselves had been committed to him, inasmuch as "the mystery" had been specially revealed to him, and he had just previously written concerning it in brief fashion. He alludes evidently to what he had written in chapter i. 19—ii. 22. An even briefer summary of it is given in verse 6 of chapter iii. where again the wonderful place given to Gentiles is emphasized. The three words in that verse have been translated, "Joint-heirs, a joint-body and joint-partakers." This may be clumsy English, but it has the merit of making us see the main thought of the Spirit of God in the verse. Now *that* was a feature, of God's purpose in blessing, wholly unknown in earlier ages: necessarily unknown, of course; for once known the order of things established in connection with the law and Israel was destroyed. It was therefore a secret hid in God until Christ was exalted on high and the Holy Spirit given below.

Now however it is revealed, and the apostle Paul was made the minister of it. It was not only revealed to him but to the other apostles and prophets also. Thus the fact of it was placed beyond all doubt or dispute. Yet the ministry of it was given to Paul, as verse 7 clearly states. In keeping with this we do not find any allusion to the mystery in any of the epistles save Paul's.

How great a theme it is, we can realize if we have at all taken in the things we have just been superficially surveying. Paul himself was so impressed with its greatness that he alludes to his ministry of it as, evangelizing "the unsearchable riches of Christ."

If we read this expression, "the unsearchable riches of Christ," in its context, we perceive that it refers, not to all the wealth that is personally His, but rather to all that which is *in Him* for His saints. Scanning chapter i, we find that the term, "in Christ," (or its equivalents, "in the Beloved," "in Him," "in whom") occurs about twelve times. In chapter ii, it occurs about six times, and in chapter iii, about three. Let us take one item only, "Blessed . . . with all spiritual blessings in heavenly places in Christ." Can we search or trace those blessings out, so that we are thoroughly masters of the whole subject? We can do no such thing. They are too big for our little grasp. They are unsearchable; and so too is all that which we have in Christ. Yet though unsearchable they may be known by us, and so they were the subject of the Apostle's ministry.

A second thing was covered by his ministry. He was commissioned to make all see, not only what the mystery is, but what is the "fellowship of the mystery," or, "the administration of the mystery." (N. Tr.). The mystery is concerning Christ and the church, and particularly concerning the place that Gentiles occupy in it, as has already been explained by Paul. The administration concerns the practical arrangements for assembly life and order and testimony, which Paul everywhere established. These arrangements were ordered by the Lord that there might be a representation, even today in the church's time condition, of those things which are true and established concerning it in God's eternal counsel.

The mystery itself was something entirely new, for from the beginning of the world up to that moment it had been hid in God. Consequently the administration of the mystery was entirely new. Previously God had been dealing with one special nation on the basis of law. Now God was calling out an election from all nations according to grace, and that which was merely national was submerged in this larger and fuller purpose. In the church of God everything has to be ordered or administrated according to these present purposes of God. The Apostle does not stop in this epistle to instruct us in the details of this divinely ordered administration; he does this in writing his first epistle to the Corinthians.

The assembly at Corinth was not walking in an orderly way, as were those at Ephesus and Colosse. There was a good deal of ignorance, error and disorder in their midst, and this furnished the occasion for the Spirit of God to enforce upon them the administration of the mystery, at least in a good many of its details, dealing with matters of a public nature which an ordinary onlooker might observe. That the point of this may not be missed we take up one detail out of the many, to serve as an illustration.

Our epistle lays it down that we, whether Jews or Gentiles, "are builded together for an habitation of God through the Spirit." This is one of the great items included in the mystery. We turn to the Corinthian epistle and we discover that this is not a mere doctrine, an idea divorced from any practical effect in the present ordering of church life and behaviour. The very opposite. Paul declares that consequently the Spirit is supreme in that house where He dwells. He dwells there in order that He may operate to the glory of God—"All these worketh that one and the selfsame Spirit, dividing to every man severally as He will" (1 Cor. xii. 11). In chapter xiv. of the same epistle we find the Spirit ordering and energizing in the exercise of the various gifts, and we are bidden to acknowledge that the instructions given are "the commandments of the Lord." The Lord, you see, is the great Administrator in the church of God, and Paul was the chosen servant to make known His administration to us.

The administration of the mystery is, we fear, very lightly brushed aside by many Christians today, even by good and earnest ones, but we are assured that they do so to their own great loss, both now and in the coming age. If we neglect any part of the truth we become undeveloped as to that part and like "a cake not turned," as Hosea puts it. Also we have to take into consideration verses 10 and 11 of our chapter, which tell us that the administration of the mystery, as worked out in the assembly, is a kind of lesson book before the eyes of angels. The lesson book of today on which the eyes of angels look down, is very sadly blotted and obscured. Yet, since angels do not die, those same eyes once looked down and saw the beauty of the manifold wisdom of God, when the excellence of the Divine administration, ministered through Paul, was first seen in the church's earliest days.

Then for a brief moment things were "according to the eternal purpose which He purposed in Christ Jesus our Lord." Now for many a long day they have mainly been according to the disconnected desires and arrangements of men, though many of the men who made the arrangements were doubtless godly and well-meaning people. May we have grace to adhere, as far as in us lies, to the administration as ordered by God, for it is evidently intended that what was "hid in God" should now be made "known by the church." At the same time let us not expect to do so without opposition and trouble, for Paul was face to face with tribulation enough, as he hints in verse 13.

Moreover we do not very easily or speedily enter into the power and enjoyment of these things. Hence again at this point the Apostle betakes himself to prayer, and is led to record his prayer that we may be stirred up by it. The prayer is addressed to the Father, and it is concerned with the operations of the Spirit with a view to Christ having His due place in our hearts. Father, Son and Holy Ghost are thus involved in it.

The Father is addressed as imparting His own Name and character to every family that will ultimately fill the heavens and the earth. The Lord Jesus is our Head, and He is also in some sense the Head and Leader of every one of these different families. It should be "every family" and not "the whole family." God will have many families, some for heaven and some for earth. Amongst the heavenly families will be the church and "the spirits of just men made perfect," i.e. Old Testament saints. For the earth there will be Israel, redeemed Gentiles, and so on. Now amongst men every family takes its name from the one who is father to it, the one from whom it derives its origin. But fatherhood amongst men is only a reflection of the divine Fatherhood.

The main burden of the prayer is that Christ may dwell by faith in our hearts, that He may be abidingly the controlling centre of our deepest affections. This can only be as we are strengthened by the Spirit's mighty power in the inner man, for naturally that which is selfish controls us, and we are fickle and uncertain. Christ dwelling in our hearts, we become rooted and grounded in love, His love not ours. Only as rooted and grounded in love can we proceed to know the love of Christ which surpasses all knowledge.

Verse 17 speaks of that which lies at the very centre of all, the indwelling Christ and the consequent rooting and grounding in love. Verses 18 and 19 pass on to the widest possible circle of blessing, love and glory. A pair of compasses may serve as an illustration. It is not easy to draw a circle except one leg be firmly fixed. With one leg fixed the circle can easily be described. So it is here. Fixed and rooted in love, the mighty sweep of verse 18 becomes possible.

If verse 19 tells us we are to know that which passes all knowledge, verse 18 infers we are to apprehend that which eludes all proper definition.

Four dimensions are enumerated, but we are not told to what they refer. The dimensions of what? Doubtless of all the great truth which Paul had been unfolding, the dimensions of the unsearchable riches of Christ. These things are only to be apprehended with all saints. We need one another as we begin to learn them. All saints should be keen to apprehend them, and they are only to be apprehended as all saints are kept in view. In these days of brokenness and division in the church of God we cannot bring all saints together, nor can we incite all saints to apprehend these things, but we can cling very tenaciously to the divine thought of all saints, and, as far as in us lies, live and act in view of all saints. They who do this are more likely than others to apprehend the mighty scope of the unsearchable riches of Christ, to know His love which is centred upon all saints, and to be filled with all the fulness of God.

The contemplation, in prayer, of such heights of spiritual light and affections and blessing moved the heart of the Apostle to worship, and the chapter closes with a doxology ascribing glory to the Father. That which he had desired in his prayer would be impossible of accomplishment were it not that there is power that worketh in us, the Holy Spirit of God. By that Power the Father can accomplish that which overwhelmingly surpasses all our thoughts or desires. Many of us, reading the Apostle's desires for us, may have said to ourselves—Very wonderful, but altogether beyond me. Yet, be it remembered, not beyond the Power that works in us. All this blessing may be really and consciously ours: ours in present possession.

The glory which the last verse ascribes to God will certainly be His. Throughout all ages the church will irradiate His glory. As the bride, the Lamb's wife, it will be said of her, "Having the glory of God: and her light was like unto a stone most precious, even like a jasper stone, clear as crystal" (Rev. xxi. 11). And all that the church is, and all that she ever will be, is by and in Christ Jesus. Christ Jesus is the most glorious Minister of the glory of God. He has wrought out the glory, and covered Himself with glory in doing it. Thus it is that we can so happily sing,

> There Christ the Centre of the throng,
> Shall in His glory shine,
> But not an eye those hosts among,
> But sees His glory Thine.

CHAPTER 4

As WE OPEN chapter iv. we pick up the thread which Paul dropped at the end of the first verse of chapter iii. In comparatively few words we have had brought before us the Christian calling in its height and fulness according to the thoughts and purposes of God. Moreover that calling has been unfolded to us, not only as it relates to us each individually, but also as it concerns us all together in our corporate or church capacity. Now comes the exhortation of a general character, and it covers all the more detailed exhortations with which the main part of the remaining chapters is filled. Still the Apostle knew right well that it is not enough to give general instructions, but that very intimate and pointed details are necessary, such as may get home to every heart and conscience. Let those who minister today take heed to this and be as wise and courageous as he.

The exhortations comprised in the first section of chapter iv. down to verse 16, have evidently in view our calling, not as individuals but rather as members of the body of Christ, the church. In the assemblies of the saints how often friction occurs! A little experience of assembly life will suffice to convince us that this is so. Here then is an immense field for the cultivation of the beautiful graces enumerated in verse 2. The lowly mind thinks nothing of itself. Meekness, the opposite of self-assertiveness, is of course the direct outcome of lowliness. Longsuffering, the opposite of the hasty spirit so critical of others, is the child of lowliness and meekness. When all these three are in operation how simply and happily do we bear with one another in love. Let us connect the love also with what we have just been seeing in chapter iii. Rooted and grounded in love, and knowing at least something of the knowledge-surpassing love of Christ, we ourselves are enabled with eyes of love, to look out on all saints, even those amongst them who according to nature are least lovable.

Amongst men we see the tendency for love to degenerate into a kind of soft amiability, which ends with condoning all kinds of things which are far from right. Thus it is not to be amongst saints, inasmuch as a very definite standard is set before us. We are to aim, not merely at agreement, for we might all be of one mind and in the sweetest agreement in favour of something entirely wrong! We are to give all diligence to keeping the unity of the Spirit—not Paul's unity, not Peter's, not yours nor mine, but rather that unity which the Spirit has produced. We did not make the unity, and we cannot break the unity. The Spirit made it and we are to keep it in a practical way in the uniting bond of peace. That is to be our constant endeavour. Our success in that endeavour will depend upon the measure in which we are marked by the beautiful features mentioned in verse 2.

If verse 2 of our chapter gives us the characteristics which, being developed in us, will lead to the keeping of the unity of the Spirit, verses 4-6 give us a series of unities which strongly support the exhortation of verse 3. The word "one" occurs seven times in these three verses.

First we have the oneness of the body of Christ, which is composed of all the saints of the present dispensation. This body has been formed by the baptism and indwelling of the one Spirit, and every member of that body shares in a common calling, which has one hope in view. Nothing that is unreal enters into this body. All is vital here in the life and energy of the Spirit.

Next we have the Lord, and the faith and the baptism that are connected with Him. Oneness is stamped upon these things connected with the Lord, equally with all that is connected with the Spirit; though the faith may be professed and baptism be accepted by some, who afterwards turn out to be nothing more than mere professors.

Then we come to God the Father, and here again oneness is pressed upon us since we all find our origin in Him. And further, though He is above all and through all, He is in all of us.

In these seven unities is found the foundation and support of the unity of the Spirit, which we are responsible to keep. It is buttressed in this sevenfold way, which is a definite testimony to its importance, as also to our frailty in keeping it. We are one, and that by the presence and action of the Spirit of God. We may fail to keep the unity, yet the unity will not thereby cease to exist, since it stands in the energy of God.

On the other hand we are great losers, and the testimony of God suffers, as we fail to keep it. The very divided state of the people of God proclaims how grievously we have failed in this respect, and it accounts very largely for the weakness, the lack of spiritual insight and vigour, which prevails. We cannot rectify the present divided state of things, but we can make it our aim to pursue the unity which is of the Spirit of God with all lowliness, meekness, longsuffering and forbearance. Only it must be the Spirit's unity. To aim at keeping any other unity, yours, mine or any one else's, is to miss the unity of the Spirit.

Moreover unity does not mean a dead uniformity. Verse 7 is plain testimony to this. We all are one, yet to each of us is given both gift and grace that is peculiar to ourselves. This thought leads the Apostle to refer to those gifts of a special yet abiding nature, which have been bestowed by the ascended Christ in proof and manifestation of His victory.

The quotation in verse 8 is from Psalm lxviii., a Psalm which celebrates prophetically the Divine victory over rebellious kings and all His enemies, which will usher in the glorious millennial age. The Apostle knew that the victory, to be publicly manifested then, had been already accomplished in the death, the resurrection, the ascension of Christ. Hence he appropriates these words from the Psalm and applies them to the ascended Christ before the day of millennial victory arrives. Having conquered Satan in death, his last stronghold, He has gone on high, having brought into subjection to Himself those who had been the slaves of Satan. Then He signalized His victory by bestowing on those, who are now captivated by Him, spiritual powers which should suffice for the carrying on of His work, even while they are yet in the place where Satan is permitted still to exercise his wiles.

Verses 9 and 10, as we notice, are parenthetical. They emphasize two things. First, that ere He ascended He had first to go down to death, where

He vanquished the power of the enemy, and even the grave. Second, that having achieved victory He is supreme in exaltation, with a view to the filling of all things.

"Far above all heavens," is a remarkable expression. In Mark xvi. we have the Divine Servant "received up into heaven." In Hebrews iv. the great High Priest is "passed through the heavens." Here the victorious Man is "ascended up far above all heavens." The very heaven of heavens is His, and it is His that He may "fill all things;" another remarkable word. Even today each believer should be filled with the Spirit as we see a little further on in this epistle. Each believer who is filled with the Spirit is necessarily filled with Christ, and consequently Christ comes out of him. If filled with Christ we display His character. The day is coming when Christ will fill all things, and consequently all things will display Him and His glory. The "all things" spoken of here is of course all things that in any way come under His headship—all things within the universe of blessing.

Verse 11 reads straight on from verse 8. The four great gifts are specified. Apostles, the men sent forth for the establishment of the church, through whom in the main the inspired Scriptures have reached us. Prophets, men raised up to speak on God's behalf, conveying His mind; whether doing so by inspiration, as in the earliest days of the church, or not. Evangelists, who carry forth into the world that great message which avails when received, to rescue men from the enemy's power. Pastors and teachers, those qualified to instruct believers in the truth revealed, and to apply it to their actual state, so that they may be fed and maintained in growth and spiritual health.

The simple meaning of the word translated, "pastor," is "shepherd," and the words, "shepherds and teachers," describe not two gifts but one. Let this be taken to heart by any who are gifted in this direction. No one can very well act as shepherd without doing a little teaching, but it is possible for a very gifted man so to concentrate on teaching that he never concerns himself to act as a shepherd; and this in practice proves very hurtful both to himself and to his hearers.

The objects in view in the giving of the gifts are stated in verses 12-15. The saints are to be perfected, qualified each to take their due place in the body of Christ. The work of the ministry is to be carried on, and thus the body be built up. And all this is to proceed until God's purpose as to the body is carried to its completion. Until then the gifts abide. The gifts in this passage, be it remembered, are not exactly certain powers conferred; but rather the men who possess these powers, who are conferred as gifts upon the church. Apostles and inspired prophets remain in the Scriptures that came from their pens. Uninspired prophets, together with evangelists and also pastors and teachers, are found in the church even to this day.

The ultimate objective contemplated in the bestowal of the gifts is stated in verse 13. We are to arrive at "a full-grown man," and that according to the measure of that which is God's purpose for us. As the body of Christ we are to be His fulness (see, i. 23) and up to the measure of the stature of that fulness we are to come. We shall arrive there in oneness—that oneness which springs from the faith fully apprehended and the Son of God really known.

Again, God's objective in connection with the gifts is set before us in verses 14 and 15, but this time not the ultimate but the immediate objective. It is that we may be marked by spiritual growth, so that instead of being tossed about, like a boat without an anchor, and at the mercy of false teachers, we may be holding the truth in love and growing up increasingly into conformity to Him who is our Head.

These objectives, whether we consider the ultimate or the immediate, are very great, very worthy of God. If we take them in we shall not wonder that with a view to them special gifts have flowed from the ascended Christ. But verse 16 completes the story by showing that the increase and growth of the body, which is the present objective, is not to be reached only by the ministry of these special gifts, but that every member of the body, however obscure, has a part to play. Just as the human body has many parts and joints, each of which supply something to the general upkeep and growth and well-being, so is it in the body of Christ.

It is very important that we bear this in mind, otherwise we easily fall into the way of thinking that the general good and spiritual prosperity of the church altogether depends upon the actions and service of gifted men. Consequently when things are poor and feeble, or altogether wrong, we can conveniently absolve ourselves from all responsibility and blame, laying all at the door of the gifts. The fact is that the healthy action of every part, down to the smallest and most unnoticed, is needful for the welfare of the whole. Let us all aim at so going forward ourselves that there may be increase of the body, to the building up of itself in love. Truly intelligence is necessary; but love, Divine love, is the great building force. God help us all to be filled with divine love.

With verse 17 we come face to face with detailed injunctions. The general exhortation occurs in the first verse of our chapter, and is of a positive character. Here the first injunction is of a negative sort: we are not to walk as do men of the world. Verses 18 and 19 give us a glimpse into the dark cesspool of Gentile iniquity which surrounded these saints at Ephesus. We see enough to discern the same hideous features as are exposed more fully in chapter i. of Paul's epistle to the Romans. Is the Gentile world of the twentieth century any better? We fear not; though the evil may be more skilfully hidden from the public eye. Still there is vanity, coupled with darkness, ignorance, blindness, and consequent alienation from all life which is of God.

Now we have learned Christ. Not only have we heard Him, and as a result believed in Him, but we have been "taught by Him," or as it may be read, "instructed in Him." He is not only our Teacher but our Lesson Book. He is not only our Lesson Book but our Example. The truth is in Jesus: that is, He Himself when here on earth was the perfect setting forth of all that is enjoined upon us. He perfectly manifested the "righteousness and holiness of truth," of which verse 24 (marginal reading) speaks.

What we have learned, then, concerns three things. First, as to our having put off the old man, which is utterly corrupt. Second, as to a complete renewal in the very spirit of our mind. Third, as to our having put on the new man, which is wholly according to God. The putting off and the putting on are not something which we are to do, as the Authorized translation would infer, but something which the true believer has done. "Your having put off . . . and having put on" (N. Tr.).

The "old man" is not Adam personally, but rather the Adamic nature and character. So too the "new man" is not Christ personally, but the nature and character which are His. The righteousness and holiness, which spring forth from, and are in entire consonance with truth, were altogether proper to Him, and like a native growth. With us they are not native but foreign, and consequently as regards us the new man is spoken of as created. Nothing short of creation would do, and nothing less than complete renewal in the spirit of our minds.

But let us not miss the point that all this is what has been arrived at in the case of the true believer. It is of the very essence of true Christianity. We are to be characterized by a walk wholly different from the rest of the Gentiles *because* this great transaction has taken place, if indeed we have heard and learned of Christ; which is equivalent to saying, if indeed we are really His.

The Apostle proceeds to lay his finger upon particular manifestations of the old man that we are to put off. Because the old man has been put off we are to put off all his features in detail. He begins with lying which is to be put off in favour of truth. The previous verse had mentioned holiness of truth as marking the new man, so we must be off with the lying which marks the old. Moreover, anger, theft, corrupt speech, and all similar evil use of the tongue, are to be put away, and kindness and forgiveness are to characterize us. We are to forgive others as we have been forgiven ourselves.

In these closing verses of the chapter we have not only what we are to put away but what we are to put on. Not lying, but truth. Not stealing, but toiling so as to have the wherewithal to give to others. Not corrupt talk, but words of grace and edification. Not anger and bitterness and heated clamour, but kind forgiveness. And all this in view of the grace which God has shown us for Christ's sake, and in view of the indwelling of the Spirit of God.

We are sealed by that Holy Spirit until the day of the redemption of our bodies and of the whole inheritance purchased by the blood of Christ. He will not leave us, but He is very sensitive as to holiness. We may easily grieve Him, and in consequence lose for the time the happy experiences that result from His presence. So may God help us to lay these practical instructions very much to heart, that we may walk not as the world, but in righteousness, holiness and truth.

CHAPTER 5

THE CLOSING WORDS of chapter iv. enforce upon us the obligation to kindness and forgiveness which rests upon all saints, inasmuch as we have been forgiven of God for Christ's sake. The opening words of chapter v. carry this thought a step further and a step higher. Not only have we been forgiven but we have been introduced into the Divine family. We are children of God and beloved by Him. Hence as dear children we are to be followers, or imitators, of God.

The imitation enjoined is not artificial but natural. Here are children playing in the market-place. They hold an imaginary court. This little maiden, arrayed in cheap finery, is impersonating a queen. She imitates queenly manners as best she can, but it is all very crude and artificial. There however is a small lad, minutely observing his father. Presently friends are smiling at him and observing how very like his father he is. His imitation is largely unconscious and wholly natural, for he *is* the son of his father, possessing his life and nature. Now it is as children of God that we are called upon to be imitators of God.

We are to walk in love. This is not natural to us as the children of Adam, but it is natural to us as born of God, for God is love. Walking in love is thus simply the manifesting in practice of the Divine nature. Hence it adds, "as Christ also hath loved us," since in Christ the Divine nature was seen in all its fulness and perfection. In His case moreover love led to action. He gave Himself for us in sacrifice to God. In this of course He stands alone, though we are to love even as He loved. He was the true burnt offering, the Antitype of Leviticus i.

Now love of the true and divine sort is altogether exclusive of the evils that spring from the flesh. Hence these things are to have no place amongst saints, indeed they are not to be even named among them. Things like those specified in verse 3 appeal to instincts deeply rooted in man's fallen nature, and we do well not only to avoid the things but also the contamination that is induced by thinking about them. We cannot talk about them without thinking of them, even if we condemn them in our talking. Therefore let us not talk about them. Nor let us allow our talk to descend to the level of foolishness or jesting. A Christian is neither a fool nor a jester, so let us not appear either in our conversation. Thanksgiving is what becomes the lips of those who are forgiven and become children of God.

56

The firm and decisive way in which the Apostle draws the line in verses 5 and 6 is very remarkable. The kingdom of Christ and of God is characterized by holiness. The unholy are outside that kingdom and subject to the wrath of God. There was to be no mistake about this, for evidently then as now there were those who wished to blur this sharp distinction and to excuse unholiness. Other scriptures indicate that one who is a true believer may fall into any of these sins, but no true believer is characterized by any of them. No one characterized by such sins is to be regarded as a true Christian whatever they may say or profess.

The true believer's attitude towards such is to be regulated by this. Whatever be their profession they have no part in the kingdom of God, and therefore we who have an inheritance in the kingdom can have no part with them. This is what verse 7 so plainly states. Notice too that the last word of that verse is *them*. We are not only to avoid the sins, but also to avoid all participation with *the sinners*. The persons as well as the evils are to be avoided. The difference between us and them is as great and distinct as that between light and darkness.

Once we were darkness ourselves. In this fact lies our danger, for as a consequence of it there is that in us which answers to the appeal of the darkness. Therefore the less we have to do with the darkness the better—whether as regards the practices of darkness, or as regards the people who themselves are darkness and consequently practice it. We who believe are light in the Lord and as a result intolerant of darkness; for as it is in nature so it is in grace. Light and darkness cannot exist together. If light comes in darkness vanishes. Light and darkness mutually exclude each other.

Being light in the Lord we are to walk as children of light. We are to be in practice what we are in actual reality. Let us carefully note this for it is a feature of the exhortations of the Gospel. The Law demanded of men that they should be what they were not. The Gospel exhorts believers to be what they are. Yet the fact that we are so exhorted shows that a contrary principle is in existence. It infers that the flesh with its tendencies is still within the believer. As the flesh is held in check and quiescent, what we really are as God's workmanship shines out.

Verse 9 explains what will shine out, for the correct reading is not, "the fruit of the Spirit," but, "the fruit of the light." Three words sum up that fruit—goodness, righteousness, truth. The opposites—evil, iniquity, unreality—should be entirely shut out of our lives. Walking thus as children of light we prove what is pleasing to God: prove, that is, not by a process of reasoning, but by experience of a practical sort. We put things to the test, and thus learn experimentally for ourselves.

The believer's life therefore may be summed up as bringing forth the fruits of the light, since he is a child of the light, while maintaining complete separation from the unfruitful works of darkness, for he is no longer of the darkness. Indeed he is to go even further and reprove them. This word, *reprove*, occurs again you will notice in verse 13. The meaning of it is not exactly, admonish or rebuke, but rather, *expose*. It is to expose, as by light, the true character of the works in question. If a believer shines out in his true character, his whole life will have that effect, just as in supreme measure his Master's did. Nevertheless of course there may be many occasions when words of rebuke are needful.

The passage we are considering puts a very solemn responsibility upon us. It is just here that friction and trouble with the world begin. People do not usually object to the kindly side of Christianity: gracious words and gracious actions meet with their approval. The trouble begins when holiness is maintained. And holiness, as these verses show, demands no fellowship with evil—neither the evil-doers (v. 7), nor their works (v. 11). When a believer walks the separated path which is here enjoined, and manifests himself as a child of light, then he must expect storms. It was thus in superlative degree with our Lord and Master. "God is Love" has always been a far more popular text than "God is light."

The peculiar quality of light is that it makes manifest all things that come under its rays. The truth of things becomes plain, and hence the one who does truth naturally welcomes the light, whilst he who does evil hates the light and avoids it. God is light in Himself; believers are only "light *in the Lord*," just as the moon is only light to us, in as far as its face is in the light of the sun. Therefore it is that we, like the moon, must abide in the light of our great Luminary, Christ Himself. This is very plainly indicated in verse 14.

This verse is not a quotation from the Old Testament, though it is probably an allusion to Isaiah lx. 1. We very easily fall victims to spiritual sleepiness, since the influences of the world are so soporific. Then we become like men sleeping amongst those dead in trespasses and sins. We are the living and they are the dead, and there should normally be the sharpest distinction between us. If we sleep amongst the dead we all appear very much alike. The call is to awake and arise that we may be in the sunshine of the Christ. Then it is that we are clear of all fellowship with the unfruitful works of darkness and, being luminous ourselves, the fruit of the light is manifested in us.

Our walk and behaviour then is to be marked by wisdom—the wisdom that seizes every opportunity of serving the Lord on the one hand, and of gaining an understanding of His will and pleasure on the other. The very essence of good service is, not merely that we accomplish work, but that what we do is according to the will of the One, whom we serve. The fact is that for this, as for all else enjoined upon us here, we need to be filled with the Spirit.

Each of us, who have believed the Gospel of our salvation, has received the gift of the Holy Spirit, as we saw when considering chapter i. It is another thing however to be filled with the Spirit, and the responsibility as to it is left with us. We are exhorted to be filled, which plainly infers that we are not filled—at all events at the moment when the exhortation is given.

The Spirit-filled believer is the subject of an extraordinary uplift. He is carried clean outside himself, centred in Christ, and enabled for the service of God in a power which is more than human. The man who is drunk with wine is carried outside himself in a way that is wholly evil. By the Spirit of God we may be carried outside ourselves in a way that is wholly good.

We get instances of the disciples being filled with the Spirit in the Acts of the Apostles—ii. 4; iv. 8; iv. 31; vii. 55; xiii. 9. These references lead us to think that the filling with the Spirit was an experience of rather an exceptional nature even in the earliest apostolic time. Still it is most evidently set before us in our chapter as something to be desired and aimed at by every Christian.

It is not only an obligation but also a very wonderful privilege. To be filled with One who is a divine Person, can that be a negligible thing? It means that He has a complete control. If we take the exhortation to heart we shall naturally ask—*How* may I be filled? What have I to do in order that I may be?

That is no small question. We may at least say this; that it is ours to remove out of the way all that hinders. The Spirit of God is *holy*. Moreover, He is sensitive. We may easily grieve Him, even by things that we allow without a bad conscience. Correspondingly we may easily be pre-occupied with things that we consider quite harmless, and yet being *pre*-occupied there is not the room for Him to *occupy* us. A good many "harmless" things will have to go out of *my* life and *yours* too, if we are to be filled with the Spirit.

The fruits of being filled with the Spirit follow in verses 19 to 21. The heart is filled with gladness which finds a spiritual outlet in song. There is a glad acceptance of all things—even adverse circumstances—with thanksgiving to the Father, in the name of the Lord Jesus Christ; and as to our relations with one another the spirit of yieldingness and submission, whilst always maintaining the fear of God. Our submission to one another must not be at the expense of true subjection to Him.

All these detailed exhortations, which have continued from verse 17 of chapter iv., have been applicable to all believers. Now we have the special exhortations, and with verse 22 the apostle turns to the wives. To them the exhortation is comprised in the one word, *Submit*. This flows naturally out of the general exhortation to submission in verse 21. The difficulty about submission is that it entails the non-assertion of one's own will. But clearly enough in the economy of things, divinely established, for this world, the subject place is allotted to the wife. Her place is typical of the position in which the church stands to Christ. Just as Christ is "Head of the church," all authority and directing ability and power being vested in Him, so the husband is "head of the wife."

Alas! in practice through the centuries, the church (as a professing body) has got far away from its true position. The church "is subject unto Christ," according to the Divine plan: it has been very insubject in its actual behaviour. It has acted for itself, and legislated as though it were the Head and not the body. Hence the confusion in church circles, so manifest on every hand. When the wife, even the Christian wife, sets aside the authority of her own husband, trouble ensues in a similar way.

The wife may however urge that she has a very awkward and incompetent husband! Too often indeed so it is. But the remedy for that is not the overturning of the Divine order. The church certainly has no such excuse, for it has an absolutely perfect Head; who is not only Head to the body but Saviour also.

Because the human husband, even the believing one, is frequently *very* imperfect, and always somewhat imperfect, an even lengthier exhortation is addressed to him. In one word his duty is *love*. It is easy to see that if the husband yields to his wife the love which is her due, she will not have much difficulty in yielding to him the submission which is his due. Obviously the greater responsibility is placed upon the shoulders of the husband. He is to love, and she is to submit; but the initiative rests with him.

When we turn from the responsibility resting upon the husband, which is the type, to the antitype, which as ever is seen in Christ, we find ourselves in the presence of perfection. The initiative indeed was with Him, and He has taken it in a most wonderful way. He not only loved the church but gave Himself for it. Moreover He has undertaken its practical sanctification and cleansing, and ultimately He will present it to Himself in glory in a perfection which is absolutely suitable to Himself.

The giving of Himself for the church took place in the past: it involved His death and resurrection. The sanctifying and purifying, of which verse 26 speaks, is proceeding in the present by means of the Word. The cleansing here spoken of is by *water*, be it noted, not by blood. The distinction is an important one. The Blood indeed cleanses, as 1 John i. 7 declares but that is in a judicial sense. The Blood absolves us from guilt, and thus cleanses us in the eyes of the great Judge of all. The water of the Word cleanses us morally; that is, in heart and in character, and consequently in all our ways. This present washing of the church by the Word is taking place of course in the hearts and lives of the saints, of whom the church is composed.

The presentation of the perfected church will take place in the future glory. It will be Christ's own gift to Himself! It will be all His own workmanship; for *He* loved, *He* gave Himself, *He* sanctified, *He* cleansed, and, as verse 29 adds, *He* nourished, *He* cherished, and finally *He* presented to *Himself*. A most wonderful work, and a most wonderful triumph, surely! Let us keep this aspect of things well in view, especially when cast down by present difficulties in the church, and painfully conscious of its sorrowful plight.

Now all these facts as to Christ and the church are to shed their light upon the relations between the Christian husband and wife. The marriage relationship is consequently set forth in the highest possible light; in a light altogether unknown to believers of Old Testament days, which accounts for the fact that many of them freely practised things which are wholly disallowed for us today. We are to walk in this light, and consequently the Christian husband is to love his wife as he loves himself—no mean standard that!—and the wife to reverence her husband.

Briefly observe three further points. First, this mystery concerns Christ and *the* church Not *a* church; no thought here of a local church, nor of any number of local assemblies. It is the church, one glorious body, and the church not viewed as a professing body, but rather as that elect body which is the fruit of Divine workmanship.

Second, the thought of the *body* comes in here; for we, who constitute the church, are spoken of as "members of His body." Yet the main thought of the passage is that of the wife, for the church's place is set forth as the pattern for Christian wives. We point this out because sometimes the fact of the church being the body of Christ is emphasized in order to maintain that it therefore cannot be in the place of the bride or wife. The fact is, as this passage indicates, that the church holds both positions.

This is made yet more plain by the third thing we point out. God's original creation of Adam and Eve was ordered in view of Christ and the church, as verses 28 to 32 show. Now Eve was Adam's wife, but she was also his body, being built up from one of his ribs. Adam's rib has no doubt provoked a good deal of sarcastic merriment amongst unbelieving modernists, who call themselves Christians. Yet here the fact concerning it clearly underlies the argument. It is nearly always thus. There is a new Testament allusion to the ridiculed Old Testament story. You cannot scrap the one without scrapping the other, if you add mental honesty and integrity to your modernism. We whole-heartedly accept both.

CHAPTER 6

WE PASS FROM the relationship of husband and wife to those of children and fathers, servants and masters, as we open chapter vi. Obedience is to mark the child, and careful nurture and admonition the father. But all is to be as under the Lord, as indicated in verses 1 and 4. This sets everything on a very high level. So also it is with the servant and the master. Their relations are to be regulated as before the Lord, as verses 7, 8 and 9 show.

All these exhortations are very important today for strong Satanic influences are sweeping through Christendom, to the denying and disturbing of all that should characterize these relationships. But the very fact that this is so presents to the believer a great opportunity for witness to the truth, by carefully maintaining the relationships in their integrity according to God's word. The opportunity for witness as servants or masters is very pronounced, inasmuch as that relationship is much in the public eye. The sight of a Christian servant marked by obedience and service with all good will, as rendered unto the Lord, is a very fine one. So also is that of a Christian master marked by an equal good will and care, in the sight of the great Master of both in heaven.

Thus far the epistle has given us a very wonderful unfolding of truth as to Christ and the church, followed by exhortations to life of a very exalted character. Now in verse 10 we come to his final word. It concerns the adversaries and the armour that we need, if we are to maintain the truth and live the life that has been set before us. We are not left at our own charges. The power of the Lord is at our disposal and we are to be strong in His might.

The adversaries that are contemplated here are not human but Satanic. They exist in the world of spirits and not in flesh and blood. Satan is their chief, but they are spoken of as principalities and powers, and also as "world-rulers of this darkness" (R.V.). We know very little about them, and do not need to know. It is enough for us that their evil design is unmasked. They are "world-rulers" for the whole world system is controlled and dominated by them, little as the human actors on the world stage may suspect it. The effect of their domination is darkness. Here is the explanation of the gross spiritual darkness which fills the earth. How often after the Gospel has been very clearly preached have we heard people express their wonder that unconverted folk have listened to it all without a ray of light entering their hearts. In this scripture, and also in 2 Corinthians iv. 4, is an explanation which removes all element of wonder from the phenomenon.

The point here however is that these great antagonistic powers exert all their wiles and energy against believers. They cannot rob them of their soul's salvation, but they can divert them from an understanding of their heavenly calling, and from a life which is really in keeping with it; and this is what they aim at doing. Now it stands to reason that we cannot meet such powers as these in our own strength. Thank God we need not attempt any such thing for all the armour that we need is freely provided of God. But we have to *take* it. Otherwise we shall not experience its value.

We are to take unto us the whole armour of God, and also we are to put it on. Then we shall be able to withstand, and to stand. The conflict here is viewed mainly as being defensive. We are set in an exalted and heavenly position by the grace of our God, and there we are to stand in spite of every attempt to dislodge us. In keeping with this the various parts of the armour specified are, with one exception, of a defensive nature. Girdle, breastplate, shoes, shield and helmet are none of them weapons of offence; only the sword is that.

The Apostle is speaking figuratively of course, for we find that each item of the armour is something of a moral and spiritual sort which is to be taken up by us: things which though given to us by God, and hence to be taken by us, are also to be put on in a practical and experimental way. The first item is truth. That is to be as a girdle to our loins. The girding up of the loins expresses a preparing for activity. All our activities are to be circumscribed by truth. The truth is to govern us. The truth is given to us by God, but we are to put it on, so that it may govern us. God's word is truth; but it is not truth in the Bible which is going to defend us, but rather truth *applied* in a practical way to all our activities.

The breastplate is righteousness. We are the very righteousness of God in Christ, but it is when we as a consequence walk in practical righteousness that it acts as a breastplate, covering all our vital parts from the blows directed by our powerful foes. How many a Christian warrior has fallen sorely wounded in the fight because there were grievous flaws in matters of practical righteousness. Chinks in the breastplate offer an opening to the arrows of the enemy.

In a normal way we hardly think of shoes as being in the nature of armour, yet inasmuch as it is with our shoes that we continually come into contact with the earth, they take on that character from the Christian standpoint. If our contact with earth is not right we shall be vulnerable indeed. What does "the preparation of the gospel of peace," mean? Not that we should be preparing the way of the gospel in an evangelistic sense (though to do that is of course very desirable) but that we ourselves should come under the preparation which the gospel of peace effects. If our feet are shod in this way we shall carry the peace of the Gospel into all our dealings with men of this world, and be protected ourselves in so doing.

Then besides all this there is faith to act as a shield; that faith which means a practical and living confidence in God; that faith which keeps the eye on Him and His Word, and not on the circumstances nor on the foes. With the shield protecting us, outside our other armour, the darts of fiery doubt flung by the wicked are averted and quenched.

The helmet protects the head, which next to the heart is the most vulnerable point in man. Salvation, known, realized, enjoyed and worked out in practice, is that helmet for us. When Paul wrote to the Philippians, "Work out your own salvation with fear and trembling, for it is God which worketh in you both to will and to do of His good pleasure," (ii. 12, 13) he was really exhorting them to take and wear the helmet of salvation.

Lastly comes, "the sword of the Spirit, which is the Word of God." This may be used both defensively and offensively. The Word of God will parry every thrust which our adversary may make; it will also put him to flight with one well directed blow. It is spoken of as the Spirit's sword, for He indited it at the outset, and He it is who gives skill and understanding in its use. Our great Example in the use of this sword is the Lord Himself, as recorded in Matthew iv. and Luke iv.

Our Lord is also our Example as to the prayer which is enjoined upon us in verse 18. Luke's gospel specially emphasizes this feature of His life. Having assumed Manhood, He took the dependent place which is proper to man, and carried it through in the fullest perfection. Hence prayer characterized His life, and it is to characterize ours. Prayer is always to be our resource, and especially so in connection with the conflict of which we have just been reading. The Word of God is indeed the sword *of the Spirit*. But just because it is we shall only wield it effectively if we are praying always *in the Spirit*. Without continued and abiding dependence on God we shall not wear any piece of the armour aright.

Our prayers are to reach that earnestness which is indicated by the word, *supplication;* they are also to be accompanied by watching. We are to be on the look-out to avoid all that would be inconsistent with our requests on the one hand, and to welcome the answer to our requests on the other. This indicates intensity and reality in our praying, so that our prayers are indeed a force and not a farce.

We are not to be circumscribed in our prayers. We have to begin with ourselves doubtless, but we do not stop there. We enlarge our requests to include "all saints." Just as all saints are needed for the apprehension of the truth (iii. 18), so the scope of our prayers is not to be less than all saints. The scope of our prayers is enlarged to "all men" in 1 Timothy ii. 1. Ephesians is however pre-eminently the church epistle and hence "all saints" is the circumference contemplated here.

Yet we are not to be so occupied with *all* that we wander off into indefiniteness. So the Apostle adds, "and *for me*." Great servant of God though he was, he desired to be supported by the prayers of others not so great as he. Only he desired prayer, not that he might be released from prison, and his circumstances eased, but that he might be able to fully accomplish his ministry though a captive. He was in bonds, yet as much an ambassador as when he was free (See 2 Corinthians v. 20).

When free he thought of himself more as an ambassador of the Gospel, beseeching men to be reconciled. Now in captivity he regards himself as an ambassador of the mystery—that mystery which he has briefly unfolded in the earlier part of the epistle. It is "the mystery of the Gospel," inasmuch as the one springs out of the other and is its appropriate sequel. If we do not understand the Gospel we cannot understand the mystery. The mystery, for instance, must be as a closed book to those who imagine that the Gospel is intended to Christianize the earth and thus introduce the millenium.

Paul's closing desires for the brethren though simple are very full. How happy must the brethren be when peace, love and faith, all proceeding from a Divine source, have free course in their midst. Then indeed grace rests upon them. Only there must be purity of heart and motive. The last words of verse 24, "in sincerity," or, "in incorruption" are a reminder to us that even in such early days, as those in which Paul was writing, that which was corrupt had found an entrance amongst those who professed to be Christian. To love the Lord Jesus Christ in incorruption is the hallmark of reality, the fruit of the genuine work of God.

PHILIPPIANS

INTRODUCTION

THE PORTION THAT now comes before us might be termed the Epistle of Christian experience. It is not characterized by the unfolding of doctrine, as are the epistles to the Romans and the Ephesians: any doctrine that it contains is brought in incidentally and not as the main theme. It is characterized by a spirit of great intimacy—for there was a very strong bond of affection between Paul and the Philippian saints—and by many personal details being given. Thus it comes to pass that in it we are given an extraordinary insight into the Apostle's inner spiritual history that is most edifying. We are permitted to scrutinize his spiritual experience that we may understand what proper Christian experience is, and discover how marvellously it worked out in a man of like passions to ourselves. Under the most disadvantageous and depressing circumstances it was a triumph.

CHAPTER 1

IN OPENING, PAUL does not present himself as an apostle, but just as a bondman of Jesus Christ. Hence we are not to regard the experience which he is led to relate as being something apostolic, and therefore beyond the reach of ordinary Christians. On the contrary it is the experience of a bondman or servant, and we all are that. He addresses himself to those at Philippi who could be spoken of as "saints in Christ Jesus." Being *in* Christ they were *set apart* for God. They had bishops and deacons in their midst, but even so these are not mentioned in the first place. These men holding office in this local assembly had a place of importance and honour, but they were not lords over God's heritage, claiming in everything the first place. Moreover, instead of there being one bishop presiding over many churches there were several bishops in this one church.

Immediately after the opening salutation Paul puts on record his joyful remembrance of the Philippian saints. They had been peculiarly marked by fellowship in the Gospel. They had had Paul very much in their hearts (for so verse 7 should read) and they had stood by him as partners, all of which was proof of the work of God within them. God had by His Spirit begun a good work in them, which had been evidenced in this way; and what God had begun He would carry to completion, which would be reached in the day of Jesus Christ.

Evidently they were marked by a great love for the Gospel and hearty fellowship with it in a practical way, and not only with *it* but also with *Paul* who was its ambassador, and so they were partakers of his grace. And they were partakers not only as to the confirmation of the Gospel by the wonderful results it produced, but as to its defence against all adversaries, and as to the bonds in which the ambassador lay. Many there are who are eager to partake in the confirmation, and possibly in the defence, who are not so eager when bonds and afflictions are in evidence. Bonds are the test, and a readiness to partake in *that* connection is a surer proof of the work of God within than much erudition as to Christian doctrine.

Verse 8 assures us how fully Paul reciprocated all the affection of the Philippians, and indeed exceeded in it. Verses 9 and 10 show us that which was the desire of his heart for them, even that they should increase continually in love, intelligence, discrimination, purity and fruitfulness. There was much about them which was delightful, but the Apostle's desire is summed up in the words, "yet more and more."

While the work of God *for* us has been accomplished once and for ever by the Lord Jesus, the work of God *in* us by His Holy Spirit is a progressive thing. That we should abound more and more in love is evidently the principal thing, for as we do our knowledge and powers of discrimination will increase. More and more we shall discern what is excellent and delight in it, and keep ourselves clear of all that would tarnish it, and consequently be filled with those fruits which are produced by righteousness to the glory and praise of God. Love is indeed the Divine nature. In that nature we are to grow as the result of God's work in us, which will continue to the end of our sojourn here, and be brought to fruition and into display when the day of Christ arrives.

When we reach verse 12 we find the Apostle beginning to refer to his own circumstances; but not as complaining or occupying our thoughts with them, but rather as showing how the God who is above all circumstances had made them work out to the furtherance of the Gospel.

What a blow it must have been to the early believers when Paul was imprisoned by the iron hand of Rome. A sudden extinguisher seemed to drop on his unparalleled labours and triumphs in the Gospel, and it must have appeared to be an unmitigated disaster. Yet it was nothing of the kind but rather the reverse, and in the succeeding verses we learn the way in which God had overruled it for good.

It was distinctly to the good that things had so fallen out as to make it manifest that Paul's imprisonment was wholly on account of the Glad Tidings. From the highest circles in Rome to the lowest it had been made perfectly clear that his bonds were on account of Christ, and not those of an ordinary malefactor.

It was even more to the good that the most of the brethren had been stirred up in a right way by his captivity. Instead of being cast down and cowed by it they were moved to a fuller trust in the Lord, and consequently were more fearless in speaking forth the Word of the Lord. There was an unhappy minority who joined in the preaching from evil motives—for they were antagonistic to Paul and hoped to stir up more trouble for him—

but at any rate they did preach Christ, and therefore God would overrule it for blessing.

Here then we get a striking glimpse of the inner life and spirit of the Apostle. His trials were very deep. Not only was his imprisonment likely to chafe his spirit, but the action of these envious and contentious brethren must have been irritating beyond measure. Yet here he is, calm, confident, gracious, without a trace of irritation in his spirit: a veritable triumph of the power of God. And the secret of it was evidently that he had learned to forget himself and view things altogether from the Divine side. What weighed with him was not how things affected himself but how they affected Christ and His interests. It might be bad for Paul, but if it was good for Christ then nothing further need be said, for *that* was the only thing that mattered to him.

As a consequence of this the Apostle could say, "I therein do rejoice, yea, and will rejoice." He rejoiced in the preaching of Christ, and he rejoiced in the assurance that all this which seemed to be so much against him would turn out to his own salvation; the Philippians helping by prayer, and the supply of the Spirit of Jesus Christ being always available for him.

Verse 19 sets before us a present salvation and one which Paul himself needed and expected to get. The nature of it becomes clear as we consider verse 20. His earnest desire and expectation was that Christ should be magnified in his body, whether by life or by death. The fulfilling of that desire would involve a salvation, for naturally we each aim at self-magnification and self-gratification through our bodies. Have we each discovered that to have the whole bent and tenor of our lives diverted from self to Christ is a wonderful present salvation? Have we ever prayed after this fashion?—

"My Saviour, Thou hast offered rest,
Oh, give it then to me,
The rest of ceasing from myself,
To find my all in Thee!"

Present salvation is found, then, in the setting aside of self and the exaltation of Christ, and not only salvation but also that which is really *life*. When the Apostle said, "For me to live is Christ," he was not announcing a fact of Christian doctrine but speaking experimentally. It is indeed a fact that Christ is the life of His saints, but here we find that the fact was translated into the experience and practice of Paul, so that his life could be summed up in one word—CHRIST. Christ lived in Paul and through Paul. He was the Object of Paul's existence, and His character was manifested in him, though not yet, of course, in perfect measure.

If life meant Christ living in Paul, death meant Paul being with Christ. Hence he adds, "to die is gain." To every Christian death when it arrives

PHILIPPIANS

IS gain, but it is very obvious that not many of us are in the abiding consciousness of that fact. When our loved ones who believe are taken from us, we console ourselves with the reflection that for them it means being with Christ, which is far better; yet we continue clinging to life in this world very pertinaciously ourselves. Have we ever been "in a strait betwixt two," as Paul was? The great majority of us would have no difficulty in deciding if the choice were left with us! We would elect at once for the alternative which is *not* spoken of as far better.

Death is gain, and Paul knew it to be gain; and he, be it remembered, had years before been caught up into the third heaven, though whether in or out of the body he could not tell. Whichever way it was, he was granted some foretaste thereby of the blessedness of being with Christ. We may take the words, "far better," as being Paul's own verdict as the fruit of that wonderful experience, as well as the revelation, as from God, of a wonderful fact.

When he says, "What I shall choose I wot not," we are not to understand that he was actually left to decide whether he was to live or die. At least, so we judge. He writes very familiarly and with much freedom to his beloved Philippian converts, and hence does not stop to say, "if the choice were left to me." He knew that it was not merely better but far better to be with Christ, yet he does not decide the point by reference to his own feelings. We see again that the only thing that mattered was, what was most calculated to further the interests of his Lord. He felt that what would be for the more help of the saints was his remaining amongst them for a little longer, and hence he had the confidence of so doing, as he says in verse 25.

Let us all be quite clear that the departure of what the Apostle speaks here has nothing to do with the coming again of the Lord. He refers to the intermediate, or "unclothed," state, to which he refers in 2 Corinthians v. 4. In that passage he shows that the "clothed" state—when we are "clothed upon" with our bodies of glory is in every way superior to the "unclothed." Yet in our passage we see that the "unclothed" state is far better than the best that we can know while still clothed in our present bodies of humiliation. What it all means in detail must of necessity be inconceivable to us in our present condition, but let us rest assured that blessedness beyond all our thoughts lies ahead of us.

It would seem pretty certain that Paul was justified in his confidence, and that he did "abide and continue" with them for a few years further with a view to their spiritual progress and joy, and give them cause for further rejoicing by his coming amongst them for a brief season.

Only there was one great desire which he had as regards them, and that equally whether he was absent from them or present with them, that they should conduct themselves in a way that was worthy of the Gospel. Not

69

only were they to stand fast; they were to "stand fast *in one spirit*." Not merely to strive for the faith of the Gospel, but to do so *"with one mind,"* and *"together."*

Here is an apostolic injunction which may well strike very deeply and acutely into our hearts. It goes a long way to explain the lack of power manifested in connection with the Gospel, whether as regards its progress amongst the unsaved or as regards the stability of those who are saved. Standing fast, you notice, comes before the striving. And the word translated *striving* is one from which we derive our word, athletics. It would seem therefore to indicate not so much a striving by word or argument in order to maintain the truth of the Gospel, as striving in the shape of actual labour on the Gospel's behalf.

In Romans xv. 30 and in Jude 3 we have the words "strive" and "contend," but there a different word is used, from which we get our word, agonize. The saints were to agonize together in prayer with Paul, and to earnestly agonize for the faith. Here we are enjoined to labour (or, athleticize, if we may coin a word) together for the Gospel, and at the beginning of chapter iv. we read of two women who did so labour together with Paul, for the same word is used there. If there were more *agonizing together* in prayer, and *athleticizing together* on behalf of the Gospel we should see *more* in the way of result.

As we proceed further in the epistle we shall discover that this oneness of mind and spirit is the main burden that was resting on the Apostle as regards the Philippians, for dissension is an evil which has a way of creeping in amongst the most spiritual and devoted Christians in various subtle ways.

When dissension is banished and unity prevails among saints the adversaries do not appear so alarming, and there is more readiness to suffer. The fact is we never need be terrified by adversaries of an open sort. The very fact that they are adversaries is to them only a token of destruction when God rises up. And when He rises up it will mean salvation for His people. While we wait for His intervention it is ours to have conflict and suffering for His sake. The Philippians had seen it in Paul, as Acts xvi. bears witness, and now they heard of the same kind of thing befalling him in Rome.

Suffering for Christ and His Gospel is here presented as a *privilege*, granted to us as believers. If we were not so sadly enervated by the dissension and disunity that prevails in the church, on the one hand, and by the inroads of the world and the spirit of the world, on the other, that is the light in which we should see it. And how immensely should we thereby be blessed!

PHILIPPIANS

CHAPTER 2

THE OPENING VERSE of chapter ii. appears to be an allusion to the supplies from the Philippians which had reached Paul by the hand of Epaphroditus. These gifts had been to him a very refreshing expression of the love and compassion that marked them, and of the true fellowship of the Spirit that existed between himself and them. As a result his heart had been filled with consolation and comfort in the midst of his afflictions. Whilst recognizing however, the immediate application of this first verse, do not let us miss its more general bearing. Christ is the source of consolation; love it is that produces comfort; the Spirit of God, possessed in common by all true believers, is the fountainhead of fellowship. These facts abide in all ages, and for us all.

These things being facts, the Apostle uses them as a kind of lever in his exhortation. The "if," repeated four times in the first verse, has really the force of "since." Since these things are so, he begs them to fill up his joy to the brim by being likeminded and getting rid of the last vestige of dissension.

Experience proves, we think, that dissension is a work of the flesh which is amongst the last to disappear, and our passage shows how great was the desire of the Apostle that it might be removed from the midst of the Philippians. Note the variety of expressions he used in setting forth his desires for them.

First of all they were to be likeminded. It is obviously a great thing when believers all think alike, yet there is also to be considered the spirit that underlies their thinking. If that be wrong mere thinking alike will not guarantee absence of dissension. Hence he adds, "having the same love." Only love can produce that of which next he speaks, "being of one accord," or, more literally, "joined in soul," which in its turn leads to all minding one thing.

When we reach chapter iii. we shall find Paul saying "One thing I do." He was a man of one object, *pursuing* one thing, instead of frittering away his energies in the pursuit of many things. Here he exhorts others all to *mind* the one thing. Only the man, whose mind is centred on the one thing of all importance, is likely to be characterized by the pursuit of the one thing. It is not difficult to see that if we are all minding the one thing, under the control of the same love, there will not be much room for dissension.

Still, even so, the Apostle has yet more to say on this point. Verse 2 does indeed bring in the great positive elements that make for practical unity, but he will also labour to exclude the elements of evil that destroy it. Hence verse 3. It is very possible for us to do many things which are quite right in themselves in the spirit of strife, as we saw in considering chapter i., where we read of brethren preaching Christ "of envy and strife." Moreover, vainglory is an evil product of the flesh which lies very deeply ingrained in the fallen heart of man. How often have we done what was right enough, but with the secret desire of gaining credit and glory amongst our fellows? Let us give our consciences time to answer, and we shall feel the keen edge of these words.

Vainglory lies at the root of a vast proportion of the strife and dissension that is distracting Christians, even those who otherwise are spiritually minded. The opposite of vainglory is that lowliness of mind that leads us to esteem others better than ourselves. *Lowliness* of mind moreover leads to that *largeness* of mind which is indicated in verse 4. If I am self-centred, aiming merely at my own interests and glory, I naturally am only considering my own things. If on the other hand I am Christ-centred, aiming at His interests and glory, I look also on the things of others. And if the things of others are really more for Christ's glory than my things are, I shall look more on the things of others than on my own.

At this point the Apostle seems to anticipate that the Philippians might wish to say to him, "You have exhorted us to be of one spirit, of one accord, of one mind. But how are we to bring it about? There is no denying the fact that differences of thought and judgment prevail amongst us. Whose mind is to prevail?"

His reply is, "Let this mind be in you"—the mind that was "in Christ Jesus." By "mind" here we have not to understand just a thought or opinion, but a whole way of thinking. Christ's way of thinking is to characterize us, and this is a very much deeper thing. If His way of thinking does characterize us we shall be delivered from dissension even though we do not see eye to eye on every point. Verses 15 and 16 of chapter iii. show this.

What then was the mind that was in Christ Jesus? We may reply in the three words that occur in verse 8, "He humbled Himself." The fact is that the mind that was in Christ is the exact opposite of the mind that was in Adam. The Lord's own words in Matthew xxiii. 12 illustrate it. There was found in Adam the self-exalting mind, and as a consequence he fell into the depths. In Christ there was found the self-sacrificing, self-humbling mind, and, as we see in this passage, He is exalted to the supreme place.

We start from the supreme heights in verse 6. He was in the form of God. Our first parents were tempted to grasp at something far above them—at becoming as gods, as Genesis iii. 5, bears witness. That place was not for them, and their grasping at it was sheer robbery. But there was nothing of that with our Lord. In His case equality with God was not something to be grasped at. It was His to start with, for He was God. He could not be higher than He was. Before Him there lay but the alternative of staying as and where He was, or of coming down in humiliation.

Blessed be God, He chose the latter. Verse 7 is the beginning of this wonderful story. Though originally in the form of God, He took upon Him another form, the form of a servant, being made in the likeness of men. This involved the making of Himself "of no reputation," or "emptying" Himself.

Years ago when the unbelieving critics of the Bible found themselves running into conflict with the words of our Lord, they invented the "*kenosis* theory" so as to be able to maintain their own denials of His words, while at the same time paying Him a certain measure of respect and homage instead of utterly rejecting Him as a fraud. *Kenosis* is a word coined from the Greek word used in this passage, with the literal meaning of "emptied," but translated, "made . . . of no reputation." The theory represents Christ as emptying Himself so fully of all that was divine that He became a Jew, just as ignorant as the majority of Jews living in His age. Hence the critic of the nineteenth or twentieth century, propounding this theory and fortified with modern learning, feels himself quite able to contradict or correct the Son of God.

Such is the *kenosis* THEORY—a web spun by the critical spiders out of their own unbelieving hearts; for *they* are the liars, and *not* the Son of God. A web which, sad to say, has served the devil's purposes only too well. Many an unwary fly has been trapped in that web. It has given them some kind of a reason for thinking exactly what they wanted to think.

Now while we turn away with abhorrence from the evil theory, we must not overlook the fact that there is a true "kenosis," a true emptying, for this passage speaks of it. If we desire to understand what it means we turn to the Gospels, and there we see what His Manhood involved, just as we also see what His Godhead involved, shining, as it did, continually through His Manhood. Just two or three examples may be cited, to illustrate what we refer to.

Having become Man, Jesus was anointed with the Holy Ghost and with power. Consequently instead of acting in the simple strength of His own Godhead He acted in the power of the Spirit. It was a case of God doing things *by* Him (Acts x. 38; Luke iv. 14; Acts ii. 22).

He is the Creator, as Colossians i. 16 so plainly states, yet in Manhood He stated that places in the coming kingdom were *not His to give* (Matt. xx. 23).

In keeping with this He disclaimed individual initiative or movement in His words and works. He attributed all to the Father (John v. 19, 27, 30; xiv. 10).

Considering these things we at once see that this true emptying, which was His own act, was in order that His taking the form of a servant might be a real thing. Were it not for this we might have jumped to the conclusion that the words, "took upon Him the form of a servant," simply meant that He took a servant's place only as a matter of form, just as the Pope of Rome is said occasionally to assume the place of a servant in washing the feet of certain poor beggars. He does it in form, but they see to it that in reality it is accomplished in surroundings of elegance and splendour. When our Lord Jesus took the servant's form, He took it *in all the reality it involved.*

Verse 8 carries the story of His humiliation to its climax. If verse 7 gives us the amazing stoop from Godhead's fullest glory to man's estate and place, this verse gives us the further stoop of the Man, who was Jehovah's Fellow, to the death of the cross. All His life was marked by going downwards, it was marked by an increasing humbling of Himself until death was reached, and that a death of extremest shame and suffering—the death of the cross.

His way of thinking then was to go down, and that way of thinking is to be in us. Only as born of God and possessing the Spirit of God is it possible for us to think in that way. Thank God, it is possible for us so to think. Then let us do so. The obligation rests upon us. Let us accept it, and let us judge ourselves by it.

The three verses which detail His humiliation are now followed by three which declare His exaltation according to the decree of God the Father. Still He takes everything from the Father's hand, and is granted a Name which is absolutely supreme. In this passage "name" is used, we judge, in the same way as it is used in Hebrews i. 4. No particular name is referred to, whether Lord, or Jesus, or Christ, or any other, but it refers rather to His fame or reputation. The once despised and rejected Jesus has such fame and renown that ultimately every created being will have to bow before Him and confess His Lordship. And when an assembled universe does Him homage, whether they do it with glad willingness or with grief under compulsion, all will be to the glory of God the Father.

In verse 12 the Apostle leaves this delightful theme and returns to his exhortation, which began with verse 27 of chapter i. He longed that their manner of life might be in everything in keeping with the Gospel, that they might be marked by earnest labour for the Gospel with oneness of mind, and courage in the presence of opposition. In the past, when Paul had been in and out amongst them, they had been marked by obedience to what was enjoined. Now let them be, if possible, even more obedient to his word since they were bereft of his personal help. Dangers threatened them from without, and there was this subtle danger threatening from dissension within, let them then with redoubled energy seek to have and manifest the mind that was in Christ Jesus. Thus would they be working out their own salvation from all that threatened. Let them do it with fear and trembling, remembering their own weakness. Once Peter thought he could work out his own salvation without fear or trembling, and we know what came of that.

This evidently is the simple meaning of this much used, and abused, verse. Can we not each apply it to ourselves? We certainly can if we will. So may God make us willing to do so. We need not shrink from doing so in view of verse 13. We are to work out our own salvation, but it is God who works in us, to the willing and doing of His good pleasure. Let us note that. God works the willing as well as the doing, and the willing comes first. Thus God's work and our work are considered as moving harmoniously together. God's work must ever take precedence of ours both as to time and importance. Yet the thing is not presented in a way that would turn us into fatalists. Rather our working is mentioned first, and the responsibility as to it is pressed upon us. The fact that God works is brought in as an encouragement and incentive.

Thus, taught of God to love His will, we do it, and if the mind of Christ be in us we do it in the right way. Not grudgingly with murmurings and disputings, but as harmless and simple children of God, bearing the character of God, whose children we are. Mankind has become a crooked and perverted generation and we are to be living in a way that presents the sharpest possible contrast. Only thus shall we be lights amidst the darkness of this world.

The word translated "shine," is a word, we are told, which is used for the rising or appearing of the heavenly bodies in our skies. This gives us a striking thought. We should appear as heavenly luminaries in this world's sky. Are we doing so? Only if we are altogether distinguished from the generation of this world, as indicated in the earlier part of the verse. Only then can we effectively hold forth to others the word of life.

There must be life as well as the testimony of our lips if the word of life is to be held forth. The word of testimony most frequently becomes the word of life to others, when it has first been translated into the life of the witness. If that were accomplished in the case of his beloved Philippian converts, Paul would have the assurance that his labours on their behalf had not been in vain. He then could anticipate abundant cause for rejoicing when Christ should appear and inaugurate His day. He could regard God's work in them, of which he had spoken in verse 6 of chapter i., as being carried to its crown and completion.

Having set before the Philippians the supreme example of the Lord Jesus, who was "obedient unto death," and having exhorted them to obedience which would mean the doing of God's "good pleasure" from the heart, the Apostle again alludes to his own case in verse 17. Though he had expressed his anticipation of still continuing amongst them for a season (i. 25) yet here he contemplates the possibility of his speedy martyrdom. Some people set great store by their "impressions" and elevate them to a certainty and authority almost, if not quite, equal to the Scriptures. This is a mistake. Paul had his "impressions" as to his future, and we quite believe them to have been justified by the event. Yet even he, apostle as he was, entertained the thought that the event *might* falsify his impressions.

The word "offered" in verse 17 is "poured forth" as the margin shows. Paul uses the same word in 2 Timothy iv. 6, when his martyrdom was impending. He alluded of course to those drink offerings which the law enjoined. A "fourth part of a hin of wine" was to be poured over certain sacrifices, before the Lord.

This being so, two very striking things confront us in verses 17 and 18. First, he calls the gifts of the Philippians, sent out of their poverty by the hand of Epaphroditus, "the sacrifice and service of your faith." That is, he considers them to be the *major* sacrifice. His own martyrdom he considers as a small quanity of wine poured over their sacrifice as a drink offering: i.e. as the *minor* sacrifice. An extraordinary way of putting things surely! We should have reversed the matter, and thought of the self denial of the Philippians as a drink offering poured over Paul's great sacrifice as a martyr.

Why did Paul esteem things in this way? Because he was looking not "on his own things but . . . also on the things of others" (ii. 4). He was a striking example of what he had urged on the Philippians, and of the worth and excellence of the mind which was in Christ Jesus. There was no affectation about Paul, no paying of mere compliments. Delighted with the grace of Christ as seen in his beloved converts, he meant what he said.

The second striking thing is that he actually contemplated his own martyrdom as calculated to provoke an outburst of rejoicing, for himself and for the Philippians—mutual rejoicing. A most unnatural proceeding truly! Not natural, but *spiritual*. The fact is, Paul REALLY *believed* what he had said as to departing and being with Christ. It really IS, *"far better."* He knew that the Philippians so truly loved him, that in spite of grief at losing him, they would rise above their own feelings to rejoice in his joy. We are afraid that we often turn Philippians i. 23, into a pious platitude. It was much more than that to Paul.

Still he was not anticipating martyrdom just at that moment, as he had already told them, and so he contemplated sending Timothy to them shortly, that he might help as to their spiritual state and also that through him he might hear of their welfare.

Now of those available just at that moment no one was quite so likeminded with himself, and so zealous for the good of the Philippians. The mass, even of believers, were characterized by seeking their own things rather than Christ's. Timothy was a happy exception to this. He was a true son of his spiritual father. The mind that was in Christ was also in him.

We are afraid that this seeking of our own interests and not Christ's is sadly common amongst believers today. No servant of God can so effectually serve the saints as he who moves amongst them seeking nothing but the interests of Christ.

So Timothy was the one he hoped to send to them before long, and indeed he hoped to be released and able to come himself. Still he wished for some speedier means of communication with them in acknowledgement of their gifts and so was dispatching back to them Epaphroditus, who had been their messenger to him, and who now became the bearer of the epistle we are considering.

We are now, verses 25-30, permitted to have a glimpse of the kind of man this Epaphroditus was, whom Paul calls, "My brother and fellow-workman and fellow-soldier" (N. Tr.). He too was like-minded, and we at once see that when just before the Apostle had said, "*I have* no man like-minded," he had meant, "I have no man amongst those who have been my immediate helpers and attendants in Rome." Epaphroditus was a Philippian and so not in view in the earlier remark.

Many there were, and *are*, who, though to be acknowledged as brothers, can hardly be spoken of as workmen or soldiers. Epaphroditus was all three, and not only so but a workman and a soldier thoroughly "fellow" to Paul. They worked and warred together with identical objects and aims. Could such testimony be rendered to anyone today? We believe it *could*, inasmuch as the New Testament informs us so fully as to the doctrine, manner of life, and service of Paul this pattern servant of God. At the same time we are afraid that in actual practice *it is rare*. Every believer is called to be a worker and a warrior. The trowel and the sword should mark us all. But do they? And are we characterized as "fellow" to Paul in our use of them?

In carrying out his service and journeying to Paul, Epaphroditus had nearly died of sickness. Twice over do we find the expression, "nigh unto death." God indeed had had mercy upon him, and averted this great sorrow both to Paul and the Philippians, yet he had not regarded his life for the sake of the work of Christ, and hence was to be honoured.

So in Epaphroditus we see another who followed in the steps of Paul and Timothy, even as they followed Christ. The mind that was in Christ Jesus was found also in him, for not only did he venture his life in order to serve his Lord, but when he had been so sick that he was near to death, he was "full of heaviness," not because of his own malady, but because he knew his brethren at Philippi had had news of his sickness and would be sorely grieved on his account. This was a fine case of a man not looking "on his own things, but . . . also on the things of others." It was un-selfishness indeed!

PHILIPPIANS

CHAPTER 3

THERE WAS REJOICING then both for Paul and for the Philippians as regards Epaphroditus; but as we enter upon chapter iii. we find where the truest and most permanent rejoicing lies for the Christian. God may, and indeed often does, give us to experience His mercy and make our hearts glad, yet on the other hand often He has to pass us through the valley of weeping. But even if circumstances are permitted to move against us, and sickness end fatally, the Lord Himself remains the same. Our rejoicing really lies in Him. "Rejoice in the Lord," is the great word for us all. In thus writing the Apostle might be repeating himself, yet the happy theme was not irksome to him, and it was safe for them. No servant of God need be afraid of repeating himself, for we take in things but slowly. Repetition is a safe process in the things of God.

Our rejoicing however must be "in the Lord." There are those who would divert us from Him, as is indicated in verse 2. In saying "dogs" the Apostle probably alludes to men of quite evil life, akin to the unclean Gentiles. By "evil workers," to those who while professedly Christian were introducing what was evil. By "the concision" he refers to the Judaizing faction, in contrast with whom are the true "circumcision" of which verse 3 speaks. The word translated "concision" means a mere *lopping off*, in contrast to the complete cutting off of death, which was figured in circumcision. The Judaizers believed in lopping off the uglier excrescences of the flesh but would not have that bringing in of death, "by the circumcision of Christ" (Col. ii. 11.), which is the truth of Christianity. The object before the Judaizers was "that they may glory in *your flesh*" (Gal. vi. 13). Men cannot exactly boast in the grosser manifestations of the flesh, so they aim at lopping them off in order to encourage more amiable and aesthetic manifestations in which to make their boast. But it is boasting in the flesh nevertheless.

Verse 3 speaks by way of contrast of what believers are, if viewed according to God's thoughts of them. We are the true spiritual circumcision, who worship by the Spirit of God, who boast in Christ Jesus, and do not trust in the flesh. We accept God's sentence of condemnation upon the flesh, and find our all in Christ. Then it is that in the energy of an ungrieved Spirit we are filled with the worship of God.

But what a lot of time is usually spent in learning not to trust the flesh, and in passing a "vote of no confidence" in it. What experiences often have to be gone through! The kind of experiences we refer to are detailed for us in Romans vii., and the lesson is one that cannot be learned theoretically, merely, it must be learned experimentally. There is no need that we should take a long time to learn the lesson, but as a matter of fact we usually do.

Paul's own case, to which he now refers—verses 4 to 7—shows that the lesson may be learned in a very profound way in a very short space of time. If ever a man was exemplary in a fleshly way, he was. Nowadays people are said to *die*, "fortified with all the rites of the church." We may say of him that for some years he *lived*, fortified with all the rites and ordinances and advantages and righteousness of Judaism. If ever educated and religious flesh was to be trusted, it was to be trusted in Saul of Tarsus. He was filled with religion and filled with the pride which was generated by his belief that all was so much gain to him.

But in that tremendous revelation, which occurred on the road to Damascus, all was reversed. He discovered himself to be outrageously wrong. His fancied advantages he discovered to be disadvantages; his religious flesh, to be rebellious flesh. All that he had counted on, trusted in, prided himself upon, came down about him with a crash. Christ in His glory was revealed to him. All that had been esteemed gain by him, he now counted loss for Christ. His confidence in the flesh was gone for ever. As soon as the three days of his blindness were over, his boasting in Christ Jesus began. In those three days his great lesson was learned.

And the lesson was learned solidly and for ever. Verse 7 speaks of the conclusion he reached on the Damascus road. "I *counted*"—the verb is in the past. Verse 8 carries us on to the day when he wrote this epistle in a Roman prison. "Yea doubtless, and I *count*"—the verb is in the present. The point reached at his conversion is confirmed and even deepened, thirty years or more later. Only now he can say what in the nature of things he could not have said at his conversion. For thirty years he had been growing in the knowledge of Christ, and the excellency of that knowledge commanded him. Compared with *that* all things were but loss, and the depth and ardour of his devotion are expressed in the glowing words—"*Christ Jesus* MY LORD."

Nor was this counting of all things but loss merely an attitude of his mind, for he adds, "for whom I have suffered the loss of all things." It is one thing to count all things as loss, and quite another to actually suffer the loss of all. Both were the experience of the Apostle. He was not unduly disturbed when he lost everything, for he had already esteemed everything as loss. Moreover, in Christ he had infinite gain, in comparison with whom all else is but refuse.

It was not that he hoped to "win Christ" as the result of giving up all things, after the fashion of those who give up possessions and retire into monasteries or convents in the hope of thereby securing their soul's salvation. It was rather that, having found such surpassing worth in Christ, such excellence in the knowledge of Him, he was prepared as to all things to suffer *loss* in order that he might have Christ for his *gain*. It was a remarkable form of profit and loss account, in which Paul emerged an infinite gainer.

All Paul's gain then could be summed up in the one word—CHRIST. But of course all this was based upon being "in Christ," and standing before God in that righteousness which is by faith in Him. Apart from that there would be no having Christ as one's gain, nor preparedness to suffer loss in this world.

How striking, in this 9th verse, is the contrast between *"mine own* righteousness" and "the righteousness which is *of God."* The one, were it possible to attain to it, would be "of the law." It would be something purely human, and according to the standard exacted by the law. The other is the righteousness in which we stand as the fruit of the Gospel. It is "of God;" that is, *divine*, in contrast to human. It is "through the faith of Christ;" that is, it is available for us on the basis of His intervention and work as presented to faith in the Gospel. And it is "by faith;" that is, it is received by us on the principle of faith and not on the principle of works of law.

Have we all taken this in? Are we rejoicing that we stand in a righteousness which is wholly divine in its origin? Do we realize that all the things of the flesh in which we might boast are so much loss and that all our gain is in Christ?

These are weighty questions that demand an answer from us each.

We may gain very considerable insight into the character of a man if we are made acquainted with his real desires and aspirations. The passage before us gives us just that insight into the character of the Apostle Paul. His desires seem to range themselves under three heads, all found in the great sentence which runs through four verses. There is no full stop from the end of verse 7 to the end of verse 11.

First, he desired to win Christ. Second, to be found in Christ, in a righteousness which is wholly divine. Third, to know Christ, and flowing out of that to know an identification with Christ, in resurrection, in sufferings, in death. We are conscious at once that this third aspiration has great depths in it. We might truly have Christ for our gain, and for our righteousness, and yet be very poor and shallow in our knowledge of Christ. "That I may know HIM," seems to have been the very crown of Paul's desires.

But then, did not Paul know Him? Certainly he did, as indeed every believer knows Him. He knew Him in fact in very much larger measure than most believers know Him. Yet there is such an infinitude in Christ, such depths to be known, that here we have the Apostle still panting to know more and more. Have we not caught at least a little of the Apostle's spirit? Do we not long to know our Saviour better—not merely to know about Him, but to know Himself in the intimacy of His love?

Our knowledge of Christ is by the Holy Spirit, and primarily through the Scriptures. Had we been on earth in the days of His flesh, we might have been acquainted with Him for a brief season "according to flesh." But even so we should have to say, "yet now we know [Him thus] no longer" (2 Cor. v. 16, N. Tr.). When His disciples spent those brief years in His company they had indeed a most wonderful experience, yet at that time they had not received the Holy Spirit and hence they understood but very little for the moment. It was only when they had lost His presence among them, but had gained the presence of the Holy Spirit, that they really knew the significance of all they had seen and heard. All that we know of Christ objectively is presented to us in the Scriptures, but we have the indwelling Spirit to make it all live in our hearts in a subjective way.

If the knowledge of the true living Christ, thus objectively presented to us, is brought subjectively into our hearts by the Spirit, it leads to a third thing; an acquaintance with Him in an experimental and practical way. To this Paul alludes in the latter part of verse 10. The order of the words is significant. The historical order in the case of our Lord was, sufferings, death, resurrection. Here resurrection comes first. Neither Paul nor any of us can contemplate sufferings or death save as we are fortified by the knowledge of the power of His resurrection. His resurrection is the pattern and pledge of ours. Indeed our resurrection altogether depends upon His.

As the Apostle realized in his spirit the power of Christ's resurrection, he looked upon "the fellowship of His sufferings" as something actually to be desired. He even desired to be conformed to His death! Until the Lord comes we can only know the power of His resurrection in an inward and spiritual way, yet the fellowship of His sufferings and conformity to His death are of a very practical nature. Paul would taste of suffering in the cause of Christ and after the pattern of Christ—suffering which should be of the same order as those sufferings which Christ Himself endured at the hands of men. He would even die as a witness to the truth, seeing Christ thus died. He actually desired these things.

Let us each take a few quiet moments to interrogate our own hearts. Do we desire these things? We fear that to ask the question is to answer it. A few of us might be able to say, "I believe that through the Lord's grace I could face these things if called upon to do so. But desire them? Well, no." The fact that Paul did desire them is an eloquent witness to the wholly exceptional degree in which Christ personally had captured his heart, and the power of His resurrection had filled him with a holy enthusiasm. The fact is, he was like a well-trained athlete running in an obstacle race with a mighty enthusiasm for reaching the goal. The earlier verses have told us how he had flung away seeming advantages as being hindrances to his course. These verses tell us that he would be detained by no obstacle, he would tear his way through the barbed wire of suffering and plunge into the watercourse of death, if in such fashion he might reach his goal.

Now this is just the force of verse 11. The Authorized version would almost make it appear that resurrection is an attainment for us, with a measure of doubt as to whether we ever get there. A better rendering is, "If any way I arrive at the resurrection from among the dead" (N. Tr.). He would get there any way, through no matter what obstacles, even through sufferings and martyrdom. And not merely is it resurrection, but resurrection out from among the dead; that is, the first resurrection, of which Christ is the firstfruits. It is while waiting for that resurrection that we are to know the power of His resurrection from among the dead, and so be walking here as those who are risen with Christ.

Verses 12 to 14 show us that the thought of a race was present to the Apostle's mind in writing. The word, "attained" in verse 12 is really "obtained" or "received" as a prize. He wished no one to think that he had already received the prize, or that he was perfected. The position rather was that he was still pursuing it. Christ Jesus had laid hold of him, but he had not yet laid hold of it. Still he was ardently in pursuit of it, stretching out like an eager athlete towards the prize of God's calling on high in Christ Jesus.

The word "high" simply means "above." The same word is used in Colossians iii. 1, where we are bidden to "seek those things which are above." The prize, of the calling to the things above, is surely that full and perfect knowledge of Christ Himself, which will be possible for us when our bodies are changed and fashioned like unto His body of glory at His coming.

Paul thirsted to know Him yet more deeply, as we have seen, while still he ran the race with the prize of a full knowledge of Him at the end. His desire was so intense that it made him a man of one thing. He was marked by concentration and intensity of purpose, suffering nothing to divert him from his aim. This feature, of course, goes far to explain the amazing power and fruitfulness that characterized his life and ministry. The weakness and lack of fruit that so often marks our lives and ministry may be very largely traced to exactly opposite features in ourselves—lack of purpose and concentration. Time and energy are frittered away on a hundred and one things of no particular value or moment, instead of the one thing commanding us. Is it not so? Then let us seek mercy from the Lord that in an increasing measure we may be able to say, "One thing I do."

This really is very much what verse 15 says. Paul rejoiced in the knowledge that others beside himself could be spoken of as perfect or full-grown in Christ: they would be like-minded with him in this matter. Others again had hardly made the same spiritual progress, and consequently might view things somewhat differently. These are exhorted to walk in the same way according to their present attainment, with the assurance that God would lead them on until they saw things in just that way in which they had been revealed to the Apostle himself. We need to take these two verses very

PHILIPPIANS

much to heart, for they exemplify the way in which the more spiritual and
advanced believer should deal with those of lesser attainments than
himself. Our natural tendency is to look down on these who may be less
advanced than ourselves, to despise them or even to attack them because
of their lack of conformity to that which we see to be right. This tendency
is specially pronounced when the advance, upon which we rather pride
ourselves, is more a matter of intelligence than of real spirituality.

Verses 15 and 16, then, reveal the spirit of a true pastor in Paul; and
in verse 17 we find that he is able to refer them to his own life and character
as an example. One is reminded of the words in which one of the poets
has described the pastor. He

". . . allured to brighter worlds,
And led the way."

In verses 15 and 16 we see Paul alluring his weaker brethren to brighter
worlds. In verse 17 we see him leading the way. Example is, as we know, an
immense thing. Paul could say to the Philippians as he did to the Ephesians
at the close of his ministry, "I have shewed you and have taught you"
(Acts xx. 20). With him there was practice as well as doctrine.

For this reason he could call upon his converts to be "followers" or
"imitators" of himself. He was to be an "ensample," that is a type or
model for them, and this was the more necessary since even in those early
days there were many walking in such fashion as to deny what is proper
to Christianity, though evidently they still claimed to be within the sphere
of Christian profession. Here we have brought before us not immature
believers, as in verse 15, nor believers in a very perverse frame of mind,
as in verse 15 of chapter i., but adversaries whose end is destruction. These
are exposed with great vigour of language.

We must not fail to notice the spirit that characterized the Apostle in
denouncing them. There was nothing petty or vindictive about him, but
rather a spirit of compassionate grief. He wept even as he wrote the
denunciation. Moreover, his care for the Philippians was so zealous that
he had often warned them before as to these men.

His exposure falls under five heads.

1. They are enemies of the cross of Christ. Not perhaps of His death,
but of His cross—of that cross which has before God put the sentence of
death on man, his wisdom and his glory.

2. Their end is destruction. This alone would make Paul weep as he
thought of them.

3. Their God is their belly; that is, their own lusts and desires governed
them: desires often of a gross nature, though, we suppose, not always such.
Always however, in some shape or form, self was their god.

4. They gloried in that which was their shame. They had no spiritual
sensibilities at all. Everything in their minds was inverted. To them light
was darkness and darkness light: glory was shame and shame was glory.

5. Their minds were set on earthly things. Earth was the sphere of their thoughts and their religion. They carried on the tradition of those of whom the Psalmist spoke, saying, "They have set their eyes bowing down to the earth" (xvii. 11).

And that tradition is still being carried on vigorously. The generation of earth-minders still flourishes. It has indeed multiplied amazingly within Christendom. The unbelievers who fill so many pulpits that are supposed to be Christian, and control the destinies of so many denominations, have an incontestible claim to this un-apostolic succession. The cross of Christ as pouring contempt on man's pride and abilities they will have none of. Man—that is to say, self—is their god. They glory in things, such as their descent from the brute creation, which if true would only be to their shame. Earth fills their vision. Believers of the old-fashioned, New Testament type they ridicule as being "other worldly." They are altogether for this world.

Now, "our conversation is in heaven." It is really our commonwealth, our citizenship. Our vital associations are there, not here, as the enemies of the cross would teach. Heaven is our fatherland, and to heaven, as a matter of fact, we are going. But before we get there a great change as to our bodies is needed, and that change will reach us at the coming of the Lord. Our bodies of humiliation are going to be transformed into the likeness of His body of glory, and the working of His mighty power is needed for its accomplishment.

So our attitude is that of looking for the Saviour, who is coming forth from the heavens, to which we belong. He is coming as One who wields a power which will enable Him to ultimately subdue all things unto Himself. Is it not a touching thought that the very first exercise of that power of His is going to be in the direction of subduing the poor bodies of His saints, whether living or in the graves, into conformity to Himself? Then in His likeness we shall enter upon all that our heavenly citizenship involves.

So, we look for the Saviour. Let us keep the eyes of our hearts directed to the heavens, for the next move of decisive importance is coming from thence.

CHAPTER 4

THERE ARE TWO words in the first verse which direct our thoughts to what has gone before: "Therefore" and "so." We are to stand fast in the Lord *therefore;* that is, because of, or in view of, what has just been stated. Well, what has been stated? Our heavenly calling, our heavenly citizenship, our expectation of that body of glory, fashioned like unto Christ's in which we shall enter into our heavenly portion. No uncertainty here! And no disappointment when the moment of realization comes! We may well stand fast in the Lord!

But we are to stand fast *so;* that is, in like manner to the way in which Paul himself stood fast as delineated in chapter iii. We are to be "followers together" of him, and have him "for an ensample," as he told us. If we too find in the knowledge of Christ an excellency that far outshines all else, we shall indeed "stand fast *in the Lord.*" Our affections, our very beings will be so rooted in Him that nothing can move us.

As we have previously noticed the adversary was attempting to mar the testimony through the Philippians by means of dissension. In verse 2 we discover that at the moment the trouble largely centred in two excellent women who were in their midst. The Apostle now turns to them, naming them with the entreaty that they be of the same mind *in the Lord.* The three words emphasized are of all importance. If both came thoroughly under the domination of the Lord, having their hearts set for Him as Paul's was, differences of mind, which existed at that moment, would disappear. The mind of Euodias as to the matter, and Syntyche's mind, would disappear and the mind of the Lord would remain. Thus they would be of the same mind by having the Lord's mind.

Verse 3 appears to be a request to Epaphroditus, who was returning to Philippi bearing this letter, that he would help these two women in the matter, for they had been in the past devoted labourers in the Gospel along with the Apostle himself, Clement and others. If they could be helped the main root of dissension would be removed.

With verse 4 we come back to the exhortation of the first verse of chapter iii. There we were told to rejoice in the Lord. Here we are to rejoice in the Lord *alway;* for nothing is to be allowed to divert us from it. Further, he emphasizes by repeating the word, that we are to *rejoice.* We are not merely to believe and to trust, we are also to rejoice.

This leads to the consideration of things that would hinder our rejoicing in the Lord. The harsh unyielding spirit that always insists on its own rights is one of these things, for it is a fruitful source of discontent and self-occupation. In contrast thereto we are to be characterized by moderation and gentleness, for the Lord is near and He will undertake our cause.

Then again there are the varied testings and worries of life, things which have a tendency to fill our hearts with anxious care. In regard to these prayer is our resource. We should mingle thanksgivings with our prayers, for we should ever be mindful of the abundant mercies of the past. And the scope of our prayers is only limited by the word, "everything."

This scripture invites us to turn everything into a matter of prayer, and freely make known our requests to God. There is no guarantee, you notice, that all our requests will be granted. That would never do for our understanding is very limited and consequently we often ask for that which, if granted to us, would be neither to the glory of our Lord nor to our own blessing. What is guaranteed is that our hearts and minds shall be guarded by the peace of God, which surpasses all understanding. Again and again when Christians have passed through trials, from which they had in vain requested to be exempted, we find them looking back and saying, "I am a wonder to myself. How I could have passed through so heavy a trial, and yet have been lifted above it into such serenity, I cannot understand."

"The peace of God," must be distinguished from "peace with God," of which we read in Romans v. 1. That is the peace in relation to God, which comes from the knowledge of being justified before Him. This is the peace, in character like unto God's own peace, which fills our hearts when having committed everything to Him in prayer, we trust in His love and wisdom on our behalf, and consequently have anxious care as to nothing.

It may also be helpful to distinguish between prayer as presented in this passage and as presented in John xiv. 13, 14. There the Lord was speaking more particularly to the Apostolic band, in their character as the representatives that He was leaving behind Him in the world, and He gives them plenary powers as regards prayer in His Name. The force of "in My Name," is "as My representatives." This praying in His Name is a tremendously responsible and solemn thing. Every cheque drawn really in His Name on the Bank of Heaven will be honoured. Only we must be very careful that we do not draw cheques for purely personal purposes of our own, under cover of drawing in His Name. That would be a kind of misappropriation of trust funds! And let us remember that in the Bank of Heaven there is a penetrating vision which can infallibly discriminate between the cheque which is genuinely in His Name and the one which is not.

Still, though there are a thousand and one matters in our lives that we could hardly present to God in prayer as being directly connected with the Name and interests of Christ, yet we have full liberty to present them to God, and indeed are bidden to do so. As we do so we may be in the enjoyment of the peace of God. We may be anxious as to *nothing*, because prayerful as to *everything*, and thankful for *anything*.

Anxious care being driven out of our hearts there is room for all that is good to come in. Of this verse 8 speaks. One can hardly exaggerate the importance of having the mind filled with all that is true and pure and lovely, the highest expression of which is found in Christ. Our lives are so largely controlled by our thoughts, and hence it says, "As he thinketh in his heart, so is he" (Prov. xxiii. 7). Hence to have our minds filled with what is true and just and pure is like a high road leading to a life marked by truth and justice and purity. We have of necessity to come into contact with much that is evil, but needlessly to occupy ourselves with it is disastrous, and a source of spiritual weakness.

But if the supreme and perfect expression of all these good things was found in Christ, there was also a very real exhibition of them in the life of the Apostle himself. The Philippians had not only learned and received and heard them, but also seen them in Paul, and what they had seen they themselves were to do. To *DO*, notice, for the excellent things that fill our minds are to come into practical display in our lives. Then indeed the God of peace shall be with us, which is something beyond the peace of God filling our hearts.

With verse 10 the closing messages of the epistle begin, and Paul again refers to the gift which the Philippians had sent him. That gift had been a cause of great rejoicing to him in his imprisonment. He knew that he had not been out of their thoughts, but they had not had opportunity to send help until this occasion of the journey of Epaphroditus. It had now arrived most opportunely; yet his joy was not primarily because it relieved him of privation, as the beginning of verse 11 shows, but because he knew it meant more fruit towards God, which would be to their credit in the coming day, as verse 17 shows.

Speaking of want or privation leads the Apostle to give us a wonderful insight into the way in which he faced his sufferings and imprisonment. These tragic circumstances had become to him a fountain of practical instruction, for he had learned to be content. To be content in present circumstances, no matter what they be, was not natural to Paul any more than it is to us. But he had learned it. And learned it, not as a matter of theory, but in experimental fashion by passing through the most adverse circumstances, with his heart full of Christ, as we see in chapter iii. Hence he was able to face changes of the most violent sort. Abasement or abounding, fulness or hunger, abounding or acute privation, all was the same to Paul, for Christ was the same, and all Paul's resources and joys were in Him.

In Christ Paul had strength for all things, and the same strength in the same way is available for every one of us. If only we exploited all that is in Christ for us we could do all things. But Paul did not simply say, "I could," but rather, "I can." It is easy to admire the wonderful fortitude, the serene superiority to circumstances which marked the Apostle, and it is not difficult to discern the source of his power, but it is another thing to tread in his steps. That is hardly possible except we go through his circumstances, or similar ones. Here it is that our weakness is so manifest. We conform to the world, we lack spiritual vigour and aggressiveness, we avoid the suffering, and we miss the spiritual education. We cannot say, "I have learned . . . I know . . . I am instructed . . . I can do," as Paul could. It is just as well that we should candidly face these defects that mark us, lest we should think that we are "rich and increased with goods," that we are picked Christians of the twentieth century, and consequently as to "spiritual intelligence" almost the last word as to what Christians ought to be.

The Apostle then was not in any sense dependent on the gifts of the Philippian saints or of others, and he would have them know it; yet though this was so he assures them, and that in a very delicate and beautiful way, that he was fully alive to the love and devotion both towards the Lord and himself that had prompted their gift. He recognized that the Philippians peculiarly shone in this grace, and had done so from the first moment that the Gospel had reached them. They had thought of him in the past, when no other assemblies had done so, both in Macedonia and Thessalonica, and now again in Rome.

The devotion of the Philippians in this respect was heightened by the fact that they were very poor. We are enlightened as to this in 2 Corinthians viii. 2. They also had been in much affliction themselves, and they had experienced much joy in the Lord. All this is very instructive for us. Oftentimes we are unsympathetic and stingy because our own experiences both of suffering and spiritual refreshment are so very shallow.

Having received of their bounty through Epaphroditus, Paul would have them know that now he had a full supply and was enjoying abundance. But their gift had not only met his need, it was in the nature of a sacrifice acceptable to God, like to those sacrifices of a sweet smelling odour of which the Old Testament speaks. This was a greater thing still.

But what of the Philippians themselves? They had further impoverished themselves, further reduced their already slender resources by their gifts in favour of an aged prisoner who could in no wise reciprocate or help them. Paul felt this and in verse 19 he expresses his confidence as to them. God would supply all their need. Notice how he speaks of Him as, "My God,"—the God whom Paul knew and had practically tested for himself. That God would be their Supplier, not according to their need, nor even according to Paul's ardent desires on their behalf, but according to His own riches in glory in Christ Jesus. It would have been a wonderful thing had God engaged to supply them according to His riches *on earth* in Christ Jesus. His riches *in glory* are more wonderful still. The Philippians or ourselves may never be rich in the things of earth and yet be enriched in the things of glory. If so we shall indeed respond, in attributing glory to God our Father for ever and ever.

It is interesting to note in the closing word of salutation that there were saints found even in Caesar's household. The first chapter told us that his bonds had been manifested as being in Christ in all the palace, and if in all the palace even to Caesar himself, we suppose. But with some of his attendants and servants things had gone further than that, and they had been converted. In a great stronghold of the adversary's power souls had been translated from the kingdom of darkness and brought into the kingdom of God's dear Son.

Such triumphs does grace effect! How fittingly comes the closing desire, "The grace of our Lord Jesus Christ be with you all. Amen."

COLOSSIANS

CHAPTER 1

THE BELIEVERS AT Colosse were far in advance of the Galatians as to their spiritual state. As we go through the epistle we shall see that there were certain important matters as to which the Apostle Paul had to sound a warning note, yet in the main they had been marked by progress, and he could speak of their "order" and of the "steadfastness" of their faith in Christ (ii. 5). They were therefore in happy contrast with both the Corinthians and the Galations, for the former were characterized by disorder and the latter by backsliding as to the faith of Christ.

Because of this, doubtless, they are addressed as faithful brethren as well as saints. All believers may rightly be called holy brethren for all are "saints," or "holy ones," that is, "ones set apart for God." Can we all be addressed as faithful brethren? Are we all going forward in faith and faithfulness? Let us take these questions to heart for the unfaithful believer is not likely to appreciate much, or understand, the truth unfolded in this epistle.

As so often in his epistles, the Apostle opens by assuring the Colossians of his prayers for them. If any word of admonition or correction is necessary, it comes with much greater power and acceptability from lips that have been habitually employed in prayer for us, than from any other. His prayers had however been mingled with thanksgivings, and both had been provoked by that which he had heard concerning them, for, as verse 1 of chapter ii. shows us, he had not yet seen and known them face to face. Tidings had reached him of their *faith* in Christ and of their *love* to all the saints.

These two things, simple and elementary as they may appear, are of extreme importance. They indicate with definiteness and certainty the possession of the divine nature—see, 1 John iii. 14; v. 1. An unconverted person may be quite attached to an individual believer here or there, who happens to strike his fancy, but he does not love "all the saints." That is quite beyond any, save the one who is born of God.

The Apostle does not inform them as to the burden of his prayers for them until verse 9 is reached. He first tells them of that for which he gave thanks. "We give thanks . . . for the hope which is laid up for you in heaven." That hope is alluded to in the course of the epistle (see, i. 27; iii. 4), but it is not unfolded in any full way because they well knew it. Tidings of it had reached them when the word of the Gospel first came to their ears. We learn from this that those who preach the Gospel should take care to emphasize not only its present effect in delivering from the power of sin, but also its ultimate effect—introducing the believer into glory. It would of course be equally a mistake to preach its ultimate effect without insisting on its present effect.

The Gospel in those days had overleaped the narrow boundaries of Palestine and was going forth into all the world. It had reached to the Colossians, Gentiles though they were, and consequently they knew the grace of God in truth. Does grace make us careless or indifferent? It does not; it works in an exactly opposite direction; it brings forth fruit. "The Glad Tidings . . . are bearing fruit and growing, even as also among you," is another rendering of this passage. Both growth and fruit-bearing are proofs of vitality. There is no stagnation and decay where the Gospel is really received.

It would appear from verse 7 that Epaphras had been the servant of Christ who brought the light to them. They had learned the Glad Tidings of the grace of God and of the hope of glory from his lips. Then verse 8 indicates that he had travelled to Rome and made known to Paul what God had wrought among the Colossians, and the depth and sincerity of their Christian love. We can see how highly Paul esteemed him. He speaks of him as a faithful servant of Christ, and at the end of the epistle we learn how truly devoted he was to the spiritual welfare of the Colossians.

The report brought by Epaphras had not only moved Paul to thanksgiving, as we have seen, but also impelled him to constant prayer on their behalf. In verse 9 he begins to tell them of that which he prayed for on their behalf. His prayer may be summarized under four heads:—

1. He desired that they might have full knowledge of the will of God, so that
2. they might walk in a way worthy of the Lord and well pleasing to Him; that so they might be
3. strengthened to endure suffering with joyfulness, and
4. be filled with the spirit of thanksgiving and praise.

But let us look a little more particularly at these things.

The will of God is to govern everything for us; hence the knowledge of His will necessarily comes in the first place. The word used for knowledge here is a very strong one really meaning *full knowledge*, and with that full knowledge they were to be filled. The apostle would not be satisfied with anything short of this. The will of God was to possess all their thoughts and fill up their horizon. This is an immensely high standard truly, but then the divine standard and objective never is anything but immensely high.

Further our knowledge is to be in spiritual understanding; that is, understanding acquired by the Spirit of God and not by a merely intellectual process. It is possible to acquire Biblical information in much the same way as one obtains historical or geographical information, and in such a case one may be able to analyse and expound the Scriptures and yet be quite a stranger to their experimental bearing and their power. Also our knowledge is to be in all wisdom. The wise man is he who is able with good judgment to apply his knowledge to the circumstances that he has to face.

So what the Apostle desired for the Colossians, and for us, is that we might gain full knowledge of God's will by the teaching of the Holy Spirit, for in that way we shall ourselves be governed by what we know and also be able to apply our knowledge to practical details in the midst of the tangled circumstances that surround us.

Now this it is that will enable us to walk worthily of the Lord, so as to please Him well. Few things are more sad than to see a believer distracted by circumstances, filled with uncertainty, vacillating this way and that. How inspiring, on the other hand, when a believer is like a ship, which though buffeted by fierce winds, blowing at times from all points of the compass, yet keeps with steadiness on its course, because the skipper has good nautical understanding of the chart, and the wisdom not only to take his observations from the sun but also to apply them to his whereabouts and direction. There is a definiteness and certainty about such an one that glorifies God. That of which we speak was exemplified in surpassing measure by the Apostle Paul himself. We have only to read Philippians iii. to see it.

This walk, worthy of the Lord and pleasing to Him, is the necessary basis of fruitfulness. We may distinguish between the "fruit of the Spirit," spoken of in Galatians v. 22, 23, and "being fruitful," according to our 10th verse. There it is fruit produced in the way of Christian *character*. Here it is fruitfulness in *good works*. The former lays the foundation for the latter, but both are necessary. Good works are the necessary outcome of a character which is really formed after Christ. Good works are works which give expression to the divine life and character in the Christian, and which are according to the Word of God. We are to be marked by *every* good work.

And in all this there is no finality while we are on earth, as the last clause of verse 10 shows. Though we may have the knowledge of His will yet we are to go on increasing in the knowledge of God, or, "by the full knowledge of God." We not only grow *in* it but *by* it, for the more we know God experimentally the more our spiritual stature increases, and the more too are we "strengthened with all might," as verse 11 indicates.

The language of that verse is very strong. It is, "all might," "His glorious power," (or, "the power of His glory,") and "all patience." We might well ask with astonishment, "Is it possible that weak and failing creatures like to ourselves should be strengthened to this extraordinary degree?" It is. The power of the glory is able to subdue all things to Himself, as Philippians iii. 21 indicates; hence it can subdue and strengthen us now. But to what end?

The answer to this question is even more astonishing. To the end that we may be able to endure all the trials of the way, not only with longsuffering but with joyfulness also. We should naturally have supposed that extraordinary strengthening would have been in view of the performing of extraordinary exploits in the service of God, of our acting like an Elijah or a Paul. But no, it is in view of suffering, sustained with endurance and joy. A few moments reflection will assure us that there is nothing less natural to us than this.

The world knows and admires that attitude of mind which is expressed by the saying, "Grin and bear it." We commend the man who faces adversity with cheerfulness, though his cheerfulness is only based on a species of fatalism and a refusal to look ahead beyond the day. The believer, who has grown in the knowledge of God and is strengthened, may be plunged into suffering, and instead of being consumed with desire to get out of it he endures with long-suffering, instead of grumbling at the Divine ways he not only acquiesces but is joyful. *Joyful*, be it noted, and not merely cheerful. His joy flows on like still waters that run deep. But then the power for this is according to the might of His glory. That glory exists today, and very shortly it is coming into display, so even now it is possible for us to "rejoice with joy unspeakable and full of glory." Read 1 Peter i. 6-9, for it illustrates our subject.

The saint who is joyful passes naturally to thanksgiving and praise. Hence verse 12 flows out of verse 11. We give thanks to God as the Father, for it is in this character we know Him, and that He has wrought on our behalf in the pursuance of His purposes of love. We give thanks for that which He *has done*. The items of the thanksgiving follow a descending scale. We work downwards from His purpose to the meeting of our need, which was necessary in order that His purpose might be reached.

Made "fit for sharing the portion of the saints in light." Not, *to be made*, nor, *in process of being made*, but, MADE. We who have believed are fit for heavenly glory, fit for that portion in the light of God's presence which is to be shared in common by all the saints of this dispensation. We may be very little able to realize what this inheritance means, but how full is the assurance that we have been made fit for it by the Father. The fitness is ours already though the inheritance is future.

In order that we might be made fit deliverance had to reach us. In our unconverted state we lay under the authority of darkness. Darkness here stands for Satan and his works, even as we have just had the word, light, used to describe the presence of God. We have been delivered from Satan's kingdom by being brought into a kingdom of an infinitely higher and better character—the kingdom of "His dear Son," or, "the Son of His love." By coming under the authority of perfect good we are delivered from the power of evil.

Again and again in the New Testament are we reminded that having believed we are brought under the Divine authority. The kingdom of God is spoken of, and in Matthew's gospel we read of the kingdom of heaven, inasmuch as Jesus, God's King, is seated in the heavens, so that He is exerting heavenly rule upon earth. Other expressions also are used as to the kingdom, but none of them give us so great a sense of nearness and affection as this which we have here. The word, kingdom, in itself might have a slightly harsh sound in our ears, but there is nothing harsh about "the kingdom of the Son of the Father's love." It speaks of authority truly, but it is authority of a perfect love, its every decree tempered by that.

Never let us kick at authority. The fact is we cannot do without it, and were never intended to do so. At the outset when man began to kick against the authority of God he instantly fell under the dark authority of the devil. It was never intended that man should be absolutely uncontrolled. If now we get deliverance from Satan's authority it is by being brought into subjection to God's dear Son. The yoke of Satan is burdensome to a degree. Those under it are like to the demoniac, who had his dwelling among the tombs, and who was always crying and cutting himself with stones. The yoke of the Lord Jesus, as He has told us, is easy and His burden is light. Our removal from the one to the other has been a translation indeed!

This translation has been effected in the strength of the redemption work of the cross. Only by redemption could we be extricated in a righteous way from bondage under the power of darkness. We have been brought back to God by blood; and by that same bloodshedding have our sins been put away, so that all are forgiven. We should not be able to rejoice in the fact of being brought back to God apart from the forgiveness of all our sins, which once stood between us and Him.

Though the glorious truth of verses 12 to 14 is stated as from God's side on a descending scale, we on our side enter into the knowledge and enjoyment of it on the ascending scale, that is, in the reverse order. We necessarily begin with the forgiveness of our sins. Then entering into the larger thought of redemption we begin to appreciate the great translation effected, and our absolute fitness for glory, as in Christ. The more we do enter into all, the more will our hearts and lips be filled with thanksgiving to the Father, from whom all has sprung.

But if the Father is the Source of all, His dear Son is the Channel through whom all has flowed to us—the One who has put all into execution at such immeasurable cost to Himself. Redemption has reached us through His blood, and when we know WHO IT IS that shed His blood, our thoughts of it are greatly enlarged. Consequently in verses 15 to 17 we are given a sight of His splendour in connection with creation. Here is a passage hard to equal whether we consider the sublimity of the thoughts expressed, or the graphic power with which they are expressed in the fewest possible words. Sublimity, graphic power and brevity are combined.

In verse 15 two words call for brief remarks. The word "Image" has the force of "Representative." The invisible God is exactly represented in Him, a thing impossible apart from the fact of Himself being God. Some are inclined to slightly demur to this on account of the second word in the verse, to which we have referred. In the word "Firstborn" they lay too much stress in their minds upon the second half of the word. "But He was *born*," they say. The word "firstborn" however besides its primary meaning has also a figurative sense (as in Psa. lxxxix. 27; Jer. xxxi. 9), meaning, the one who takes the supreme place as holding the rights of the firstborn. That is the sense in which it is used in our passage. The Lord Jesus not only stands forth as the Representative of all that God is, He also stands forth absolutely pre-eminent over creation. All creation's glory and its rights are vested in Him, for the simple reason that He is the Creator, as verse 16 states.

In the very first verse of the Bible creation is attributed to God, and it is a remarkable fact that the word used there for God is a plural word, *Elohim*. It is the more remarkable inasmuch as the Hebrews employed not only the singular and the plural but had also another number, the dual, signifying two, and two only. Their plural words therefore signified *three* or more, and when we turn to the New Testament we find that there are *three* Persons in the Godhead. We also discover that of the three Persons creation is always attributed to the Son.

It is so here; and in verse 16 this great fact is stated in a threefold way, three different prepositions being used, *in, by* and *for*. In our Authorized version the first preposition as well as the second is *by*. Literally, however, it is *in*. If you turn up this passage in Darby's New Translation you will find footnotes which instruct us that *in* signifies "characteristic power:" that "He was the One whose intrinsic power characterized the creation. It exists as His creature." They instruct us also that *by* signifies that He was "the active Instrument," and that *for* signifies that He is "the End" for which creation exists.

You will notice too the comprehensive way in which the creation is described in this passage. Heaven as well as earth is brought into view. Things invisible are contemplated as well as things visible; and the invisible and spiritual powers are spoken of under four heads. What may be the real distinction between thrones, dominions, principalities and powers we do not know, but we do know that they all owe their very existence to our Lord Jesus. Twice over in this one verse is it stated that He is the Creator of "all things." Consequently He is before all both as to time and place; and all things hang together by Him. The stars pursue their appointed courses, but they only do so because directed by Him.

It is not difficult to see that the Creator, having entered into the midst of His own creation by becoming Man, He necessarily stands in the creation as Head and Firstborn. In verse 18 however, we find that He is both Head and Firstborn in another connection. He is the Head of the body, the church, and that church is God's new creation work. He is the Firstborn from among the dead; that is, He holds the supreme rights in the resurrection world. Consequently in all things and in every sphere He has the first place.

What glorious truth is this! How wonderful that we should know Him as Firstborn in this twofold way, both in connection with the first creation and the new creation! Only our relation with Him according to the new creation is far more intimate than ever it could have been according to the old. In all creation He is of course Head, in the sense of being Chief, and it is in that sense that He is spoken of as, "the Head of every man," in 1 Corinthians xi. 3. He is Head to the church in another sense, illustrated by the human body. An organic and vital union exists between the head and the other members of the body, and just so does a vital union exist between Christ and His members in new creation.

Further, He is "the Beginning." He existed in the beginning, as we are elsewhere told, but that is another thing. Here He *is* the beginning, and that beginning is connected with resurrection as the next words show. The resurrection of the Lord Jesus was the new beginning for God. All that God is doing today He is doing in connection with Christ in resurrection. All our links with Him are on that footing. Let us very prayerfully consider this point, for except we lay hold of it with spiritual understanding we shall fail to appreciate the true nature of Christianity.

In the risen Christ, then, we find God's new beginning, but let us now notice the important truth that follows in verses 19—22. There had to be a complete settlement of every liability incurred in connection with the old creation. Unscrupulous men may sometimes open a business and having incurred heavy liabilities, close it up without any attempt at meeting them. Then they depart elsewhere and propose to open up a new business! Such a practice is universally condemned. God ever acts in strict righteousness. By His death the Lord Jesus has wrought a settlement as regards man's sin in the old creation. Then in His resurrection God commenced anew.

Verse 19 tells us that all the fulness of the Godhead was pleased to dwell in the Son when He came forth to do His mighty work, and by the blood of His cross the Godhead aimed at so effectually making peace that the basis might be laid for the reconciliation of all things. And we may safely add that what the Godhead aims at the Godhead always accomplishes.

The effect of sin has been that man has lapsed into a state of enmity with God, and hence the earth is filled with strife, confusion, disharmony. In the death of Christ a clearance has been effected judicially by judgment falling on that which created all the trouble. The disturbing element being removed peace can ensue. Peace being established reconciliation can come to pass.

Now peace *has been made*. No one has "to make their peace with God." Nor could they make peace with God if they had to do it. Christ is the

Maker of peace. He made it, not by His life of singular beauty and perfection, but by His death. We of course are to enjoy the peace, and that is what is spoken of in Romans v. 1. "Being justified by faith *we have* peace with God." By faith we have the peace in our hearts, and what a wonderful peace it is! Here however the point is the making of the peace at the cross. The only possible basis for the peace enjoyed *inside* us is the peace made *outside* us when the blood of the cross was shed.

Peace having been made the reconciliation of all things is coming. We must not, however, imagine that this means the salvation of everybody, for a qualifying clause is immediately added. The "all things" is limited to "things in earth or things in heaven." When it is a question of bowing the knee to Jesus, there are included "things under the earth," but they are not included here. The world of the lost will have to submit. They will be broken but not reconciled.

It is perfectly evident that reconciliation has not yet been reached as to things on earth. Yet believers are already reconciled as verse 21 states; and in that verse we find a word that helps us to understand what reconciliation really means—a word that describes the state which is the exact opposite of reconciliation—*alienation*.

Manifold evil has engulfed mankind as the result of the incoming of sin. Not only have we incurred guilt but we lie under a terrible bondage. Again not only are we in bondage but we have been utterly estranged from God, in whom all our hope lies. We needed justification in view of our guilt. We needed redemption in view of bondage. And because we were so wholly alienated from God we needed reconciliation. The alienation, be it observed, lay wholly upon our side. The enmity existed in our minds towards God, not in God's mind towards us; and the enmity and alienation expressed itself in wicked works. Hence we may say that, whilst there *is* a sense in which God needed reconciliation, we needed it in a twofold way.

Reconciliation was effected "through death,"—the death of Christ. His death is the stable basis on which it rests, needed by God and needed by us. We however needed more than this. We needed the mighty work in our hearts by which the enmity should be swept out of them for ever. As a result of it all God looks down upon us, as in Christ, with complacency and delight; whilst we, sensible of His favour, look up to Him with responsive affection.

God only has full delight in that which is perfect. But then the effect of the death of Christ is that we can be presented "holy and unblameable and unreproveable in His sight." Cleared are we from everything which formerly attached to us as the fallen children of Adam, for "in the body of His flesh through death" the judgment of all that we were has been executed. That same death provides the basis for the coming reconciliation of all things in heaven and on earth.

COLOSSIANS

What a glorious prospect this is! There are things in heaven which have been touched and tarnished by sin, and these are to be reconciled, though the angels that sinned have been cast down to hell, and so do not come within its scope. Everything upon earth has been wrecked. Yet a day is coming when everything within these two spheres will be brought into complete harmony with the will of God, and bask for ever in the sunlight of His favour, responding in every particular to His love. Well may we cry, Lord, haste that day! Well may we ponder deeply upon such themes, for the more we do so the more will dawn upon us the wonder of the death of Christ.

All that we have been considering supposes of course that we are really and truly the Lord's. Hence the qualifying "If" in verse 23. Many there are who, hearing the Gospel profess to believe and yet at some later time they totally abandon their profession. They do not "continue in the faith grounded and settled," they are "moved away from the hope of the Gospel"; and thereby they make manifest that they had not the root of the matter in them. The words, "yet now hath He reconciled," do not apply to such.

Again in this verse does the Apostle emphasize the vast scope of the Gospel, even "every creature which is under heaven," just as in verse 6 it is stated as "all the world." The point here is of course not that it had then been actually preached to every creature, but that the sphere of its operations was no less than every creature. Of that Gospel Paul had been made a minister. A further ministry, that of the church, was his also, as stated in verse 25.

The Apostle introduces the subject of his second ministry by a reference to his sufferings. He was in prison when he wrote and he speaks of his sufferings as, "the afflictions of Christ." That was their character. They were certainly afflictions *for* Christ, but the point here seems to be that they were in character Christ's afflictions, of the same kind as He endured in His wonderful path on earth, though far less as to degree. Needless to say the Lord Jesus stands absolutely alone in His atoning sufferings in His death. There is no allusion to those here.

The sufferings which rolled in upon Paul's flesh were endured for the sake of the whole church, and that church is the body of Christ. In his imprisonment the Apostle was filling up the cup of his afflictions, and that on behalf of the church in its widest sense—we mean, not only for the church as existing on earth in his day, but for the church through the ages to the finish of its earthly history, including ourselves. He suffered that the truth as to the church might be made abundantly plain and established, and out of his sufferings sprang these immortal epistles which instruct us today. In this way his ministry as to the church is made available for us today.

A "dispensation," or "administration" was given to him of God that thereby he might "fulfil" or, "complete" His Word. This does not mean that Paul was to write the last words of Scripture, for, as we know, John did that. It means that the revealing of the mystery alluded to in the succeeding verses, was committed to him, and when that was made known the last item of revelation was filled in, the circle of revealed truth was complete.

In Scripture a "mystery" does not mean something mysterious or incomprehensible, but simply something which up to that time had been secret or hidden, or at all events only known to the initiated. The mystery spoken of here had been completely hidden in earlier ages, and now is only made manifest to God's saints. It concerns Christ and the church, and more particularly the bringing in of the Gentiles in one body. This side of it is more definitely unfolded in the epistle to the Ephesians. In verse 27 of our chapter it is said to be "Christ in you, the hope of glory." Read the verse and you will see that the "you" here means "you Gentiles." Formerly God had dwelt for a brief time in the midst of Israel, and then again the Messiah had appeared for another brief season amongst Jews in the land, but that Christ should now be found in Gentiles was an altogether new and unprecedented thing. It was a pledge of the glory to come, for Christ will be all and *in all* in that day.

It is not easy for us to imagine how revolutionary a doctrine this appeared to be when first announced. It completely set aside the special and exclusive position of the Jew and this was its chief offence in their eyes, arousing their furious opposition. The maintaining of this it was that had brought imprisonment and such suffering upon Paul.

On the other hand Paul knew its great importance as being the characteristic truth for this dispensation. Every dispensation of God has truth which gives character to it, and this is the truth which characterizes the present dispensation. Only as instructed in it are we likely to be "perfect" or, "complete" in Christ. Hence the Apostle laboured mightily in making this truth known according to the working of the Spirit of God in him.

CHAPTER 2

NOT ONLY DID Paul labour in teaching this great truth, but he laboured also in prayer, and this the more now that he was restrained from his former activity by prison walls. His prayers were so intense that he describes them as conflict. In this conflict he was led out specially on behalf of those he had never met face to face, such as the Colossians, the Laodiceans and others. He wanted them to come to a full knowledge of this secret and to have their hearts knit together in the process, for in this full knowledge lay the full assurance of understanding.

In Hebrews x. we read of "the full assurance of faith," the faith that simply takes God at His word. That is something with which we are entitled to *begin* our career as believers. Full assurance of understanding marks *maturity* of spiritual intelligence. Entering into the understanding of the mystery, the last segment of the circle of truth falls into its place, the whole becomes intelligible and luminous, the vastness and wonder of the whole Divine scheme begins to dawn upon us, and a very wonderful assurance takes possession of our hearts.

We must not leave verse 2 without noticing that word, "their hearts . . . knit together in love." In the mystery of God all the treasures of wisdom and knowledge are hid, and by a full knowledge of it the full assurance of understanding is obtained, but it is when divine love reigns amongst the saints that the full knowledge of the mystery becomes a simple thing. A believer isolated from all Christian companionship might so study his Bible in dependence on the Spirit's teaching as to gain a very good *mental* grasp of it, but he could not grasp it *experimentally*. We never understand it fully until we have some experience of what it means.

Here lies the reason, without a doubt, why the mystery is so little understood today. The true church of God is so sadly divided that there is very little knitting together in love. We cannot remedy the divided state of the church but we can walk in love towards our fellow-saints as far as we know them; and as far as we do this so far shall we have our hearts expanded to embrace this truth—so far shall we enter into our place in the body of Christ, instead of thinking, as so many do almost exclusively, of a place in some body of Christians, or some denominational organization.

In the first century they had not to face difficulties springing from the divided state of the church, but there were difficulties nevertheless as verse 4 indicates. Already men were going about beguiling believers. Let us take especial note that they were doing so "with enticing words." Smooth, elegant, persuasive speech is the chief stock-in-trade of deceivers. How often have simple and unsuspecting folk said of some propagandist, "Oh, but he must be all right: he spoke so beautifully!" When a little subsequent investigation showed that he was as far from being "all right" as could be.

The Apostle proceeds to warn them more in detail as to these deceivers whose teachings would altogether turn them aside from any understanding of the mystery. Before doing so however he joyfully acknowledges the good that marked the Colossians, and he exhorts them to further progress in the right direction.

The good that characterized them we have in verse 5. In the first place they were orderly. In this they contrasted happily with the Corinthians, who were in a very disorderly state. Evidently both in their assembly life and in their private lives they had been subject to the apostolic instructions. In the second place there was a steadfastness about their faith. They were like soldiers who had firmly withstood the shock of battle. Every assault upon their faith had failed.

Verses 6 and 7 indicate that the best preventive against evil is progress in the right direction. Having received Christ as their Lord, they were to "walk in Him," that is, to put into practice what they knew of Him and of His will. Having been rooted in Him they were to be built up in Him, and thus established so firmly in the true faith that they were like vessels filled up to the brim with it, and overflowing with praise and thanksgiving. Let us all take note that it is when our knowledge of the truth comes out in our *practice* on the one hand, and in our *praise* on the other, that we are really established in it.

But when a frontal attack fails the enemy will try an assault upon the flank. What cannot be accomplished by open and bold denials may perhaps be achieved by subtle insinuations, by sly subtractions, or even better still, by apparently harmless additions to the faith of Christ—additions which nevertheless do nullify much that is vital. Such has ever been the plan of the devil, and Paul's watchful eye saw signs of danger for the Colossians in this way. Consequently the rest of the chapter is taken up with earnest and loving warnings, together with unfoldings of truth calculated to fortify them against the dangers.

The Apostle's warnings seem to fall under three heads. This may be seen by looking at verses 8, 16 and 18, each of which opens with a word of caution as to the activities of men. The activities run in different directions, but all are antagonistic to the truth. In the first case the danger comes from philosophy. In the second from Judaism. In the third from superstition. All three dangers are tremendously alive and energetic today, particularly the first and third.

The word "spoil" in verse 8 does not mean *to mar*, but rather, *to capture as spoil*, or *to make a prey of you*. It describes the kind of thing that will happen to you if instead of progressing in the faith of Christ you submit to the teachings of philosophers. It is a strong way of putting it, but not one whit too strong. In the ancient world the Greeks were the great philosophers. They had no knowledge of any revelation from God, and in its absence set their minds to work on the problems presented by man and the universe. In result their teachings were but empty deceit, all of them framed according to man and his little world.

Even in Paul's day some were found who wished to accommodate Christian teaching to Grecian philosophy, and this meant the virtual destruction of faith. In our day the same kind of thing has taken place. The philosophy of today differs in many ways from that of the ancient world. Two terrible features characterize it: firstly, it pursues its investigations and theorizings not in ignorance of any revelation from God at all, but in rejection of the revelation that has been brought to their notice; secondly, it all too frequently has seized upon the terms used in God's revelation, the Bible, and then having emptied them of their Scriptural meaning has filled them with another meaning suited to their own purposes. A very deceitful process, this! When the Apostle coupled together *philosophy* and *vain deceit* he wrote as a prophet indeed!

Philosophic teachings, whether ancient or modern, are brought in professedly to supplement the simple teachings of the Gospel and lead us on to more perfect knowledge. In reality they destroy the Gospel. Christ is the test of all teaching. Is it according to Christ?—that is the test. And why is Christ the test? Because the whole fulness of the Godhead dwells in Him, and we ourselves are "complete" or "filled full" in Him. We need go outside Him for nothing.

There is a strong likeness between verse 19 of chapter i. and verse 9 of our chapter; only there it refers to that which was true of Him in the days of His sojourn on earth, whilst here it is stated as being true of Him today. It is hardly possible to imagine a stronger statement of His deity, and yet it plainly infers that He still is Man in saying, "bodily." If then we are rooted and built up and filled full in such an One as He, it would be manifestly very foolish to turn aside to the philosophizings of poor little human brains that ere long will be eaten of worms.

Verse 11 adds another important consideration. We are circumcised in Him as well as complete in Him. Now circumcision is a thorough cutting off. The circumcision of Christ was His cutting off by death. In His death He put off all connection with the old order of things; He died to sin, and lives to God, as Romans vi. 10 puts it. A spiritual circumcision, "made without hands," has reached us by means of His death, which to us has been "the putting off the body of the flesh"—the words, "of the sins," should not be included in the text. Death has come in between us and the flesh, and consequently we are cut off from the teachings of man and his world.

If verse 11 speaks of death, verse 12 brings before us burial and resurrection. Burial is the completion and ratification of death. That which goes to corruption must be put out of sight. We are buried, be it noted, *in baptism*. In submitting to that ordinance we go to our own funeral. But we go into burial·in view of resurrection, for we are risen with Christ through the faith of that which God did, in raising Him from the dead. In these two verses we are instructed in the true force of the death and resurrection of Christ and also of our baptism—what God sees in them. And we are entitled to see in them what He does. The application of all this comes later in the epistle.

As we commence verse 13 we pass from that which has been accomplished in Christ to something accomplished in us. As to our spiritual state we were dead; dead in our sins—what we had done; dead in the uncircumcision of our flesh—what we were. But now quickened—made to live—together with Christ; our new life being of the same order as His.

Resurrection put us in a new world, and quickening endows us with a new life. Neither the one nor the other however brings us release from the guilt of our sins. We *are* released however. All our offences are forgiven. But that brings us back to the cross.

The cross blotted out our sins truly, but it did more than this: it blotted out also the whole system of legal ordinances which had been against us. The law was not blotted out: far from it, for it was vindicated and magnified in the death of Christ. On the other hand we died from under the law in His death, and we are now under grace, with all the old legal ordinances—samples of which are found in verse 16—set aside. The language of verse 14 may need a word of explanation. The word translated "blotted out" is one "used for annulling a decree of law." The idea of "handwriting" is that of "obligation to which a man is subject by his signature." Paul used a very graphic figure. We had bound ourselves by our signature to Jewish ordinances, but the document has been nullified in the death of Christ. As far as we are concerned it was nailed to the cross when He was nailed to the cross. In these words of course Paul particularly had Jews in view.

The cross is viewed in still another light in verse 15, so that we have it here presented in three connections. We may summarize them thus:—

v. 11. The cross in relation to ourselves, and in particular the flesh.
v. 14. The cross in relation to legal ordinances.
v. 15. The cross in relation to the spiritual forces of evil.

Whatever these spiritual powers may be, from Satan downwards, in the cross the divine triumph has been manifested. On the surface it looked like being the triumph of the powers of evil. Really it was their undoing. This being so we can see that when verse 10 spoke of the Lord Jesus as "the Head of all principality and power," it was stating something which is true not only upon the ground of creation, but also on the ground of what He accomplished at the cross.

The truth of the cross as unfolded in verse 11 had special reference to what had preceded, that is, the warning as to the snare of philosophy. Today we should speak of it not only as philosophy but as rationalism also—the worshipping of human intellect and human reasonings. Immediately we discern in the cross our circumcision—our cutting off—a clean sweep is made of rationalism, as to any authority it possessed over us. It influences us no more.

The cross as presented in verse 14 is the basis of the warning uttered in verse 16, as indicated by the word, "therefore." There were plenty of Judaizing enthusiasts who would take them to task as to their observance or non-observance of ordinances, but they were not to be moved, nor to pay attention to them. Five classes of ordinances are specified, those relating to meat, drink, feasts, new moons, sabbaths. These things are all shadows of things to come, as we are told also in the epistle to the Hebrews, but the body—that is, the substance—is of Christ.

If any are disposed to ask in what way these things have to say to us today inasmuch as there is no active Judaizing party at work in the church at present, the answer is that they are still very much to the point. The reason why there is not much active Judaizing is that the professing church has been for many centuries so largely Judaized. But have you never met the Seventh-day Adventists? If so you may thank God. But if you have, take special note of the way in which this Scripture negatives their propaganda, the spear-head of which is their insistence on the Jewish sabbath. They will judge you as to the sabbath, if you will let them. The word here is not exactly "sabbath days," but rather, "sabbaths," as covering sabbaths of all kinds whether of days or years.

The sabbath as a legal and Jewish ordinance is set aside, but that of course does not touch the fact of one day in seven being set apart by God from the creation as a day of rest. This is a mercy from God which we do well to esteem very highly.

We come in verse 18 to what we may call the ritualistic snare. We shall easily see that it is a snare if we revert to the truth of the cross as it was presented to us in verse 15. The only angels that desire to have our homage are evil ones. The holy angels always refuse human worship, ascribing all worship to God. See, for instance, Revelation xix. 10 and xxii. 9. Now the unholy angels have been despoiled and vanquished at the cross. Who then would wish to worship them? Oh, what light does the cross shed! What deliverance it effects!

There is another very powerful consideration. We are entitled as members of the body each one of us to be "holding the Head." Thereby we maintain an intimate and worshipful contact with Him. The figure of the human body is evidently before the mind of the Spirit, and the head is considered as the seat of all supply for the body. The supply and the increase may reach us *through* the "joints and bands," yet it all comes *from* the head.

It is of the utmost importance that we should take up our privilege and learn what it means to hold the Head. Once we have learned that, we shall be rendered proof against the seductions of ritualism. If I am accorded the right of access to the presence of a real potentate, and privileged to hold intercourse with him, you will not find me presenting my requests to, or expecting to receive from, one of his footmen. The footman may be a very fine fellow, and very gorgeous to look at in his golden-braided uniform, but you will not catch me doing my obeisance to him.

Someone may wish to observe that by doing homage to the footman we should at least be showing what very humble people we are. But is this the procedure laid down? It is not! Then after all we are only doing our own will; and this is self-will, the exact opposite of humility. This may serve as an illustration of what is said in verse 18.

Angels have been purposely hidden from our eyes lest we should give them the place that belongs to God. They are amongst the things not seen. Their would-be worshippers are puffed up by the mind of their flesh. The opening of the verse has been translated, "Let no one fraudulently deprive you of your prize, doing his own will in humility and worship of angels." This makes the whole position very clear. The procedure all looks very humble. It is really self-will, a thing very hateful to God. And those who fall a prey to it may indeed be true believers but being fraudulently diverted from Christ they lose their prize.

The fact of the believer's identification with Christ in His death and resurrection has already been before us in verses 11 and 12. We have now to see that it is not a mere doctrinal notion, something existing only in the region of theory. It is a FACT, and intended to exert a very potent influence upon our lives.

In verse 20 we get the words, "dead with Christ"; in verse 1 of chapter iii., the words, "risen with Christ." So complete was the identification that His death was our death, His resurrection was our resurrection. It may be remarked however that in both cases there is an "if." Yes, but not as expressing doubt but rather as furnishing the basis of an argument. *If* this, *then* that. It really has the force of "since." Certain things are incumbent upon us since we have died with Christ: and again certain other things should mark us since we have been raised with Christ.

Since we have died with Christ our true interests lie clean outside the world and its rudiments, or, elements. Having died out of the world system we cannot proceed as though we are alive in it. That is the argument of verse 20. The world, and particularly the religious world, has its many ordinances concerning the using or not using of perishable material things. According to these ordinances we should not handle or taste or touch this or that. But if we really understand our identification with Christ in His death we find ourselves outside the world where ordinances have their sway, and that of course settles all such questions for us in a very decisive way. There were many ordinances connected with the law of Moses, which was given to curb men in the flesh. They have no validity as regards men who are dead with Christ.

But the point here is not so much as regards Jewish ordinances but rather those that are "after the commandments and doctrines of men"; ordinances which never did have any divine sanction at all. Such are the ordinances which ritualism enforces upon its votaries today.

In our Bibles verse 21 and the first part of verse 22 are printed in brackets. In the New Translation all verse 23 save the last six words is printed in brackets also. This makes the sense of that verse clearer. The words in the first bracket give us samples of the ordinances which the Apostle had in mind. The words in the second bracket tell us certain things which characterize these ordinances. They have an appearance of wisdom, being marked by "will worship," (i.e., voluntary worship) and humility and the neglecting of the body instead of giving it the honour which is due. And then the words not enclosed in brackets read, "subject to ordinances . . . after the commandments and doctrines of men . . . to the satisfying of the flesh."

What a searching condemnation of ritualism it is! All these elaborate ordinances may look like the voluntary rendering of homage in great humility. The asceticism connected with it looks very lowly. The dress, the girdle of rope, the poor food and the fastings and neglect of the body may appear to be very holy and very wonderful; but in point of fact it is all according to purely human teachings and all ministers to the satisfaction of the flesh. In true Christianity the flesh is disowned and refused. In ritualism it is fostered and gratified. That is the condemnation of ritualism.

CHAPTER 3

THE COUNTERPART TO our identification with Christ in His death is our identification with Him in His resurrection. The effect of the one is to disconnect us from man's world, man's wisdom, man's religion. The effect of the other is to put us into touch with God's world and with all that is there. The first four verses of chapter iii. unfold the blessedness into which we are introduced.

There are things which find their centre in Christ seated in heavenly glory. They are "things above," that is, things which are heavenly in character. On these things our minds and affections are to be set, and not on earthly things. At the present moment Christ is not in manifestation here, He is hid in God. Now He is our life, and all the hidden springs of our life are consequently hidden with Him in God. The day approaches when He will be manifested, and then we shall be manifested with Him in glory. It will be quite clear in that day where our real life is found.

It is, alas! not nearly so clear today. Yet our life today lies just exactly where it will then. This is what makes this truth so very practical. The unbeliever necessarily lives and moves and has all his thoughts in "things on the earth." As a fallen creature estranged from God he knows nothing else. Still there is a very great danger of our getting absorbed with earthly things. Hence the need for these exhortations.

The fact is we have an altogether new sphere of life. Our interests centre in the right hand of God, and not in our homes or businesses, however important these may be in their place as furnishing us with occasions for serving the will of God. We set our minds upon things above, not by reposing in arm-chairs indulging in dreamy and mystical imaginings as to things that may be in heaven, but rather by setting our minds supremely upon Christ, and seeking in all things the furtherance of Heaven's interests. The British ambassador in Paris sets his mind upon British things by seeking British interests in French circumstances, and not by continually sitting down to try and recall to his memory what British scenery is like.

As risen with Christ, then, we are lifted into His heavenly interests and permitted to seek them while still on earth. A position of extraordinary elevation, this! How little do we go about as those who are risen with Christ into another region of things, and that a heavenly one! How much do we get our minds clogged with earthly things!

The Apostle recognized how great and how many the hindrances are and hence he exhorted us to mortify certain things. The "members which are upon the earth," of which he speaks in verse 5, are not of course the actual members of our bodies. The term is used metaphorically as indicating certain moral, or rather immoral, features of an earthly nature which characterized us more or less in our unconverted days. We now have heavenly interests and therefore these purely earthly features are to be mortified; that is, put to death.

Put to death is a strong and forcible expression. Our tendency is to parley with these things, and sometimes even to play with them and make provision for them. Our safety however, lies in action of a ruthless kind. Sword in hand, so to speak, we are to meet them without any idea of giving quarter. We should rather meet them after the fashion of Samuel who hewed Agag in pieces before the Lord.

But there are other things besides those specified in verse 5, which we must have done with, and these are mentioned in verses 8 and 9. It is not now, "Mortify," but, "put off." Once we lived wrapped up in these things as in a garment. When men looked at us that is what they saw. But they are to be seen no more. The ugly garment that once characterized us is to be visible no more. Another garment is to be put on as we shall see when we arrive at verse 12.

Notice how much the things mentioned in verses 8 and 9 have to do with our tongues, and consequently with our hearts which express themselves thereby. Sins of the tongue are terribly common even among Christians. We all know the kind of words that are provoked by anger, wrath and malice. Would any true believer blaspheme? Hardly, yet how very easily it is to fall into speaking of God and of divine things in a light and irreverent way. How easy too it is to utter unsavoury things with our lips, even if we do not go so far as "filthy communications." And what about lying? An Ananias or a Sapphira may still be found. And we may go further and assert that every one of us who possesses a sensitive conscience knows right well that it is no easy thing to stick to absolute and rigid truth in all our utterances.

Truth, however, is incumbent upon us because we have put off the old man and have put on the new. This is what we have done in our conversion, and the exhortations to put off and put on in verses 8 and 12 are based upon it. Conversion means that we have learnt to judge and condemn and refuse the old order of man and his character, and to put on the new man which is God's creation and partakes of His character. We do not for one moment say that we understood this or realized it at the moment of our conversion. But we do say, in the light of this Scripture, that this is what was really involved in our conversion, and that it is high time that we do understand and realize it.

In this new man the distinctions of this world—whether national, religious, cultural or social—simply do not exist. Christ is everything, and in all who have put on the man, for the new man is a reproduction of Himself.

Just what the old man is and what the new man is, is not easy to grasp, and still less easy to explain. In both expressions we have a certain character of man personified. In the one you have the Adam character, in the other Christ. Only it is not just idealism but a real transaction. The Adam order is judged and we have done with it and put on Christ and consequently the character of His life. We put it on however not just as a man may don a new coat, but rather as a bird dons a new dress of feathers after moulting. The new character grows naturally out of the new life we have in Christ.

In verses 12 to 15 we find portrayed the character that we are to put on. It is just the opposite to those things that we are to put off according to verses 8 and 9. We are to put off the characteristics of the old man because we have put off the old man. We are to put on the characteristics of the new man because we have put on the new man. What we *are to be* hinges entirely upon what *we are*. We are the elect of God—if indeed we are believers—holy and beloved of God. From this flows what we are to be. Grace always works thus—first what we are, then what we should be.

In these verses CHRIST is in evidence. It is His character that we are to wear. If a standard is set as to the forgiveness we are to accord to others it is, "as Christ forgave you." The peace that is to rule in our hearts is "the peace of Christ," for so it should read, and not "the peace of God," as in our Authorized Version.

Also the word, "quarrel," in verse 13 is really "complaint," as the margin of a reference Bible shows. Have we ever heard of any Christian having a complaint against another? Ever heard of a complaint! we should reply. Why the air is frequently thick with complaints! The difficulty would be to discover any Christian company without them! Well, see what is enjoined upon us in connection with such—forbearance and forgiveness; and that after the pattern of Christ Himself. For this we need the humbleness of mind, the meekness and long-suffering mentioned in verse 12, as well as the charity, or love, which verse 14 enjoins. Love is the bond of perfectness for it is the very nature of God.

The peace of Christ is that of which He spoke in the upper chamber the night before He suffered. "My peace I give unto you," He said. It is that rest of heart and mind which results from perfect confidence in the Father's love and perfect subjection to the Father's will. In our chapter we are reminded that we are called to this peace in one body. Consequently, the peace ruling in all our hearts, an atmosphere of peace pervades the whole body. The closing words of the verse, "and be ye thankful," are significant.

The men of this age are peculiarly marked by unthankfulness—see, 2 Timothy iii. 2. They see the hand of God in nothing, and if perchance things go well with them they only say "My luck was in." It is our privilege to see the hand of God in all things, and, walking in His fear, to trace His ways with us in a thankful spirit.

The peace of Christ is followed by, "the word of Christ," in verse 16. His word gives us all the direction we need and it is to dwell in us, to have its home in our hearts. Further it is to dwell in us richly. Our hearts and minds are to be filled with it in all wisdom. We are not only to know it but also to know how to apply it to all the problems that life presents to us. And we are to be so filled with it that it overflows from us, and we communicate it the one to the other. In our every-day dealings the one with the other we are to be able to instruct each other in that which is His will, and also to warn each other against all that would divert us from His will.

Further we should be marked by praise and song. Only our hymns and songs are to be spiritual in their character, and the Lord is to be the Object before us in them—they are to be "to the Lord." Moreover we must be careful as to our own spiritual state even in our singing. Our songs are to be with grace in our hearts. Singing which springs from a mere spirit of jollification is nothing worth. When the heart is filled with a sense of grace then we can sing to the pleasure of God.

Finally every act and detail of our lives is to be under the control of the Lord, and hence done in His Name and in the spirit of thanksgiving. This comprehensive word closes these more general instructions. The next verse begins to take up things in a more particular way.

It is worthy of note that the instructions of this epistle are not confined to the laying down of general principles, but come down to very practical and personal details. We might have supposed that when spiritually minded believers were in question, such as the Ephesians and Colossians, nothing would be needed beyond principles, and that they might be safely left to make all needful applications themselves. It is however, just in these two epistles that we get full details as to the conduct that befits the varied relationships of life. We are told exactly how we should behave, in the full light of Christianity.

COLOSSIANS

We cannot go through the world without having many and varied relations with our fellow-creatures. Most of our testings and trials reach us in connection with those relations, and hence it is God's way to leave us after conversion in the same old relationships, only teaching us how to fulfil them in the light and power which the knowledge of Christ brings. We are not set to the task of putting the world right. That will be done effectually and speedily by the Lord when He takes up the work of judgment. We are left to bear effectual witness to what is right by acting rightly ourselves.

Though the relationships of life are so many, and varied in detail, they may, we believe, be all condensed under the three heads that we find in the verses before us—(iii. 18—iv. 1). There is, first, the *marriage* relation. Second, the *family* relation, which springs out of the marriage relation. Third, what we may term the *industrial* relation, which springs out of the fact that hard work is decreed to be man's lot as the result of his fall.

The organization of life in this world, according to God, is based upon marriage. If we read Matthew xix. we shall find the Lord opening out the truth, first upon marriage, then upon children, then upon possessions. Our passage deals with marriage, children, work, in that order. We make bold to say that NEVER was it more important for Christians to fulfil these relationships in a Christian way, for never have these divine institutions been more fiercely assailed than just now. Being bulwarks of that which is good the devil aims at their destruction, and every weapon is used from a "modernism" which has all the appearance of being scholarly and refined to the "communism" which practices "free love," turns the children on the streets to prowl about in droves, and alternately encourages the work-man to destroy private property on the one hand, or shoots him for complaining of his miserable pay and food, on the other. We may incidentally remark just here that without a doubt "modernism" and "communism" are but varying phases of the same great devil-inspired movement. The same basic principles are common to both.

In all our relations two parties are involved. It is so here. The marriage relation is taken up as between wives and husbands; the family as between children and parents; the industrial as between servants and masters. Each of the three relationships, as instituted by God, involves this, that one party shall assume the lead and the other shall be subject. Moreover, this is not a point which is left for negotiation and arrangement as between various individuals entering upon the relationship. It is a matter which is settled by the Word of God.

In each of the three cases those who have the place of subjection are addressed first. Subjection becomes the wife; obedience, the child. In the case of the servant there is to be not only obedience but heartiness and integrity. The most striking thing about the exhortations in each case is the way everything is to be done as in the sight of the Lord. This lifts the whole matter on to the loftiest plane. The wife is subject, but it is, "in the Lord." This implies that the prime reason for her subjection is that it is the Lord's appointment. She is subject to her husband as expressing her subjection to her Lord. It is to be hoped of course that her husband bears such a character that subjection to him is no hardship but a pleasure. But even were it otherwise she would still be subject, seeing it is to the Lord.

The same principle applies to the children and to the servants. They are to consider what is pleasing to the Lord. We must remember that the servants contemplated here were bondmen—they were practically slaves. There was very little or no profit for themselves in all their labour. Yet they were to work exactly as if they were working for the Lord. And indeed they were working for Him, and they will ultimately receive from His hands a full reward for their labour, though they might never get as much as a "Thank you" from a churlish master. "Ye serve the Lord Christ," is what the Apostle says.

Subjection, we must remember, does not necessarily imply inferiority, but it does imply the godly recognition of the divinely established order.

Moreover, God's arrangements are never lop-sided. If there is a word of instruction and guidance for those who have the subject place, there is equally a word for those who take the lead. In each case the Spirit of God puts His finger upon the weak spot. The husband is exhorted to love. Mere natural love can easily turn to bitterness, but this can never happen when his love is a reflection of the divine. If the husband is marked by love the wife has no difficulty in being subject.

So with the fathers, they are not to provoke or vex their children. Discipline is necessary and good, but, if not itself controlled by love, it may easily become excessive and vexatious to the utter discouragement of the child.

CHAPTER 4

IN THE THIRD case, that of the masters, the prominent thought is not that of love but of righteousness. Every Christian master should be continually asking himself in regard to his servants, "What is just? What is fair?" And further he is to remember that he himself is a servant with his Master in the heavens—a Master who has laid it down that, "With what measure ye mete, it shall be measured to you again."

Here, then, are six items of instruction which if obeyed would go far towards producing a heaven upon earth. Family discord and industrial discord would be a thing of the past! But the point here is that we, believers, should anticipate the blessedness of the millennial day, and carry out God's will in our several relationships, while waiting for the day when God's will shall be done on earth as it is in heaven.

Verses 2 to 6 of chapter iv. bring us back to exhortations of a more general sort; first as regards prayer, then as regards the relations of the believer with the unconverted.

We are to pray, and not only so but to persevere in it, and to watch God's dealings that we may not miss His answers to our requests, nor fail to render thanks to Him for grace received. Moreover our prayers are not to be mainly of a personal or even selfish nature. Paul urged the Colossians to intercession on his behalf, that he might make manifest that "mystery of Christ" to which he had alluded in the epistle. He wanted them to be intercessors on behalf of the work of God, and thus taking a share in the conflict connected with it.

We are very, very weak today in this matter of prayer. Modern life is organized on the principle of rush, and prayer gets crowded out all too often. Again, what about persevering? When we deeply desire a thing we do persevere, but how often are we creatures of very shallow desires! Our sympathies are called forth on some point and we join in a prayer—but that is the end of it! We soon forget and there is no perseverance.

In verse 5 the unconverted are spoken of as "them that are without." There are those within the Christian circle and those without it, and it is very important that we should be right in our relations with those without. We are set in a place of testimony in regard to them. First our general behaviour towards them is to be marked by wisdom. That being so we are sure to have opportunities for witnessing which we are to redeem by seizing them as they present themselves.

It is one thing, however, to seize an opportunity, and another to use it to best advantage. Words *not* fitly spoken are often more to be deplored than no word being spoken at all. Our words are to be always with grace. Never are we to descend to the censorious, or the bitter, or the cutting remark. But then on the other hand our words, while full of grace, are not to aim at merely pleasing men. They are to be seasoned with that which salt represents—the pungent quality of truth. Grace and truth were found in our Lord and they should mark those who are His, even characterizing their words.

The standard here set is a very lofty one. We come far short of attaining to it. Yet let us not lower the standard in our minds. Let us maintain it at its full height as seen in Christ, and let us press on toward it.

With verse 7 the closing messages and salutations begin. They present many points of interest. Tychicus, of whom the Apostle writes so warmly, was evidently to be the bearer of this letter to the Colossians. Onesimus, who is called "a faithful and beloved brother," was the run-away slave, with whom the epistle to Philemon is concerned. What but the grace of God can turn a defaulting and absconding slave into a faithful and beloved brother in Christ? So Tychicus carried the letter to the Colossians and Onesimus the letter to Philemon when they travelled to Colosse together. Philemon does not appear in our chapter, as is natural, seeing there was the special letter for him. But Archippus appears in both letters.

At the time of writing Paul had with him Aristarchus, Mark and Justus. He was able to speak of each of them in high terms as workers for the Kingdom and as a comfort to himself. It is most encouraging to find Mark mentioned in this way since the glimpses we have of him in the Acts are so unpromising. It shows how one who was a failure at the beginning of his service was yet thoroughly recovered to complete usefulness. So much so that he eventually became the writer of the second Gospel which specially portrays the Lord as the perfect Servant. An illustration, this, of how the power of God can ultimately make us strongest in that very thing wherein at first we were weakest.

Epaphras also was with Paul but he was "one of you," that is, a Colossian, and so not "of the circumcision." Separated as he was from his own people he yet had a great zeal for them and he was fervently labouring on their behalf. This labour was accomplished in prayer.

Prayer, you see, is labour: or rather, it may be labour.Epaphras carried it to such a point that it was truly labour for him, and *continued* labour too, since Paul bears witness that it was always his practice. The word translated "labouring" really means striving or combatting. Epaphras though absent from his friends was engaged in a real prayer combat on their behalf, the object of which was that they might stand in the will of God, perfect and complete.

It is a great thing to have a full knowledge of the will of God; that the Apostle desired for the Colossians in verse 9 of chapter i. It is a greater thing to stand perfect and complete in that will. Standing in it implies that we are subject to it and characterized by it, according to that which is said in verse 10 of chapter i. It is evident that the desires and prayers of Epaphras, for the saints of Colosse and neighbourhood, ran exactly parallel with the prayers of Paul for them.

Laodicea was in the neighbourhood. It is mentioned in chapter ii. 1, as well as three times in our chapter. The very name has a sad sound about it in view of what the Lord has to say to this church in Revelation iii. 14-22. In spite of the prayers and conflict on their behalf of a Paul and an Epaphras, in spite of the circulation of Apostolic epistles in their midst, it fell to the lowest depths. The "epistle from Laodicea," was no doubt an epistle which just at that time was being circulated from assembly to assembly.

This epistle to the Colossians and the Laodiceans sets forth exactly that truth which, had it been heeded by the Laodiceans, would have preserved them. It sets forth the glory of Christ, the Head of His church. It exhorts them to "hold the Head." Alas! they heeded it not; and the epistle to them sent from Patmos reveals them as supremely self-satisfied, and Christ, their Head, entirely outside their door.

We are, as regards the flesh, no better than they. So let us take to heart the warning with which they furnish us.

Let us also accept the word of admonition given to Archippus as applicable to ourselves. Has the Lord given a service to you? Then take good heed to perform it, however insignificant it may appear to be. Non-fulfilment of the service means laziness, which at once opens the door to decline and spiritual disaster. Nothing can preserve us but that grace, which is the closing word of the epistle.

1 THESSALONIANS

INTRODUCTION

IT SEEMS TO be generally admitted that this was the first of all Paul's inspired epistles to be written. If any desire confirmation of this they will do well to read the third chapter of the Epistle and then compare it with Acts xvii. The Epistle was written just after Timothy had returned from his visit to Thessalonica, paid while Paul was at Athens; and hence when he wrote it the Apostle's labours at Corinth had barely begun and he had not even visited Ephesus. In any event read the early verses of Acts xvii. for the historic details there found give much point to various details in the Epistle.

The fact that the Thessalonians were believers of not many months standing—just young converts—imparts a peculiar interest to this epistle. It is most encouraging to see how many things are true of even the youngest believers in Christ, and also how much grace and devotedness may mark them if their simplicity be unspoiled.

Paul's labours at Thessalonica were very brief; at the end of about three weeks they were cut short by a riot. Very solid work was done however, as this first chapter bears witness. We may take it as certain that intense Satanic opposition is always a sign that a real work of God is proceeding. The rioters called Paul and his friends, "These that have turned the world upside down," and this designation was not far from the truth. The truth was that the world itself was completely upside down, and the labours of Paul and others were setting men right side up before God. The world itself was left in its upside down condition, but many in Thessalonica were converted out of the world and set in right relations with God. These converts became the church, or assembly, of the Thessalonians.

CHAPTER 1

THEY WERE NOT formally incorporated as "a church." Had some ceremony been usual the sudden and violent ending of Paul's work in their midst would have precluded it. No, they became the church, that is, the "called-out-ones," of God by the very act of God in calling them out of the world through the Gospel. The Apostle can own them, young converts though they were, as an assembly of God, gathered in the happy knowledge of God as Father, and in subjection to Jesus as their Lord. To know the Father is the characteristic feature of the babe in Christ, according to 1 John ii. 13. To acknowledge Jesus as Lord is the way into salvation, according to Romans x. 9. 10.

Paul looked back with much thankfulness to his brief sojourn in their midst, and now absent from them he remembered them continually in prayer. From verse 3 to the end of the chapter he recounts that which he had seen in them of the working of the power of God, and thus there is furnished for us a striking picture of the wonderful effects produced in character and in life when men are soundly converted.

It is worthy of note that the first place is given to the character that was produced IN them, a character summed up in three words, faith, hope, love. Character however can only be discerned by us as it expresses itself in our actions and ways, hence their work and labour and patience (or endurance) are referred to. Their "work of faith" was evident to all, in keeping with that which James writes in his epistle, "I will shew thee my faith by my works." Note that both here and in James ii. the works spoken of are the works of faith, whereas in Romans iv., a chapter erroneously supposed by many to be in conflict with James, the works spoken of are "the works of the law"—an entirely different thing.

If faith comes to light in its works, love is expressed in labour. It is characteristic of love to labour unsparingly for the good of its object, as we all know. Hope too, expresses itself in patient endurance. Only when men become hopeless do they readily give up: they endure as long as hope is like a star shining before their eyes.

These things were clear and distinct in the Thessalonian believers, and led Paul to the confident conclusion that they were amongst the elect of God. It was not that, when he stood up in the synagogue at Thessalonica those three Sabbath days, he could have put a mark on the back of each who would believe before he began to preach, as having private access to the Lamb's book of life and knowing in advance the names of those who were chosen of God. Paul's knowledge was arrived at from the opposite direction. Knowing the powerful way in which the Gospel reached them and the results produced in them by the Spirit of God he had no doubt in his conclusion that they were chosen of God.

In this connection notice the opening words of the Apostle in his first epistle to the Corinthians. In their case he can only thank God that grace had visited them by Christ and that they were a gifted people. The possession of gift does not however of necessity mean that its possessor is a true believer, as witness the case of Judas Iscariot. Hence the searching words of warning he utters in the latter part of his ninth and the opening of his tenth chapter. To them he spoke of being "a castaway," because of the element of doubt there was in his mind as to some of them, in spite of their gifts. The Thessalonians were in happy contrast to this.

There are "things that accompany salvation" (Heb. vi. 9), and the "labour of love" is specified directly after as one of them. In our passage three things are mentioned and the labour of love is one of them. No gifts may be manifested, but if these things are present we can be sure that salvation is possessed, and that the people in question are the elect of God.

If verse 3 gives us the fruit produced in these believers and verse 4 the Apostle's confidence on beholding this fruit, verse 5 indicated the way in which the fruit was produced. Firstly, the Gospel reached them in word: it was boldy preached by Paul. Secondly, his preaching was supported by his devoted and holy life. Thirdly, and largely as a consequence, the Gospel came in power and in the Holy Spirit. The Holy Spirit wrought mightily through the Word. The Apostle alludes in much detail to what manner of man he was amongst them in his second chapter.

The Gospel also came to them "in much assurance." This is very significant when we turn back to Acts xvii. and note that the particular form that Paul's preaching took in their city was that of reasoning with them out of the Scriptures; showing them that when the true Christ of God appeared He must die and rise again, and that these predictions had been so perfectly fulfilled in Jesus that the conclusion was irresistible—Jesus is the Christ! In other words, amongst these people he had very specially based his gospel proclamation and appeal upon THE WORD OF GOD; hence the MUCH ASSURANCE in the converts.

Let us take good note of this. If an Apostle, able himself to give forth inspired utterances, appealed to the Scriptures with such solid and lasting result, we, who have only the Scripture to appeal to, may well make it the basis of all we preach. "Preach the Word," is the great word for us. There is no assurance outside it. The preacher may persuade us that things are as he states, upon the strength of his personal assurances. The converts may tell us that they have every assurance because of the happy feelings that they experience. But there is as little *real* assurance in the one as in the other. We can only really be *assured* of anything as we have the Word of God for it.

In verses 6-8 we find what the Gospel made of these who received it. We saw in the first place the three-fold character it produced *in* them. Now we see the three-fold character it stamped UPON them. They had been made into "followers . . . of the Lord," "ensamples [or patterns] to all that believe," and they "sounded out," like trumpeters or heralds, thus advertizing the Word of the Lord.

Paul himself was a pattern man (see, 1 Tim. i. 16), hence he could rightly ask believers to follow him. Even so, it was only because of the fact that he followed Christ; so that it was indeed the Lord whom they followed. In this connection it is recorded that, though they now followed with joy begotten of the Holy Spirit, they had first known the power of the Word piercing into the conscience and producing repentance toward God with its accompanying affliction of heart. It is ever thus. The deeper the work of repentance the brighter the joy and the more sincere the discipleship of the convert. Let those who preach the Word aim at a deep work in heart and conscience rather than at showy and superficial results and they will not fail of their reward in the day of Christ.

Following the Lord comes first; it was because of their discipleship that they became examples to their fellow-believers in surrounding provinces. Paul could point to them and say, "That is the kind of thing that the grace of God produces where it is received as the fruit of a deep work of repentance towards God." This is indicated by the words, "so that," at the beginning of verse 7. The little word "for" which opens verse 8 shows us that what follows is also connected with this matter. Their evangelistic fervour also made them an example to others. They not only received the Word to their own blessing but they sounded it forth to others, so much so that their faith in God became notorious not only in the nearer districts but further afield. The whole work of God was so effectually advertized by its wonderful effects in these people that there was no need for the Apostle himself to say a word.

Nothing so effectually advertizes the Gospel as the transformed lives of those who have received it. This fact has been often noted by careful observers, but here we find that Scripture itself recognizes it. Conversely nothing so effectually stultifies the proclamation of the Gospel as breakdown and sin on the part of those who profess to have believed it. In the light of this, and of the sad conditions prevailing in the Christianized nations, can we wonder that the evangelist in these lands finds himself confronted by hard and difficult conditions today? May God give help to each one of us so that our lives may tell in favour of the Gospel and not against it.

In the closing verses we find a third thing. Not now the character wrought *in* them, nor the features stamped *upon* them, but that which was being done BY them. Their conversion was in view of service to God and patient waiting for Christ.

"Ye turned to God from idols." Here we have a Scriptural definition of conversion, which is not only a turning, but a turning to God and consequently from idols. Idols are not only the ugly images venerated and feared by the heathen, but also *anything*, whether elegant or ugly, *which usurps in the heart of man that place of supremacy and dominance which belongs of right to God alone.* Idols are before the face of every fallen sinner, charming his heart, and God is behind his back. Conversion takes place and lo, God is before his face and idols are behind his back!

Converted to God our lives are to be now spent in His service. Has it ever occurred to you what an extraordinary favour it is, and what a tribute to the power of the Gospel, that we should be permitted to serve Him at all? An earnest worker in a slum district notices very definite signs of repentance in one of the worst occupants of a thieves' kitchen one Sunday evening. He very greatly rejoices, though with trembling. Yes, but how would he feel if early on Monday morning the poor thing arrived on his doorstep and with many tears avowed her thankfulness for the blessing received and announced her desire to express her gratitude by entering his service—cooking his meals and dusting his house? Stamped upon her he sees disease, dirt, degradation and, until yesterday, drink. What would he say? What would *you* say?

We have not overdrawn the picture. What we were morally and spiritually just answered to the case supposed. And yet we have been brought into the service of the thrice-holy God as redeemed and born again. But then how mighty must be the moral renovation which the Gospel effects! And even so, remembering that we still have the flesh in us and are consequently very liable to sin, how great a favour it is that we should be taken into the high and holy service of God. We are actually permitted to serve His interests, His purposes and plans made before the world began. If we realized this there would be no desire to shirk His work. We should eagerly and joyfully run to fulfil it.

While we serve we wait. We are saved in hope of the fulness of blessing which is yet to be introduced. We are not left to await death, which is our departure to be with Christ, but to await His coming for us. We await God's Son from the heavens. This is as far as the Apostle goes for the moment: when we reach chapter iv. we shall find disclosed what is involved in this statement.

However we will not anticipate; for the moment we will only note that it is God's Son who is coming, that He is coming from the heavens where now He is seated, and that His name is Jesus, whom we know as our Deliverer from the coming wrath. The verb is not in the past tense—"delivered"—as in our Authorised Version. It is rather, "Jesus, who delivers us" or "Jesus, our Deliverer." The point is that Jesus who is coming from heaven will deliver us from the wrath that is coming.

Again and again in both Testaments the word wrath is used to denote the heavy judgments of God which are coming upon this earth. We do not for one moment deny that in several New Testament passages the meaning of the word is enlarged to take in the penal judgment of God which stretches out into and embraces eternity. Still the main use of the word is as we have indicated, as may be seen if the book of Revelation be attentively read. Men and nations are heaping up to themselves wrath against the day of wrath, and the opened eye can see that day of wrath approaching with silent and stealthy tread.

What a joy it is for the believer to know that though wrath is coming Jesus also is coming, and coming as Deliverer! Before wrath swoops like an eagle upon its prey Jesus will come and we shall be delivered out of the very spot where the wrath is going to fall. For the details of this wonderful event we must wait. Meanwhile we can rejoice that the event itself is a glorious certainty and fast approaching.

1 THESSALONIANS

CHAPTER 2

IN HIS FIRST chapter the Apostle had alluded to "what manner of men" he and his fellow-workers were among the Thessalonians when they first arrived amongst them with the Gospel, and intimated that the power which had accompanied the message was largely connected with the unblameable character of the messengers. He returns to this subject at the opening of chapter ii.

Paul and his friends found at Thessalonica a door opened of the Lord, and they consequently gained a most effectual entrance into their midst. This was the more striking as they had just come from suffering and shameful treatment at Philippi as recorded in Acts xvi. However far from being cowed by this they had such confidence in God that again they boldly spoke forth the Word. The power of it was such that some even of the Jews believed, "and of the devout Greeks a great multitude, and of the chief women not a few" (Acts xvii. 4). Thus did God grant to His faithful servants a time of much encouragement after severe suffering and before they were plunged into further troubles in Thessalonica itself. We must remember of course that the violence at Philippi did not mean that but little was accomplished in that city. On the contrary, Paul's Philippian converts were among the brightest trophies of grace.

The Apostle puts it on record in verse 2 that he preached the gospel "with much contention." By contention we must not understand heated argument. The expression is literally, "in much agony," or "conflict." The New Translation renders it, "with much earnest striving." Paul preached in an agony of spiritual conflict that the truth might be effectual in his hearers! No "take it or leave it" gospel was his! He was not the mere theologian or Christian philosopher contented with the truth correctly stated in his lectures; nor was he the dreamy mystic wrapped up in himself and in his own impressions and experiences. He was a man with a message, and burning with zeal, and in agony of mind to effectually convey it to others.

What amazing power this must have given him! He may have been weak as to bodily presence and contemptible as to his powers of utterance—"rude in speech" as he elsewhere says—yet the inward agony of spirit with which he spoke must have made his "rude" words like a whirlwind. Multitudes were converted under them, and still greater multitudes were lashed into fury against him! Where do we see power like this today? We hear Gospel addresses that may be characterized as good, clear, sound, striking, intelligent, eloquent, sweet. But they do not achieve much either in conversions or in stirring up the powers of darkness. Yet the need is as great and the energy of the Holy Spirit is the same. The difference lies in the character and calibre of the messengers.

119

1 THESSALONIANS

In verses 3 to 6 we are given a glimpse of what Paul and his helpers were NOT, and thereby we may learn the things that are to be studiously avoided by every servant of God. First of all every element of deceit and unreality must be put away. It has been very rightly said that,

"Thou must be true thyself,
If thou the truth would'st teach."

Not only so but all thought of pleasing men must be banished. Any service we have had committed to us, however small it be, has been given of God and not by man. Hence to God we are responsible and He tries not only our words and acts but also our hearts. Paul was put in trust with the Gospel in an altogether exceptional measure, but the three words, "PUT IN TRUST" may well be written upon all our hearts. We must never forget that we are trustees.

If we bear it in mind we shall of course avoid the use of flattering words, and the cloak of covetousness, and the seeking of glory from men, of which verses 5 and 6 speak. These three things are exceedingly common in the world. Men naturally seek their own things and hence are ruled by covetousness, though they may disguise it under some kind of cloak. Glory from man is also very dear to the human heart; and, whether they pursue possessions or glory, they find flattering words a useful weapon, for by them they can often curry favour with the influential. All these things were utterly refused by Paul. As a servant of God, with God for his Judge and God for his Witness, they were altogether beneath him.

The positive characteristics of Paul's ministry come before us in verses 7 to 12, and it is worthy of note that he begins by comparing himself to a nursing mother and ends by comparing himself to a father. We may find it difficult to imagine how this exceedingly forcible man could have been gentle, "as a nurse would cherish her own children," but so it was. Physical force is usually brutal. Spiritual force is gentle. There was plenty of the former to be seen in Thessalonica when "the Jews which believed not, took unto them certain lewd fellows of the baser sort . . . and set all the city on an uproar," yet it all ended in nothing. Paul's gentleness, on the contrary, left lasting results. It was the gentleness begotten of an ardent love for these young converts. He cherished them; that is, he kept them warm, and how could he do this except his own love was warm. It was so warm that he was ready to impart to them not the Gospel only but also his own soul or life. He would have laid down his life for them.

However he was not called upon to do that. What he did was to labour with his own hands by night as well as by day in order that, being self-supporting, he might not be any charge upon them. He refers to this again in his second epistle, and from Acts xx. 34 we glean the astonishing information that he not only met his own needs in this way but also the needs of those that were with him. Elsewhere he speaks of "night and day praying exceedingly," and we know how abundant were his labours in the gospel.

120

Under these circumstances we may well marvel that this extraordinary man could find any time for his tent-making, but somehow the thing was done and thus he made the Gospel of Christ without charge, although the Lord had ordained as a general rule that those who preach the Gospel should live of the Gospel. It is very evident that manual labour is honourable in the sight of God.

To all this the Thessalonians were witnesses. Himself marked by holiness and practical righteousness he had been able to charge them that they should follow in his steps and walk in a way that was worthy of God—the God who had called them that they should be under His authority and enter into His glory.

What has occupied us thus far has been the manner of life that characterized Paul and his fellow-labourers: with verse 13 we turn again to that which marked their converts in Thessalonica. Receiving the Word of God through channels such as these men were, they received it as the Word of God. This verse plainly indicates that the Word of God may be received as the word of men, and that it is not one whit less the Word of God if it be so received. If you happened to get hold of a camera with a defective lense you would find the subjects of your films strangely, and often grotesquely, distorted. You must not however blame the objects which you photographed. The objects were all right though your subjects proved all wrong. We must learn to distinguish between the *objective* and the *subjective*, as the Apostle does here. The objective Word of God was presented to the Thessalonians and the subjective impression made in them was according to truth. Had they received it as the word of men its effect upon them would have been but transitory. Receiving it as the Word of God it operated in them powerfully and produced in them just those effects that had been seen when first the Gospel had been preached in Judaea. Though tested by persecution they stood firm.

The seventeenth of Acts shows us how quickly the storm of persecution burst in Thessalonica. The house of Jason was assaulted and Jason himself and certain other brethren haled before the magistrates; the instigators of the riotous behaviour being Jews. The Apostle here shows them that they had only been called upon to suffer like things to the earlier converts in Judaea, and that the Jewish instigators of their troubles were true to type. This leads him to sum up the indictment which now was laid against them.

Of old God's great controversy with the Jews was on account of their persistent idolatry. Of this the Old Testament prophets are full. The New Testament adds the even greater charge that they "killed the Lord Jesus." Added to this they drove out the Apostle by their persecutions and, as far as in them lay, forbad the going forth of the Gospel to the Gentiles. They refused to enter the door of salvation themselves and as far as possible they hindered others doing so. How striking is the description of this unhappy people, "They please not God, and are contrary to all men."!

It is pretty evident that the nations generally are contrary to the Jew. Verses 15 and 16 of our chapter shows us the reason why. They themselves are contrary and nationally they lie under the Divine displeasure, hence nothing is right with them, though of course God is still saving out of them "a remnant according to the election of grace" (Rom. xi. 5). Earlier they had been under trial. Even after the death of Christ an offer of mercy had been made to them consequent upon the coming of the Holy Spirit, as recorded in Acts iii. 17-26. Their official answer was given by the martyrdom of Stephen and by the persecution of Paul who was raised up directly after Stephen's death to carry the light of salvation to the Gentiles. They would have slain Paul also had not God intervened in His providence to prevent it. (See, Acts ix. 23 and 29). As a consequence the wrath long withheld had been definitely loosed against them. They will not have paid as a nation, the last farthing, till the great tribulation has rolled over their heads. But nothing now can stay God's dealings against them in wrath.

Against this dark background how beautiful is the picture which verses 17 to 20 present. The Apostle, who was hurried out of their midst under cover of night, was filled with ardent longings towards them. As his spiritual children, begotten of the Gospel, he looked upon them as his hope, and joy and crown of rejoicing. The links that bound them to him were of the tenderest, most spiritual nature. If he looked on, he anticipated having them as his glory and joy at the coming of the Lord. Looking back he recognized how Satan had worked to keep them sundered on earth, as to bodily presence.

This passage plainly indicates that Satan is permitted to harass and hinder the servants of the Lord; yet comparing the story with the history recorded in Acts it is very evident that God knows well how to over-rule Satan's hindering work for good. Satan hindered Paul from returning just then to Thessalonica, but God led him to Corinth; and He had much people in that city!

Notice also how happily Paul looked forward to reunion with his beloved Thessalonian converts in heaven. His words would have been meaningless had he not expected to know them each and all in that day. The saints of God will know one another when they meet at the coming of Christ and in His presence.

CHAPTER 3

BUT IF PAUL had been hindered from coming personally—very likely by the violence of the persecution raised against him by Satan—he had sent Timothy to comfort and encourage them. Here again, in opening chapter iii., we see in Paul the marks of a true father in Christ. He was at Athens, a peculiarly hard and difficult city, a place where more urgently than in most he felt the need of the support and encouragement afforded by like-minded fellow-labourers, yet would he sacrifice himself and be left alone in order that Timothy might shepherd the souls of these young believers, and establish them just when Satan was aiming at their overthrow by means of afflictions. The trial of their faith had not come as a surprise for he had forewarned them about it, even though his stay amongst them had been so short.

From this let us learn that it is not right nor wise to hide from the youngest convert that tribulation from the world is the normal lot of the Christian while on earth. There are abundant joys in Christianity, but not of a worldly order. In the world we are to have tribulation, so let us not misrepresent the case, thinking thereby to get more converts. Let the truth be faced and we shall thereby not lose one *true* convert, though plenty of make-believe ones may be checked—to their own good and our good also. As to tribulation, we all of us have to say in our turn, "it came to pass, and ye know."

In raising persecution against believers Satan is always aiming at their faith. He would weaken it and destroy it if possible. Notice how, as a consequence, faith is emphasized by Paul in this passage. He sent Timothy to comfort "concerning your *faith*." He sent to "know your *faith*." Timothy returned and brought "good tidings of your *faith*," and as a consequence he was comforted "by your *faith*." Faith is the eye of the soul. It gives spiritual vision. Paul knew that, as long as the unseen things of faith were real to them, the persecution would only produce spiritual enrichment and invigoration, just as a cold douche which would be hurtful to an invalid is invigorating to a man in full health. Faith is a vital link between the soul and God and if it be weakened, everything about the believer is weakened. Satan knows this right well.

When faith is maintained in the hearts of believers they "stand fast in the Lord," and this was a great joy to the apostle. It comforted him in all his afflictions. So deeply did he feel about the Thessalonians, exposed as they were to such trials so soon after their conversion, that until he knew how they had been sustained in them he was like a man at the point of death. The good news he got through Timothy brought him back to life. This is the figure he uses when he says, "Now we live, if ye stand fast in the Lord."

Though faith was so brightly maintained in these Christians, yet there was need that it be perfected, as verse 10 shows. Something was lacking as to it in this sense—that as yet they were unacquainted with the whole circle of truth that had been revealed. What they did see by faith, they saw very clearly; but they did not as yet see all there was to see. The apostle earnestly longed to meet them again and bring before them those parts of God's truth which as yet they knew not. In this Epistle he reveals to them something of which as yet they were in ignorance, as we shall see when considering chapter iv.

While as yet he was hindered, his desire was that they should increase and abound in love one toward another. God alone is the Object of faith. He is also the Object of love, but love to Him can best be practically expressed by love to those born of Him, as we are reminded in John's Epistle. Moreover the Christian should be an overflowing fountain of love toward all men. The Thessalonians were this, and it explains how they became such effectual advertisements of the gospel, as we saw when considering chapter i. Only they were to increase more and more.

Thus would they be established unblameable in holiness in view of the coming of the Lord. Holiness and love are evidently closely connected. As love is operative in our hearts towards God and his people, so we hate what He hates and are preserved unblameable before Him. The grand goal before us is the coming of the Lord Jesus with all His saints. Mark that preposition *"with."* When He comes in His glory we are to be with Him. How we reach His presence above, so as to come forth from heaven in His company when He appears, is not yet plainly indicated in the Epistle; but this verse alone should have assured the Thessalonians, and should assure us, that when He comes not one will be missing. It will be with ALL His saints.

CHAPTER 4

As WE OPEN the fourth chapter of this epistle we find the Apostle turning to exhortation and instruction. The earlier chapters had been largely occupied with reminiscences both as regards the work of God, wrought in the Thessalonians, and also the behaviour and service of Paul and his fellow-workers in their midst. Now the Apostle addresses himself to the present needs of his much-loved converts.

In the first chapter he had been able to say about them much that was highly commendatory, but this did not mean that there were no dangers and difficulties confronting them, nor that they were beyond the need of further advancement in the things of God. On the contrary they were as yet but babes. There was much they had yet to learn as to the truth and much they needed to know as regards the will of God for them. A great word for them, and for all of us, is that with which verse 1 closes—"more and more."

In the first place they were to abound more and more in all those practical details of life and behaviour which are pleasing to God. During his short stay in their midst Paul had succeeded in conveying to them an outline of the walk that pleases God though of course there was much to be filled in as to detail. It is one thing however to *know* and quite another to *do*, and we are set here to please God in all our activities and ways. The will of God is our sanctification, that is, that we should be set apart from all that defiles in order that we may be wholly for God, and the Apostle had given them definite commandments as from the Lord in keeping with this.

Do we pay sufficient attention to the commandments of the Lord Jesus and of His Apostles which we find so plentifully in the New Testament? We fear that the answer to this question is that *we do not*. There are indeed some believers who have a rooted objection to the idea that any commandment has application to a Christian. The very word they will have none of. It has, they feel, so exclusive a connection with the law of Moses that to bring any kind of commandment to bear upon a Christian is to at once put him under law; and we Christians are, as they rightly remind us, "not under law but under grace."

In this however they are mistaken. Under grace we have been brought into the kingdom of God. The Divine authority has been established in our hearts, if indeed we have been truly converted; and though love is the ruling force in that blessed kingdom yet love has its commandments no less than law. The law issued its commands without furnishing either the motive or the power that would ensure obedience. Only love can furnish the compelling force that is needed. Still the commands of love are there. "This is the love of God, that we keep His commandments: and His commandments are not grievous" (1 John v. 3). Under law men were given commandments on the keeping of which depended their life and position before God. Under grace the believer's life and position are assured in Christ, and the commandments he receives are to shape and direct that new life in a way that will be pleasing to God.

In the New Testament we have, thank God, many plain commandments of the Lord covering all the major matters of life and service. There are however many minor matters as to which the Lord has not issued any definite instructions. (A comparison of three verses, viz., 1 Corinthians vii. 6 and 25; xiv. 37, might be helpful at this point). These omissions are not by oversight but of set purpose. It is evidently the Lord's purpose to leave many things to the prayerful exercises of His saints; they must search the Scriptures to discover what pleases Him and judge by analogies drawn from His dealings of past days. This is in order that they may be spiritually developed and have "their senses exercised to discern both good and evil." As to such matters each of us must seek to ascertain God's will and be fully persuaded in our minds.

This we fully admit; but let us not therefore overlook the plain commandments of the Lord where He has spoken. Some Christians are, we fear, rather apt to practice self-deception in this matter. They seem much exercised about a certain point. They seek light. They pray very piously. Yet all the while if they opened their Bibles there would stare them in the face a plain commandment from the Lord upon the very point in question. Somehow they manage to ignore it. In that case all their prayers and exercises are of but little worth, and indeed savour of hypocrisy.

We have enlarged a little upon this point because of its importance. Turning again to our Scripture we notice that having stated that God's will for His people is, in a general way, their sanctification, the Apostle specifies one sin which is the deadly enemy of any such thing. This particular sin was exceedingly common among the Gentile nations, so common that it was thought nothing of at all, and it was only when the light of Christianity was shed upon it that the real evil of it became manifest. Amongst the Christianized nations of today it is looked upon with far less abhorrence than it was fifty years ago; a definite witness this to how far they have turned aside from even the outward profession of Christ. Verses 3 to 7 are all concerned with this particular sin. Let us each carefully read these verses and take home to our hearts the Apostle's pungent words.

The word *sanctification* really occurs three times in these verses, but it has been translated "holiness" in verse 7, where it is put in contrast with uncleanness. To sanctification we have been called and if we ignore this we shall find serious consequences in three directions.

In the first place we have to reckon with the Lord, who will deal with us in His righteous government of His saints. If another has been wronged He will constitute Himself the Avenger of their cause. Secondly there is God to be reckoned with. It may seem as if the wrongdoer is merely despising or disregarding the rights of a man, but in reality he is disregarding the rights of God. Thirdly, there is the Spirit of God to be considered, and He is the *Holy* Spirit—the word for holy coming from the same root as the words for sanctification in the verses above. The Spirit being given, He sets us apart for God.

With verse 9 Paul turns from this sin which so often masquerades falsely under the name of love, to brotherly love, which is the real article as found among the people of God. As to this he gladly acknowledges there was no need of his exhortations for they had been taught of God to do it. It was the very instinct of the divine life in their souls. The only thing he has to say to them is that they should "increase more and more." Here again we meet with these words. There is to be more and more happy obedience to the commands of the Lord, and more and more brotherly love amongst the people of God. LOVE and OBEDIENCE—these are the things! And more and more of them! How happy shall we be if thus we are characterized!

It is very significant how we pass from brotherly love to the very homely instructions of verses 11 and 12. Before now brotherly love has been

126

known to degenerate into unbrotherly interference with one's brethren. Well, here we have the wholesome corrective. "Seek earnestly to be quiet, and mind your own affairs and work with your own hands," as one translation renders it.

The Apostle now (verse 13) approaches the matter which was apparently the main reason for the writing of the epistle. They were at that moment in a good deal of sorrow and difficulty as to certain of their number who had died. They were well aware that the Lord Jesus was coming again, indeed they were expecting Him very soon, and this made these unexpected deaths very mysterious to their minds. They felt that in some way or other these dear brethren of theirs would be losers. The Saviour would come and the glory would shine *without them!* It was a very real grief to them, but it was a grief founded upon ignorance and it only needed the light of the truth to dispel it for ever.

"I would not have you to be ignorant, brethren," says the Apostle, and he forthwith instructs them in the very details which they needed to know, perfecting in that particular matter that which was lacking in their faith.

The first thing he assures them is that God will bring these departed saints with Jesus when He comes again. In the last verse of chapter iii. he had spoken of "the coming of our Lord Jesus Christ with ALL His saints" and here he fortifies this assurance. The *"all"* includes those who "sleep in Jesus" for it is as certain that such will be brought with Christ as that Jesus Himself died and rose again. The death and resurrection of Christ are to faith the standard of absolute truth and reality and certainty. All parts of the truth are equally certain and the Apostle desired them to realize this.

This most definite assurance, comforting as it must have been, would not solve the difficulty existing to their minds as to how it was to be accomplished. *How* were these departed saints to be found in Christ's glory so as to come with Him at His advent? *In what way* would this great change be accomplished? This question is answered in the succeeding verses, and the Apostle prefaces his explanation with the words, "This we say unto you by the word of the Lord." By this he indicated that he was conveying to them something as a direct and fresh revelation from the Lord, and not merely restating something that had been previously revealed. The item of truth which he makes known to them was just that which they needed to complete their understanding of the coming of the Lord.

When the Lord comes the saints will be divided into two classes—(1) "we which are alive and remain" (2) "them which are asleep." Evidently the Thessalonians to begin with had not contemplated the possibility of there being this second class at all. Even later they probably imagined that the first class would form the majority and the second the minority; and hence there would be the tendency to treat the second class as a negligible factor. Verse 15 corrects this tendency. The fact was, as the Apostle assures them, that the saints in class one would not "prevent"—that is, "go before" or "have precedence over"—those in class two. If there was to be any precedence given at all it would be accorded to class two as verse 16 shows, for there it is stated that "the dead in Christ shall rise *first*."

Verses 16 and 17 then speak of the coming of the Lord Jesus *for* His saints. They reveal to us just how He is going to gather them to Himself so that subsequently He may come *with* all of them as the last verse of chapter iii. stated. Unless the distinction between the coming *for* and the coming *with* is seen no clear view of the Lord's coming is possible.

How emphatic is that statement:—"The Lord *Himself* shall descend." In that supreme hour He will not act by proxy but come Himself! He will descend with an assembling shout. Myriads of angels will serve, for the archangel's voice will be heard. The hosts of God will be on the move, for the trumpets of God shall sound. Yet all these will be subsidiary to the mighty action of the Lord Himself. Verse 16 gives us His sudden descension from heaven into the air, and the exertion of His power, the utterance of the voice that wakes the dead.

The last clause of verse 16 and verse 17 give us the response that will be at once found in the saints. The first effect of His power will be seen in the resurrection of the dead saints. Then they, with those of us who are alive and remain until that hour, will be caught up to meet the Lord in the air and so be for ever with Him. How simple it all is; and, thank God, as certain of accomplishment as simple.

We notice of course that this Scripture does not give us *all* the details connected with this blessed hope. We might wish to enquire for instance in just what condition the dead in Christ are raised? This we find answered very fully in 1 Corinthians xv. That chapter also informs us of the change that must take place as to the bodies of all saints who are alive when He comes. We must be changed into a spiritual and incorruptible condition ere we are "caught up." That chapter also tells us that all will take place "in a moment in the twinkling of an eye," which assures us that though the dead in Christ shall rise *first*, the precedence they are granted will be a matter of but just a moment.

In verse 17 observe the word "together." The Thessalonians sorrowed and so often do we. Being taught of God to love one another their hearts were torn when death snatched some from their midst. We too know what these wrenches are. We do not sorrow as those who have no hope, nor did they. The life-giving voice of the Son of God is going to reunite us. We shall meet Him, but not in ones or twos or in isolated detachments. We shall be caught up TOGETHER.

> *"What a chorus, what a meeting,*
> *With the family complete!"*

Notice also that we are going to *meet* the Lord. The word used here only occurs thrice elsewhere in the New Testament, viz., in Matthew xxv. 1 and 6, and Acts xxviii. 15. In each case it has the meaning of "going forth and returning with." When the brethren from Rome "met" Paul that was exactly what happened. They went forth as far as Appii Forum and having met him they joined his company and returned with him to Rome. Just so shall we all meet our Lord in the air. Joining His company—never to part from Him—we shall subsequently return with Him when He is manifested to the world in His glory.

Are not "these words" enough to comfort all our hearts; enough indeed to fill them with abiding joy?

CHAPTER 5

THE FIRST AND second verses of chapter v. stand in very direct contrast to verses 13 and 15 of chapter iv. As to the coming of the Lord Jesus for His saints—that which is commonly spoken of as "the rapture"—they had been ignorant, and consequently they were in needless difficulty and sorrow, and the Apostle wrote to them "by the word of the Lord" to enlighten them. But as to "the times and the seasons" they were not at all ignorant and there was no need for Paul to write to them on that subject.

We must not fail to notice the distinction which is thus made between these two parts of prophetic truth. It is possible to be quite ignorant as to the rapture while being well informed as to the times and the seasons. Plainly then they are two different things, quite distinct from each other. Were the rapture an essential part of the times and seasons, then to be wholly ignorant of it would mean partial ignorance as to them. The Thessalonians however were quite ignorant as to it, while being so well instructed as to them that the apostle could say you "know perfectly" and "have no need that I write unto you."

The times and seasons have to do with the earth and not heaven, as Genesis i. 14 shows us. The term is used in Thessalonians to indicate not the various divisions of earth's history as regulated by the heavenly bodies but those larger divisions, each characterized by its own special features as regulated by God's moral government of the earth. In the past fresh seasons have been introduced by such events as the flood, the redemption of Israel from Egypt and the giving of the law, the overthrow of David's line of kings and the passing of dominion into Gentile hands. Another season yet to come is to be introduced by the Lord Jesus assuming His great power that He may reign. That will be "the day of the Lord."

The rapture of the saints is however disconnected from these earthly seasons. It is not just an item on the programme of earthly happenings. It will be the Lord calling up His saints to heaven for the enjoyment of their heavenly portion. The church—composed of all the called-out saints of the present dispensation—is heavenly in its calling and destiny. It does not belong to the earth, which is the reason why its translation from earth to heaven is not included in the programme of earthly events. There is no hint consequently of the rapture in Old Testament Scripture. A right understanding of this matter furnishes us with a key that unlocks much dispensational truth, which otherwise must remain closed to our minds.

The day when the Lord shall have His rights and dominate the whole situation is certainly coming. Its arrival will be unexpected, sudden, inevitable, and unerring in its effects. It will come, as all God's dealings have come, in the most appropriate time and manner possible, and it will mean destruction for the ungodly. Just when men are saying "Peace and Safety" then the judgment will fall. Conditions amongst the nations are such that peace is an urgent necessity. Modern teachings, both scientific and religious, are such that men feel increasingly secure from supernatural happenings. In the minds of the people *God* has been reduced to a nonentity by the popular doctrine of evolution; so they fear nothing from that quarter. To their minds the only danger that threatens is from *man*. Man, wonderful man, has sought out many inventions, but unfortunately his marvellous discoveries in chemistry coupled with researches in other directions are capable of being turned to the most diabolical uses. Now if only peace can be maintained amongst men safety is assured.

When men congratulate themselves on having achieved this desirable end then God will assert Himself and the day of the Lord arrive. The world will be overtaken by it like those who are asleep in the dark; but not thus is it going to be with believers. *Today* the world is asleep in the dark; *today* the believer is a child of light, and in the light.

The contrast between the believer and the world, as given to us in verses 4 to 8, is very striking, and we do well to ponder it. The world is in darkness. The world is asleep. The world is even "drunken," intoxicated with influences that are from beneath. This was never more apparent than it is today when multiplied means of inter-communication spread new ideas and influences with great rapidity. Think of the potency with which the one word *"evolution"* has drugged the *minds* of men! No opiate for the *body* ever yet discovered can compare with it!

The believer is not *in* darkness nor is he *of* the darkness. He is a child of light and of the day. He has been begotten, so to speak, of the light which reached him in the Gospel, and he partakes of the character of that which gave him birth. Hence, though he is in the world, which is in darkness, he is not in darkness himself; rather light divine surrounds his going. He is a child of the coming day and hence he knows where he is going and what is coming.

Upon this is based the exhortation to shake off anything like sleep that we may watch and be sober. As a means to this sober watching we are to be characterized by faith, love and hope. These virtues, if in active exercise, will be to us like breastplate and helmet, protecting both heart and head in this day of conflict. Though children of light we are surrounded by the darkness of the world and ugly blows may fall upon us, struck from out the darkness.

The hope which is ours is the "hope of salvation." The Christian is *never* spoken of in Scripture as hoping for forgiveness of sins, but he *is* as hoping for salvation, for salvation is a word of large meaning, embracing the final deliverance which shall reach us at the coming of the Lord. For that we hope; that is, we await it with expectation. It is certain to arrive in its due season for there is no element of uncertainty in hopes which are founded on God and His word.

The Christ-rejecting world is appointed to wrath when the vials of His judgment will be outpoured on earth. Details as to this solemn time we find in the book of Revelation. We however have been appointed to obtain salvation by our Lord Jesus Christ. God's appointments are always kept to time. They never fail. Wrath for the world and salvation for the saints are alike sure.

That salvation is going to reach us by our Lord Jesus Christ acting as described in chapter iv. 16, 17. His people shall be taken by Him out of the place where the judgment is going to fall, just as of old God removed Enoch before death reached him or the flood came. In more places than one the Old Testament bears witness to the way in which God shelters his people from judgment. He may do it by safely housing them and carrying them through it, as once he did with Noah, and as He will do with a godly remnant of His people Israel when soon His judgments are abroad in the earth. He may do it by removing them from the very scene of judgment, so that they never see it, as with Enoch in the past and the church in the future. But He always does it.

When we thus "obtain salvation," it will reach us righteously for the One who will bring it to us has died for us, as we are reminded in verse 10. The object He had before Him in dying for us was that we might "live together with Him." How full of comfort and edification is this wonderful truth.

From chapter iv. 13, to chapter v. 11 is one long paragraph, and the close of it brings us back to where it started. Jesus died for us that He might have us with Him. He will put the finishing touches to His design when He raptures the saints into His presence whether they are awake on earth or sleeping in their graves.

Let us all ponder the words that "*we should live together with Him,*" so that their sweetness may deeply penetrate our souls. He *died* that we might *live*. But not only is life before us, but life *together with Christ*. We noticed the word "together" at the end of chapter iv. It was delightful to discover that in the resurrection day we should be *united* with all the saints—and *reunited* with those we knew on earth—in order to meet the Lord. It is more delightful still to know that as one united company we shall for eternity enjoy life together with Him. All that life means, its pursuits and joys, we are to share with Him. We shall *have* His life so that we may be capacitated to *share* His life in that day. Even today we may share His thoughts, His joys, though not in the wonderful fulness of this glad tomorrow.

With verse 12 the closing exhortations begin. There were evidently no officially appointed elders at Thessalonica. Hence the apostle's desire that they should *know*—in sense of *recognizing*—those in their midst who were qualified as such and doing the work of elders. They were not only to know them but to listen to their admonitions and esteem them in love. The carnal mind, which is by nature insubordinate, would take advantage of the absence of any official appointment to flout their spiritual authority; but thus it was not to be.

How clearly this shows that the thing of all importance is *moral quali-fication* and *authority* as given of God, and not *official sanction and appointment*, even when such can be ministered through an apostle. The latter without the former is but an empty husk. What is it when even the official appointment has nothing apostolic about it? And Scripture is quite silent as to apostolic powers and authority being transmitted from generation to generation.

If the Lord raises up godly men with shepherd instincts to care for the spiritual welfare of His people we should thankfully recognize and profit by them, even though apostolic power to appoint them be lacking. This, we believe, is just our position today. Let us beware of spurning such spiritual guides. It is not difficult after all to discern between those who are but tiresome meddlers with other people's affairs and those who care lovingly for our spiritual welfare in the fear of God.

In verses 14 to 22 we have a series of important exhortations couched in very brief terms. It is very evident that the church of God is not intended to be a community wherein everyone may go as they please. It is rather a place where spiritual order under divine authority is maintained. This is as we should expect, remembering that it is God's house. Warning, comfort and support are to be administered as occasion arises. Patience is to be exercised. Good is to be pursued. Joy, prayer and thanksgiving are to be the happy occupations of the saints, and that abidingly.

Nothing is to quench the believer's joy for it is occasioned by that which is eternal. Prayer is to be unceasing for the need is continuous, and access to the throne of grace is never closed on God's side. Prayer, and that attitude of soul of which prayer is the expression, is to be habitual. As for thanksgiving it should be rendered to God "in *everything*," inasmuch as we know that "all things work together for good to them that love God." Moreover it is God's will that we should be a thankful people, so that He may "inhabit" our praises, according to the spirit of Psalm xxii. 3. These things are all intensely individual.

Verses 19 to 22 refer more to matters which concerned the assembly of God's saints, where the Spirit of God operated and made known the mind of God. There, in those early days, He was accustomed sometimes to speak and act in supernatural ways,—see Acts xiii. 2; 1 Corinthians xii. 7-11; 1 Timothy iv.1. He also, in a more general way, made His voice heard in the ministry of the prophets, as contemplated in 1 Corinthians xiv. The Thessalonians were not to attempt to regulate the action of the Spirit in the assembly or they would quench His action. It is not for us to control the Spirit, but for Him to control us. Prophesyings were to be given their due place of importance and yet, seeing that such a thing as prophecy of a spurious sort was not unknown, everything they heard was to be "proved;" i.e., *tested*, for though they had not as yet the written New Testament, they had the Old Testament and the verbal instructions of the apostle. Having tested what they heard they were to "hold fast" all that was good and "abstain from" or "hold aloof from" evil in all its forms.

Reading the exhortations do we not feel that a very lofty standard is set before us? It is so indeed, and that it may be reached we need to be set apart for God; and God Himself, the God of peace, must be the Author of our sanctification. The Apostle's desire was that God might work to this end; the *whole* man, spirit, soul and body being brought under His power. Thus they would be sanctified *wholly*.

In as far as we are really set apart for God, in spirit, in soul and in body we shall be preserved blameless. At the coming of the Lord Jesus we shall be removed altogether from the scene of defilement and we shall no longer have the flesh within us. But how cheering is verse 24! In spite of all the breakdowns and defections upon our side God has called us to this blameless condition in glory and He will not fail to achieve His purpose with us. He will do it!

To this end what is needed but that the grace of our Lord Jesus Christ should be with us? With a benediction to this effect the epistle closes.

2 THESSALONIANS

CHAPTER 1

THE SECOND LETTER to the Thessalonians was evidently written not long after the first, while still they were young in the faith and the more likely to be misled by false teachers, especially in matters pertaining to the coming of the Lord. The opening words are almost exactly the same as in the first letter; Paul again associating with himself the same two fellow-labourers.

The condition of this assembly still gave great joy and thankfulness to the Apostle. Their spiritual health was good, in spite of the persecutions and tribulations that were pressing upon them; we had almost said, *because of* their persecutions and troubles. The world being actively antagonistic to them, they were not for the moment, being tested by its seductions. The very pressure that it was exerting against them had the effect of welding them together.

In verses 3 and 4, growing faith and abounding love are brought into intimate connection with persecution and tribulation, and not without good reason. Not only was their faith growing, but growing *exceedingly;* not only was love there, but love was *abounding*. In this the Apostle greatly rejoiced as being the sign of spiritual vitality and progress, though he had nothing to say in this epistle as to their knowledge or gifts. In contrast to this, he acknowledged the knowledge and gifts of the Corinthians in his first letter to them, whilst he had nothing favourable to say as to their faith and love; and in them he could not boast, for they were carnal. Have we all grasped the significance of this? To what do we look if we desire to see spiritual advancement in one another?

The scripture shows us that real faith is a living thing. It is like a living tree, with its roots striking down into the soil of the knowledge of God. Faith is spiritual eyesight, and as we proceed our sight should grow clearer and its range be increased. As we know God better we trust Him more.

We must notice that in this second epistle Paul makes no allusion to their *hope*, though he does mention their patience, which is one of its fruits. The reason for this is, apparently, that adversaries had made further attempts to confuse their minds as to things to come in a way calculated to impair their hope, and that for the moment they had succeeded. How they did it, and how the Apostle countered their efforts by this epistle, we shall see more clearly as we proceed. That which follows—verses 5 to 10 of this first chapter—was evidently penned with a view to setting matters rightly before their minds. The attempt had been made to delude them into thinking that their present troubles were a sign that the day of the Lord was already come. This will be seen, if verses 1 and 2 of chapter ii. be read. The word translated "at hand" at the end of verse 2 is really "present."

In verses 5 to 10 the public appearing of the Lord Jesus is presented as being the reversal of previously existing conditions; a complete turning of the tables, we may say. The Thessalonians were suffering tribulation, the men of the world being their troublers. When the Lord Jesus appears, He will recompense the world with tribulation and His saints with rest. In so doing, He will be acting in *righteousness*.

It is not difficult to see that it will be an entirely righteous thing for God to presently recompense the persecutors of His saints with tribulation. It is not quite so easy to see how the entrance of the saints into the coming kingdom can be connected with righteousness, for we should surely disclaim any thought of merit and protest that grace alone could bring us into the kingdom of God. The thought in verse 5 however, appears to be that though all is of grace yet God desires to put His saints in possession of His kingdom, as those who are counted worthy of it. Hence He permits the persecutions and tribulations, which produce in them the fortitude and patience which He loves and can righteously reward. In this patience and faith under trial was seen a manifest token that God's judgment was righteous in assigning them to the coming kingdom and its rest.

The description of the public appearing of the Lord Jesus, given in verses 7 to 9, is indeed terrible. When He is unveiled from the heavens, nothing will be lacking which is calculated to strike fear into the hearts of rebellious men. Vengeance will fall upon those who do not know God and who do not obey the Gospel. Everlasting destruction from the presence of the Lord, will be the penalty inflicted. Many attempts have been made to avoid the plain and evident force of the two words, "everlasting destruction," but when all is said and done the fact remains that destruction does *not* mean annihilation, and everlasting *does* mean lasting for ever, and this whether we consider the Greek original or the English translation.

Let us notice that the Gospel is a message from God which we are to OBEY. We are so apt to think of it as a kindly invitation which we are to accept, and to present it only in that light to others. Consequently, they think of it only as an invitation which they may decline, or at least defer indefinitely, without any very serious consequences; and that is to them a very fatal mistake. All who hear the Gospel, are responsible to render to it in response *the obedience of faith*.

Notice also that there can be no worse fate than to be consigned to eternal ruin away from *the presence of the Lord*. We saw in considering the first Epistle that to live together with the Lord is the very height of bliss. The converse holds true. There can be nothing worse than to be banished for ever from the presence of the One who is the Fountain-head of life and light and love.

The appearing of Christ will however have two sides. He will be glorified in taking vengeance on the ungodly. He will be also glorified and admired in all those who have believed in that day. The preposition here, you will notice, is not *by* but *in*. He will certainly be glorified and adored by us, but the point here is that He will be glorified in us. In that day, the saints will shine forth in His likeness as His handiwork. Men and angels will look at them and glorify Him, inasmuch as all that they are will be the fruit of His work.

Nowadays, all too often we are to His discredit. Of old, the accusation had to be laid against Israel that, "the name of God is blasphemed among the Gentiles through you." (Rom. ii. 24). and the same indictment has to be brought against those who profess to be the people of today. But in that day, what will be displayed, will not be our crookedness or our peculiarities but the grace and power of Christ reproduced in us. In us men will see the glorious effect of the mighty work of God.

What a wonderful calling this is! No wonder the Apostle earnestly desired that God would count them worthy of it, by fulfilling His good pleasure in them now, promoting the work of faith with power in their hearts and lives. In this way the name of the Lord Jesus would be glorified in them now, and not only in the coming age. If He is to be glorified in us then, it is surely right that we should be concerned about it that He is glorified in us now.

The last verse of this first chapter emphasizes this, and adds the fact that not only is He to be glorified in us in the coming age but we are to be glorified in Him, for we shall then be shining in a glory not our own but His. This will be "according to the grace of our God and the Lord Jesus Christ." Nothing but the grace of God could produce so wonderful a result as that.

CHAPTER 2

WITH THE OPENING verses of the second chapter we reach the matter which was the occasion of the writing of this epistle. Mischief-makers had been at work, endeavouring to persuade the Thessalonians that they had already passed into the day of the Lord, though they knew well that the day of the Lord brought heavy judgments with it, and that it would come as a thief in the night. (See, 1 Thess. v. 1-3). Those who were attempting to lead them astray evidently reasoned that the persecutions and trials into which they had been plunged were judgments, which proved that the day of the Lord was upon them.

Now all this was simple deception, as verse 3 states, and the methods to which these adversaries stooped, hoping thereby the more effectually to deceive, were in keeping with their false teaching. They pressed their ideas upon the Thessalonians, "by spirit" "by word" and even "by letter as from us." Not only did they assert it by word of mouth, but they gave out their teachings as having been received by inspiration of the Spirit of God. The Spirit of God, did give inspired utterances in the early Christian assemblies, as the Acts of the Apostles bears witness, but there were also to be found false utterances proceeding from a spirit or spirits, which were not the Spirit of God, as indicated in 1 John iv. 1-6. These deceivers might claim that they had received their teaching from a spirit. If so, it was from a spirit who was not the Spirit of God. They went however, one step further than this. They even sent a letter to the Thessalonians which purported to be from the Apostle Paul. By a species of forgery, they tried to make it appear that their erroneous ideas had his sanction. Satan is not at all careful as to the means he uses to attain his ends. Crooked teaching can be quite appropriately supported by crooked behaviour.

Some however, may wish to ask what was the importance of the point at issue? The persecution and trial were there. Did it after all matter so much whether it signified the arrival of the day of the Lord, or whether it did not? How often we find large issues of a practical sort hinging upon points of doctrine that look small enough! It did matter very much indeed. If the day of the Lord were really present then the truth that Paul had been led to reveal to them, in the latter part of chapter iv. and the opening of chapter v. of his first epistle was very evidently overturned. That day had stolen a march upon them, and overtaken them as a thief. Is it nothing to have the Word of God discredited?

Further, it would mean that here were believers left on earth to suffer tribulation, which came as retribution from the hand of God. Their heavenly hope would be dimmed, and they left to face the fearful things about to come on the earth. Was this a small matter? No, indeed.

How did the Apostle meet this deceptive teaching? He met it in two ways. First, by reminding them of the truth he had already established in his first Epistle. Second, by giving further clear instruction as to the day of the Lord, and the order of its events.

He besought them not to heed the error, by the coming of the Lord Jesus and by "*our gathering together unto Him.*" To what does he refer in these words? Clearly to that, as to which he instructed them in verses 15 to 17 of the fourth chapter of His first epistle. If we are to gather together to Christ in the air, before the coming of the day of the Lord, how can we find ourselves on earth suffering its throes? In the light of the truth that had already reached them the Thessalonians ought never to have listened to these deceivers. But then of course, they were only recent converts—but babes in Christ—and consequently not yet much skilled in discerning the drift of the teachings they heard. Many of us may be like them, and if so it will help us to see that the truth is one consistent whole, so that we must never be shaken by new teachings, if they are at variance with the foundations laid by God in our hearts at an earlier period.

With verse 3 his further instruction begins. Not only is the Church to gather together to Christ in the air, before the day of the Lord arrives, but there are also two great events to first of all materialize upon the earth itself. They are both mentioned in verse 3. There is to be a "falling away" or, "an apostasy" first. Also "the man of sin" must be manifested. The former is a *movement*, the latter is a *man*.

All history teaches us how movements and men, are linked together, and in that order. First comes a movement, created all too frequently by the god of this world; then presently, a man appears who brings the movement to a head and in whom it reaches its highest expression and finality. Ancient imperialism reached its head in Nebuchadnezzar: the French republican movement in Napoleon; whilst the modern Fascist movement has been headed up in Mussolini. Thus history will repeat itself on a much grander scale before the day of the Lord arrives.

Let us be clear as to what apostasy means. It is not just a course of backsliding, a growing cold on the part of Christians, as a result of which the world invades the church, dragging into its bosom a whole train of attendant evils. It is rather a complete forsaking of the truth of God, a total abandonment of the ancient foundations of the faith. There have been all too often in the history of the church distortions and perversions of truth, which might be compared to the transplanting of shrubs and the lopping of trees which largely spoil the effect of an otherwise beautiful and symmetrical garden. Apostasy is not like that. It is rather like a landslide of such dimensions that the whole garden is obliterated.

The idea is still quite widely held that the Lord will not return until the world has been prepared for His advent by the preaching of the Gospel and the conversion of most, if not all, its inhabitants. There is no support for this idea in the passage we are considering, but quite the contrary. The fact is, that what will precede His advent in glory is a total abandonment of the faith by those who formerly professed to hold it. This apostasy will pave the way for the revelation of a great personage, who will be the direct representative of Satan, called here "the man of sin," for in him sin will find its highest expression. This man will be marked by the most arrogant self-exaltation. He will oppose God by claiming himself to be God. A claim such as this would be impossible amongst people calling themselves Christian—it would merely excite ridicule— were the way not prepared for it by the apostasy.

The apostasy then will be of such a nature that the minds of men will be prepared to accept such gigantic claims on the part of a mere man as quite possible and reasonable. The deification of man will be the logical and reasonable outcome of the movement. This throws a flood of light as to what the main drift of the apostasy will be. God will be dethroned and man will be enthroned!

Let us survey great Christendom today in the light of these facts. Without a doubt we see very ominous signs of the approach of the apostasy. The coming events cast their shadows before. The whole drift of "advanced" religious thinking and teaching is in the direction which this scripture indicates. If God be admitted at all into the scheme of their thinking, He is relegated to the far distance and evolution is made to entirely fill the foreground. Evolution is only the flimsy creation of their own minds, yet they have endowed it with wonderful powers and mankind is supposed to be the very crown and fruition of all its workings. Man therefore is to them of supreme importance and not God. Moreover, they expect that evolutionary processes will not stop with man as he is today, but continue until a super-man will be produced. How simple and natural then it will be to acclaim the man of sin when he appears as the super-man long expected!

The Apostle had warned the Thessalonians of these things when he had been with them on that brief first visit, preaching the Gospel amongst them. We may wonder that he found time to speak of such a matter to them in so short a visit, and that he thought it appropriate to do so within not many days of their being converted; but so it was. Paul knew right well that "the mystery of iniquity" was already at work, as he tells us in verse 7. The meaning of this is that "iniquity" or "lawlessness" in its "mystery" or "secret" form was even then moving in men's hearts. The lawless self-assertion which is to blaze forth in the light of day at the end of the dispensation was there at the beginning, though hidden in the dark. Hence the warning was necessary.

It is much more necessary then for us upon whom the end of the age is come. Let us take heed to it.

Have we all got clearly fixed in our minds thus far that the apostasy and the revelation of the man of sin must precede the day of the Lord? Human evil must reach its flood-tide height before the Lord deals with it in judgment.

If we have this clear, we shall not have difficulty in seeing that the coming of the Lord for His saints and our gathering together unto Him in the air must precede full-blown apostasy. The true saints of God never apostatize. As long as the true church of God is here a witness is maintained on earth in the energy of the Holy Spirit, and the apostasy in its fulness is hindered—its chariot wheels drive heavily, for the brake presses hard against them.

When the brake is suddenly taken off by the rapture of the saints to heaven, the chariot will bound forward to the final crash that awaits it.

In verse 8 the man of sin is referred to as "that Wicked," or more literally, "the *lawless* [one]." The phrase in verse 7, "the mystery of iniquity," is more literally, "the mystery of *lawlessness*." Reading it thus, it is more easy to catch the connection. Lawlessness is the very essence of sin. It is the refusal of all controlling authority and restraint, and therefore in deadly opposition to God. The lawlessness, which has long been at work in

Christendom in a mysterious or hidden way like a suppressed fire, is going to blaze forth in the lawless one.

But this will only be when the saints of God are removed from the scene of conflict by the coming of the Lord for them. At present the forces of evil are under restraint—*restraint* is the meaning of the two words *withholdeth* and *letteth* in verses 6 and 7. There is *"He* who restrains" and also *"what* restrains." The former doubtless refers to the Holy Spirit of God, who is at this time personally upon earth as He never was before and will not be again. The latter, we believe, refers to the presence of the church on earth; the church being the house of God wherein the Holy Ghost is dwelling.

We have probably but little conception of how great is the restraint placed upon the working of lawlessness by the presence of the saints of God. They may be poor and feeble but the Spirit of God who indwells them is almighty. Occasionally this restraint is manifested in quite unmistakable style, as when, for instance, a spiritist seance has been a failure because of the presence in the building of some definite and earnest Christian. This we believe has happened more than once. Have not many of us noticed how the flow of ungodly conversation in a room or office is stopped by the sudden entrance of an out-and-out servant of Christ?

When the Church is raptured to heaven, and therefore the Holy Spirit no longer has a *house* on earth, the consequences will be very serious and very immediate. The repressed lawlessness will burst forth in the lawless one and for a brief moment the working of Satan will have full scope. This coming lawless man will be inspired by Satan and exhibit his energy in every particular. Notice how sweeping are the expressions used. Satan will support him with ALL power, even to signs and wonders of falsehood, so that EVERY possible deceit of unrighteousness will be brought to bear upon men who have been left behind to perish.

This tremendous energy of Satan will continue but for a short time. The lawless one being revealed on earth, he will be speedily dealt with. The Lord Jesus being revealed from heaven, He will utterly destroy him, casting him alive into the lake of fire, as Revelation xix. 20 shows. How appropriate it is that this utterly lawless and disobedient man, the very personification of Satanic energy, shall be dealt with personally by the Lord Jesus, the wholly subject and obedient Man, the personification of the power and majesty of God. No intermediary shall be allowed to intervene in that conflict!

We must also notice how just are all the dealings of God with men. Those who will fall a prey to all this deceit of unrighteousness, are just those who when they heard the truth did not love it. Loving not the truth, they did not believe it, rather they had pleasure in unrighteousness. And now the deceit of unrighteousness captures them; they believe the lie, and they all fall under the judgment of God. Formerly God sent them the truth, the Gospel was sounded into their ears by men who preached it "with the Holy Ghost sent down from heaven" (1 Peter i. 12). Now God sends them a strong delusion. He does for them what of old He had to do for rebellious Israel, when He "blinded their eyes, and hardened their heart" (John xii. 40; and see Acts xxviii. 26, 27). Is God unrighteous in acting thus? On the contrary; He is acting in righteousness of the strictest and most exact kind.

These verses should act as a check upon those Christians who seem to be so very desirous of possessing miraculous powers, particularly in the directions of "healings" and "tongues." Let them note that though there were such miraculous displays in the energy of the Holy Spirit at the beginning of the dispensation, it is predicted that at its close there shall be a great display of similar powers, but of a spurious and Satanic kind. We are now near its end and it is significant how there has been a revival of strange happenings which purport to be miraculous and divine. We do not assert that *all* these happenings have been spurious and Satanic, but we do say that *many* have been and that if we do not test them all in very exact fashion by all the Scriptures we may easily be woefully deceived.

If we review for a moment the first twelve verses of our chapter we shall see then that directly after the coming of the Lord *for* His saints there will be,

1. A great movement in the realm of HUMAN thought, resulting in the falling away or apostasy, and culminating in the man of sin.

2. A great movement in SATANIC realms, resulting in an intense concentration of the powers of darkness, and culminating in great displays of lying wonders, so artfully staged as to utterly deceive apostate men.

3. A great movement of GOD'S government and power, resulting in His shutting such men up in their delusion and unbelief, and culminating in His public intervention in judgment through the glorious appearing of the Lord Jesus.

There will be first the *catching away* of the true saints of God. Then the *falling away* of corrupt and forsaken Christendom. Lastly the *sweeping away* of the whole nauseous thing in the judgment of God.

No hope is held out here for Gospel-rejectors. No second chance after the coming of the Lord for His people is hinted at. The solemn statement is, "that they ALL might be damned who believed not the truth but had pleasure in unrighteousness."

How delightful is the contrast of verse 13 with verse 12. The Thessalonian believers—and ourselves also—have been chosen of God to salvation, a salvation which will be consummated when the Lord comes for us, and we obtain His glory. To this we were called by the Gospel. In believing that Gospel we believed *the truth* and so from the outset we have that which fortifies us against *the lie* which those who perish believe, deceived by Satan.

The "sanctification of the Spirit" does not refer to the progressive work of the Spirit in the hearts of believers, conforming them more and more to the will of God. It refers rather to that setting apart for God which is achieved by the initial operations of the Spirit of God in the souls of men, operations which have in view His indwelling us when once the Gospel is believed. By this sovereign work of the Spirit we have been sanctified.

In view of this the word to us is "stand fast." We are to hold the apostolic "traditions" or "instructions." The Thessalonian believers had these instructions in two ways—by word of mouth and by the written epistle. We have them in one way only. Let us take therefore the more earnest heed to the apostolic *writings*. We have indeed a good hope through grace, so we may well be comforted and established.

CHAPTER 3

FINALLY, THE THESSALONIANS were to pray for Paul himself, and that not only in regard to his personal safety but in regard to the work with which he was entrusted. The history recorded in Acts xvii. shows us how greatly prayer for his safety was needed at this juncture, yet he gave the first place to the work. The word had had full course amongst the Thessalonians and consequently it had been glorified in the wonderful results it produced in them. Paul asked prayer that thus it might be wherever he went. He prayed unceasingly for his converts but he was also not ashamed to ask for their prayers for himself. The most advanced saint or servant may well be thankful for the prayers of the youngest convert or the humblest believer.

As to the Thessalonians themselves the Apostle had confidence in the Lord concerning them that they would be governed by his directions, only he desired that the Lord Himself might direct their hearts into the enjoyment of God's love and into the patience of Christ. This is what we all want, and especially so seeing that the end of the age is upon us. If our hearts enter into Christ's patience, as He waits at God's right hand, and are tuned into sympathy with Him, we shall not chafe at what to us may seem a long delay. God's love will meanwhile be our enjoyed portion and we shall be able to display it to others while passing through the world.

From verse 6 of this third chapter and the succeeding verses it is evident that the erroneous ideas concerning the coming of the Lord, which had been pressed upon the Thessalonians, had already borne evil fruit. It is ever the way that evil communications corrupt good manners. Some amongst them had become fanatical in their minds, under the impression that the day of Christ was upon them, and had thrown up their ordinary employment. Having done this they began to expect support from others.

They became disorderly busybodies, doing nothing themselves and preying upon others who quietly went on with their work.

As to this the Apostle was able to hold himself up as an example. He had laboured night and day for his own support, though he might justly have been chargeable to them. God had ordained that "they which preach the Gospel should live of the Gospel" (1 Cor. ix. 14). Yet he had not claimed this right. As to all others the divine rule is, "that if any would not work, neither should he eat."

In verse 12 we have Paul's word to these busybodies. He commands them to work for their own living. Then in verse 13 he turns to the rest of the assembly at Thessalonica and tells them not to be weary in well-doing, We can well imagine how tired they must have got of these disorderly brethren who were continually trespassing on their kindness. If now they were to be relieved of this burden let them not cease their benevolence but still be hearty and cheerful givers in the interests of the Lord.

Verses 14 and 15 give instructions in case any of the disorderly brethren were contumacious and refused obedience to God's word through the Apostle's letter. Such were to be disciplined. The displeasure of God was to be manifested in His people withdrawing their companionship. The offender would thereby be made to feel the unenviable notoriety of his isolation. His links with the world *without* were broken and now there would be no happy companionship *within* the Christian circle. This would be a well-nigh impossible position and calculated to bring him to his senses. He was not however to be put right outside the Christian circle as though he were an enemy, which was the dealing that had to be taken with the offender of whom we read in 1 Corinthians v.

All this should be done that peace might reign in their midst. Only the Lord Himself however could really give this. Paul desired that it might be theirs at all times and in every way.

As the Thessalonians had been troubled with an epistle falsely represented as coming from Paul, he was very careful that there should be no doubt about the authenticity of this epistle which really did come from him. This explains verse 17.

1 TIMOTHY

INTRODUCTION

THE EPISTLE BEFORE us is the first of a group of four which were written by the Apostle Paul to *individuals*. They were all written rather late in the Apostle's life of service, when declension was becoming pronounced in the church, and consequently the heart of that devoted man turned more especially to reliable and trusted disciples who stood firm when others began to slip. This imparts a certain general resemblance to the four, though each has its own clearly marked features.

We might perhaps characterize them as follows:-

1 Timothy. The Epistle of *godliness.*
2 Timothy. The Epistle of *courage.*
Titus. The Epistle of *sobriety* and *soundness.*
Philemon. The Epistle of *Christian courtesy.*

At any rate godliness—or *piety* as some translate the word—is stamped very distinctly upon the epistle we are now to consider, as any concordance will show. It becomes a very urgent necessity when spiritual life is on the decline.

CHAPTER 1

IN HIS OPENING verse Paul presents his apostleship as proceeding from God our Saviour—not from Jesus our Saviour, as we might have put it. He is going to bring before us the *living* GOD as both Saviour and Preserver (ii. 3; iv. 10) and so he commences on this note, and presents the Lord Jesus to us as our hope. When declension sets in it is well for us to know a living God as our Preserver, and to have our hopes centred not in churches, bishops, deacons, nor in a man of any kind, but in the Lord Himself.

Having saluted Timothy in verse 2, Paul at once reminds him of the responsibility resting upon him as left at Ephesus during his absence. Already some were beginning to teach things which differed from the truth as already laid down. These strange doctrines were of two kinds, "fables" (or "myths") and "genealogies." By the former term Paul indicated ideas imported from the heathen world, even though they were the refined speculations of Grecian schools; by the latter, ideas imported from the Jewish world in which genealogy had played so large a part. Timothy however was to abide in what he had learned of God and exhort others to do likewise, since the end of what was enjoined was love springing out of a pure heart, a good conscience, and unfeigned faith. This was that which God desired to see in His people.

The certain result of turning aside to fables or genealogies is questionings (verse 4) and vain jangling (verse 6). Christendom has largely turned aside to the teaching of fabulous assertions in the name of science on the one hand, and on the other to genealogies connected with religious succession, apostolic and otherwise, with all the ritualism based thereupon, consequently the religious arena is filled with questioners and resounds with the uproar of vain jangling. What God aims at producing, and does produce where *the truth* holds sway, is love, and what is ministered is "God's dispensation which is in faith." The A. V. reads "edifying" but evidently the correct reading is "dispensation" or "house-law"—the alteration of one letter in the Greek word makes the difference. Love furthers all those things that God has ordered as the rule of His house.

The "commandment" of verse 5 has nothing to do with the law of Moses. The word is virtually the same as the one translated "charge" in verse 3. Verse 5 states the object Timothy was to have in view in the charge which he observed himself and enjoined upon others.

There were those at Ephesus who were enamoured of the law and desired to be teachers of it, and this leads the Apostle to indicate the place that the law was designed to fill, of which these would-be law-teachers were entirely ignorant. The law was not enacted for the righteous but for sinners. Hence to strenuously enforce it upon those who were righteous, because justified by God Himself, was not a lawful use of it. Paul does not pause in this passage to state that which the law of Moses was designed to effect. It was given to bring in *conviction of sin*, as is stated in Romans iii. 19; v. 20; and Galatians iii. 19.

The law itself is "holy and just and good" (Rom. vii. 12) whatever men may do with it. Verse 8 of our passage states that if lawfully used it is good in its practical effects. If wrongly used, as by these law-teachers, it works mischief, though perfectly good in itself.

Let us all be very careful to use the law lawfully. It is a most potent instrument of conviction for sinners. It deals unsparingly with the terrible list of sins given in verses 9 and 10, but besides all these there were other things which the law did not specifically mention but which were contrary to all sound teaching, and the Apostle alludes to these at the close of verse 10. Only notice that he does not say, "contrary to sound doctrine *according to the holy standard established by the law*" but, "*according to the glorious gospel of the blessed God*," for the gospel sets before us a standard of conduct more lofty than the law.

The law did not set forth the *maximum*, the utmost possible that God could expect from man, but rather the *minimum* of His demands, if man is to live on the earth; so that to fall below the standard set, in one item on one occasion, was to incur the death penalty. Now however the gospel has been introduced and Paul was entrusted with it. He speaks of it as the "glorious gospel," or more literally, "gospel of the glory" of the blessed God.

There is for the present moment but one gospel, though spoken of in various passages as the gospel "*of God*," "*of Christ*" "*of the grace of God*" *"of the glory of Christ"* and as in this verse. So also the one and the same Holy Spirit is variously characterized in different passages. This is in order to teach us the depth and wonder residing in both, the many-sided characters that they wear. How striking then is the character in which the gospel is presented to us here, and how suitable to the subjects in hand!

What could exceed the moral filth and degradation of those who had come short not only of the law, but of "the glory of God" (Rom. iii. 23)? Their portrait appears in verses 9 and 10. Then in verse 11 comes "the gospel of the glory of the blessed God" followed in succeeding verses by the dark picture Paul gives of himself as an unconverted man. Look before and look after and we see nothing but the shame of cursed and unhappy man. Into the midst comes the glad tidings of the glory of the blessed, or happy, God. A contrast indeed!

The Old Testament has told us that, "it is the glory of God to *conceal* a thing" (Prov. xxv. 2) so that busy and inquisitive men are baffled in their researches again and again. Our New Testament passage tells us that it is also the glory of God to *reveal* Himself in the magnificence of His mercy to rebellious sinners; and the latter glory is greater than the former. If any ask, what is glory? We may answer, it is *excellence in display*. The Divine excellence may be displayed in such a way as to be visible to the eye, but on the other hand it may not; yet the glory of a moral and spiritual sort which reaches the heart by other channels than the eye is no less wonderful. When Saul of Tarsus was converted a glory smote him to the earth, blinding his eyes, but the glory of that exceeding abundant grace of our Lord "with faith and love which is in Christ Jesus" (verse 14) opened the eyes of his heart without dazzling the eyes of his head, and that is the glory spoken of here.

The sin of Saul of Tarsus abounded, since full of ignorant unbelief he aimed in his injurious antagonism directly at Christ Himself, by blasphemy and the persecution of His people. Hence he was, and he felt himself to be, the chief of sinners. The abundance of his sin was met however by the super-abundant grace of God. Did ever the glory of divine grace more brightly shine than when the rebel Saul encountered the risen Saviour? We think not. Yet we all owe our salvation to the same glad tidings of the glory of the blessed God. We all have reason to sing,

> *Oh! the glory of the grace*
> *Shining in the Saviour's face,*
> *Telling sinners from above,*
> *God is light, and God is love.*

By the time this Epistle was written not a few crisp statements of truth had passed into sayings. "Christ Jesus came into the world to save sinners," was one of these. It is endorsed as faithful and worthy of all acceptation— hall-marked as it were—by the Apostle's own experience as the chief of sinners. No sinner is beyond the grace and power of a Saviour, who could deliver such an insolent, persecuting blasphemer as he.

How all this shows up the folly of such as were desiring to be law-teachers, and landing their votaries in vain jangling. How weak and beggarly is all that beside this!

Now the astonishing mercy extended to Paul was not shown him for his sake alone but that there might be set forth the extent of divine long-suffering. His was a pattern case showing the full extent of the Lord's dealings in mercy, lifting him from the depths of verse 13 to the heights of verse 12.

Think for one moment of his conversion as recorded in Acts. Jesus had just been made Lord and Christ in resurrection. The early apostolic witness was rejected in the martyrdom of Stephen. Saul played a directing part in that outrage and proceeded forthwith on a career of violent persecution. From His lofty seat in heaven, clothed with irresistible might, the Lord looked down upon this outrageous little worm of the dust and instead of crushing him in judgment converted him in mercy. Thereby He gave a most striking delineation of His gracious ways and of the extent to which His long-suffering would go.

Henceforth Paul becomes a pattern man. Not only a pattern *of* mercy but a pattern *to* believers. He exemplifies and shows forth the truth in its practical workings in the hearts and lives of the people of God. It is because of this that again and again in his epistles he calls upon his converts to be followers of himself.

The recalling and recital of these wonders of mercy greatly moved the heart of the Apostle and led him momentarily to break the thread of his subject and to pen the doxology of verse 17. We find the same kind of thing elsewhere, as for instance, Romans xi. 33-36, where the Apostle utters his doxology moved by the consideration of the wisdom of God; or Ephesians iii. 20, 21, where he is moved by the love of Christ. In our passage he is moved thereto by the mercy of God.

The more majestic the Person who shows the mercy the greater the depth of the mercy displayed. Hence the Apostle views God in the height of His majesty and not in the intimacy of relationship. True, God is our Father as revealed to us in Christ. We *do* stand in this tender relationship as His children; still He is, "the King eternal, immortal, invisible, the only wise God" and this enhances the wonder of the mercy which He showed to the Apostle and to us. In response to such mercy Paul ascribes to Him honour and glory to the ages of ages.

Surely we too feel impelled to join in the doxology and add to it our hearty "Amen!"

In verse 18 the Apostle returns to the main theme of the epistle. In verse 3 he had referred to Timothy's position at Ephesus: he had been left there to charge some against turning aside from the truth. In verse five he had shown what is the end or object of all the charges which God commits to His people. Now he comes to the charge which is the burden of the present epistle from the beginning of chapter ii. to the end of chapter vi.

Before starting his charge to Timothy he reminds him of three things that might well emphasize in his mind the weight and importance of what he was going to say. First, that he had been marked out beforehand by prophetic utterance for the important service that he had to fulfil. Timothy was indeed a very distinguished servant of God, and we might at once feel inclined to excuse ourselves on the ground that we are not at all what he was. That is true. But while this fact may possibly preclude us from doing much in the way of enforcing God's charge upon other Christians it in no way exempts us from the obligation to read, understand and obey the charge ourselves.

Second, that only by holding faith and a good conscience could the faith of God be preserved in its integrity, and with the preservation of that faith the charge was concerned. Have we all digested this fact? We all recognize the doctrine of "justification by faith" but do we equally recognize the doctrine of "faith-preservation by faith"? Our little barque is launched upon the ocean of truth by faith, but do we now successfully navigate that ocean by intellect, by reason, by scientific deductions? Not so, but rather by faith and the maintenance of a good conscience. The Scriptures are the chart by which we navigate but the discerning and understanding eye which alone reads the chart aright is not intellect nor reason but FAITH, though when faith has done its work the chart discloses to us things which satisfy and overpower the highest intellects. Conscience is our compass, but a conscience that has been dulled and tampered with is as useless as a compass which has been demagnetized.

How do we maintain a good conscience? By honestly obeying that which we see to be the will of God as revealed in His Word. Disobedience will immediately give us a bad conscience. If we let go faith which enables to discern the truth, and a good conscience which keeps us in practical conformity to it, we soon make shipwreck of the faith.

In the third place Timothy was reminded of two men whose history was like a warning beacon. They had let go faith and a good conscience and had gone to such lengths in error that Paul brands them as blasphemers and in his capacity as an apostle had delivered them to Satan. This was something beyond excommunication, which is an act of the church, as may be seen in 1 Corinthians v. 3-5. This delivering unto Satan was an apostolic act, and carried with it terrible consequences, as may be seen in the case of Job in the Old Testament.

1 TIMOTHY

CHAPTER 2

IN THE LIGHT of these solemnizing considerations Paul commences his charge to Timothy in verse 1 of chapter ii. His first exhortation is significant. In the end of chapter iii. he tells us that the church—to which Timothy belonged, and to which we belong—is the "house of God" for God is dwelling today in the midst of His redeemed people. Now it was always God's intention that His house should be called "an house of prayer for all people" (Isa. lvi. 7). The temple in Jerusalem should have been this, as our Lord's words in Mark xi. 17 show, and how much more so the house in which God dwells today? Only at the present time God's house has taken such a form that all nations do not come to it in order to pray, but rather the believers who form the house being also the household, "an holy priesthood" (1 Pet. ii. 5), they take the place of prayer and intercession with all men in view.

The great mass of mankind is wholly out of touch with God. In Paul's day the majority were worshippers of dumb idols and it is not otherwise today. How important then that we Christians should be busy in this service which is exclusively ours. In it we have immense scope for the only limit set is *"all* men" and then again for "kings and for *all* that are in authority." We are to pray for all such and to give thanks as well. God is "kind unto the unthankful and to the evil" so we may well render thanks on their behalf.

Our prayers for those in authority have a good deal of reference to ourselves: it is that we may be permitted to live godly lives in quietness and tranquillity. Those who compose God's house should carry upon them the stamp of godliness, and although times of persecution may be overruled of God for the promotion of courage and endurance amongst His people, yet it is in times of quietness and rest that most they are edified and established, as Acts ix. 31 bears record.

But in praying for all men generally our requests are to be purely evangelic. The God whom we approach is a Saviour God who desires that all men should be saved and come to the knowledge of the truth. Have we come to the knowledge of the truth ourselves? Then we have found it to be salvation and we are put into touch with a Saviour God and His character is stamped upon us. He desires the salvation of men and so do we. In our case the natural outlet for our evangelic desires is *prayer*.

The expression of God's loving desire for men is far different, being found in *the ransom gift of Christ*. God indeed is one—this fact was made manifest in the Old Testament, in contrast to the many gods of the heathen—the Mediator between God and men is equally one, the Man Christ Jesus. The priestcraft of Rome has built up in the minds of its votaries an elaborate system of many mediators, but here is one sentence of Scripture which demolishes its system at one blow.

Long before Christ appeared the hearts of men yearned for a mediator. The book of Job is evidence of this, for that patriarch felt the immense gulf that lay between God and himself. "He is not a man as I am" was his complaint, "neither is there any Daysman betwixt us, that might lay his hand upon us both" (ix. 32, 33). The One who takes up the part of Daysman or Mediator must Himself be God to fully represent God, and must be Man to rightly represent man. The Man Christ Jesus is He. Being Man we have no need of further men to come in as subsidiary mediators between Him and ourselves.

And then, oh wonder of wonders! the Mediator became the Ransom. Being Man He could rightly offer Himself as the ransom price for men, and being God there was infinite value in the ransom price that He offered. Hence none are excluded on God's part. His desires for the salvation of men embrace all: the ransom work of Christ had all in view. This is one of those Scriptures that states the scope and bearing of the death of Christ rather than its actual realized effects. All are not saved, as we know sadly enough, but the blame of that lies upon their side and not upon God's. The tidings of Christ's ransom work are the subject of gospel testimony in the appointed season. Now is that appointed season and the Apostle himself was the great herald thereof in the Gentile world.

All this has been brought before us by the Apostle to enforce upon us how necessary it is that prayer for all men, and not only for ourselves and our own small interests, should mark the church of God if it is to rightly set forth the God whose house it is. But who are to actually voice the church's prayers? The answer is, the men. The word used in this eighth verse is not the one which means mankind, the human race in general, but that which means man distinctively, the male, as contrasted with the female.

Verse 8 then brings before us that which is to characterize Christian men, and verses 9 to 15 that which is to characterize Christian women. The men are to be marked by holiness and the absence of anger and doubting, or "*reasoning*" as it more literally is. But then the reasoner usually becomes a doubter so that there is not much difference between the two words. Any breakdown in holiness, any allowance of anger or reasoning is an effectual barrier to effectual prayer, and indicates that there is but little sense of the presence of God.

The women too are to be sensible of the presence of God. Those addressed are spoken of as "Women professing godliness" or more literally "Women professing the fear of God." The woman living in the fear of God will not run after the extremes of fashion but rather adorn herself in the modest and quiet way of which verse 9 speaks. Moreover she will practice good works and also be content to take the place which God has assigned to her. That place is governed by two considerations, according to this passage. First, there was God's original act in creation giving priority and headship to the man. This is mentioned in verse 13. Then there is that which happened at the fall when Eve took the leadership and was deceived, and of this verse 14 speaks.

There is not the slightest ambiguity about this passage. There is really no doubt as to what it teaches. Nor is there any uncertainty about the reasons given for woman's place of subjection and quietness in God's house. Those reasons have nothing to do with any peculiar prejudices of the Apostle as a Jew or as a bachelor, as some would have us believe. They are founded in God's original order in creation, and in that order confirmed and perhaps accentuated as the result of the fall. Genesis iii. 16 is explicit in naming two results which were to follow for the woman consequent upon her sin. The second of those two results is alluded to in the verses we have been considering, while the first result is alluded to in verse 15 of our chapter, and in connection with that a gracious proviso is attached, no mention of which is found in Genesis iii.

The modern *feminist* movement must of necessity come into violent collision with the instructions here laid down, and end by rejecting this small portion of the Word of God. This rejection may seem to the unthinking a comparatively harmless thing. But is it so? There is the allied *modernist* movement which comes into equally violent collision with the truth of the virgin birth of Christ, with His atoning death, with His resurrection. There is just as much reason—or just as little—for conceding the point in the one case as in the other. True, we may not have the slightest wish to concede the point to the modernist, and we may have a good deal of feeling as to matters raised by the feminist but to be swayed by such feelings is to stand on dangerous and uncertain ground. Are we then to virtually say that we believe what commends itself to our way of thinking and what does not we reject? Away with such a thought!

May all our readers stand honestly and happily and altogether upon the authority and integrity of the Word of God.

CHAPTER 3

THE THIRD CHAPTER is a continuation of the same general theme as occupied us in our reading of the second chapter; viz., the behaviour that becomes believers as being in the house of God. That this *is* the general subject is plainly stated in verse 15 of our chapter.

Now God is a God of order and hence in the Christian assembly where He dwells all things are to be done "decently and in order" (1 Cor. xiv. 40). For the furtherance of this the two offices of Bishop and Deacon had been established in the church, and are referred to in this chapter.

From the first verse it would appear that there were some at Ephesus who were aspiring to become bishops. The Apostle acknowledges that what they aimed at was a good work but he insists in this connection upon the all-importance of character. It is not that the bishop *may* have all the spiritual qualifications that he mentions, but that he *must*. Moreover, before he is appointed to take care of the church of God he must have proved his fitness for such a work by the way in which he has governed the far smaller and humbler sphere of his own household. He must not be a novice, one who though possibly well on in years is only a beginner in the things of God, else being lifted up with pride in his new-found importance he may fall into the very fault that caused the overthrow of Satan at the beginning. Diotrephes, who is spoken of in 3 John 9 and 10 would seem to be an illustration of what is meant.

In many of the primitive churches bishops or elders were officially appointed, in others they do not appear to have been. But even if duly appointed the one thing that would confer real weight upon them would be the character of Christian godliness that Paul here describes. Who would be disposed to pay attention to their exhortations otherwise, or submit themselves to their shepherd care and direction in spiritual things? Moreover there was the outside world to be considered, as verse 7 states. The world has sharp eyes and quickly hurls reproach if there is the least ground for it; and to accomplish this the devil lays his snares.

The word translated "bishop" simply means "overseer." The word "deacon" means "servant." There are many services to be rendered in the church that are not primarily of a spiritual nature, such as those mentioned in Acts vi. But if men are to handle such ordinary matters as these in the service of God they need to possess very definite and high spiritual qualifications, and to be tested first ere they begin.

The wives of deacons are specially mentioned in verse 11. This is doubtless because diaconal service was of such a nature that they not infrequently took part in it. Phebe, for instance, was "a servant [*deaconess*] of the church which is at Cenchrea" (Rom. xvi. 1), and was highly commended by the Apostle.

We must remember that bishops and deacons were to possess this sterling Christian character inasmuch as they were to set an example to the mass of believers who looked up to them. Hence all of us reading this chapter today must accept these verses as delineating the character which God desires to see in us. Can we read them without feeling rebuked? How about that greed of money, or the slander, or even the being double-tongued—the saying of one thing in one direction and quite another thing in another direction? Pretty searching considerations, these!

The service of a deacon might seem a very small matter, but nothing in God's service is really small. Verse 13 definitely states that such service faithfully rendered is the way to higher and larger things. This is clearly illustrated for us in the subsequent history of two who are mentioned in Acts vi. 5. Stephen advanced to become the first Christian martyr: Philip to become a greatly used preacher of the Gospel, the only man designated an evangelist in Scripture (See, Acts xxi. 8). Every true servant of God has begun with small and humble things, so let none of us despise and shirk them, as naturally we are inclined to do.

Notice that phrase in verse 7, "them which are without." At the beginning things were quite sharply defined. A man was either within the church of God or part of the great world without, for the church and the world were visibly distinct. Now, alas! it is otherwise. The world has invaded the church and the lines of demarcation are blurred. Not blurred, of course, to God's view, but very much so to ours. It is consequently far more difficult for us to understand how wonderful a place is God's house and the conduct that becomes it.

Verse 15 tells us that the house of God is the church of the living God. We are evidently to understand that the fact of our being a part of the church, and therefore in the house, is not a mere idea void of practical significance. The living God dwells there and He has said, "I will dwell in them, and walk in them" (2 Cor. vi. 16). He scrutinizes everything and He operates there as is illustrated in Acts v. 1-11. Hence we should be marked by suitable conduct.

Then again, the church is "the pillar and ground [or, base] of the truth." Pillars had a two-fold use. They were largely used as supports, but they were also commonly erected not to support anything but to bear an inscription as a memorial. The reference here is, we believe, to the latter use. God intends that the truth shall not only be stated in the inspired words of Scripture but also exemplified in the lives of His people. The church is to be like a pillar reared up on its base on which the truth is inscribed for all to see, and that in a living way for the church is "the church of the living God."

The church then is not the authoritative teacher and interpreter of truth as Rome claims but the living witness to the truth which is authoritatively set forth in Scripture. To differentiate between these two things and to keep them in their right relative places in our minds is of extreme importance. AUTHORITY *lies in the very word of God which we have in Scripture alone*. The living witness to what Scripture sets forth is found in the church, but at the present moment that witness is sadly obscured though it will be perfect and complete in glory. Compare verses 23 and 21 of John xvii, and note that what the world has failed to "believe" now it will "know" when the church is perfected in glory.

If verse 15 speaks of the church as the witness to the truth verse 16 gives a wonderful unfolding of that which lies at the heart of truth, the very

revelation of God Himself, spoken of as "the mystery of godliness." There is no thought here of godliness being a mysterious thing. The force of the sentence is rather—that beyond all question great is the hidden spring from whence flows such godliness as is here taught. The godliness displayed by saints in different ages was always in keeping with such knowledge of God as was available to them, and never went beyond it. The New Testament unquestionably indicates a higher type of godliness than the Old Testament. But why? Because we now have not a partial but a full revelation of God.

The godliness then which the Apostle enjoins is only produced as we know God. In the revelation of God lies its great "mystery" or "secret." It is a secret because made in a way not appreciated by the world but only by believers. "God was manifest in the flesh" in Christ, but in seeing Him unbelievers found "no beauty that they should desire Him," only believers in seeing Him saw the Father. Verse 16, then, is a condensed summary of the way God has revealed Himself in Christ.

The verse is one that baffles the profoundest meditation—as we might expect. It consists of seven terse statements, six of them summarizing the great revelation. The first of the six shows us God manifested in Manhood, and the last shows us the Man Christ Jesus, in whom God was manifested, received up into glory. The intervening four give us various ways in which the reality of that manifestation was realized.

God was "justified in the Spirit." Compare with Romans i. 4. The resurrection justified Jesus, declaring Him "Son of God with power according to the Spirit of holiness" when the world had crucified Him as an impostor. After all, He *was* God manifested in the flesh.

"Seen of angels." Had angels ever really seen God before? Certainly not as they saw Him when the great outburst of angelic praise took place at Bethlehem.

"Preached unto the Gentiles" or "proclaimed among the nations," for He had been so really manifested in historic fashion as to become the subject of gospel witness among the peoples who had been far from the actual scenes of His manifestation.

"Believed on in the world." Not *by* the world, notice, but *in* the world. Though the world knew Him not yet His manifestation was not an intangible something existing only in the subjective consciousness of the onlookers or hearers, but something real and objective, verified by competent witness and hence received by those in whom faith existed.

The one who knows by faith this real, true, historic Christ, the true God manifested in flesh, and who as Man has gone up into glory, possesses the secret of a life of godliness. No unbeliever can possibly be godly though he may be of most kindly and amiable disposition as a natural man.

1 TIMOTHY

CHAPTER 4

VERSE 1 OF chapter iv. must be read in connection with the last two verses of chapter iii. God dwells in the church as His house by the Holy Spirit and the church is the pillar on which the truth is inscribed. Now the indwelling Spirit speaks in defence of the truth, warning of the devices of the devil to be expected in the latter times, and He speaks expressly, there is no indefiniteness about His utterances.

When the Apostle wrote the Holy Spirit was still giving inspired messages through prophets, as we see in Acts xiii. 2. The apostles and prophets who were the vehicles of inspiration belonged to the foundation of the church (See, Eph. ii. 20) and inspiration has ceased, though we have as the result of it the Holy Scriptures. Still though He no longer speaks in that authoritative way He abides with us for ever and His direction may often be perceived by those who have eyes to see.

The Spirit's warning in the first three verses has often been taken as applying to Romanism. We believe that the reference is rather to that deliberate trafficking with demons which we see today in spiritism. It is true that Rome imposes celibacy on her clergy which looks like a fulfilment of the opening words of verse 3. Spiritism advocates both celibacy and vegetarianism as necessary if anyone aspires to be a good "medium," and this fulfils both parts of the verse.

The Holy Spirit then warns us that His speaking will be imitated by unholy and seducing spirits, their object always being to turn away from the faith. They may pose as being very cultured, and as wishing to refine our food on aesthetic grounds, and this may be all that is in the mind of their dupe, who acts as the medium, yet the unclean demon who manipulates the dupe has other thoughts and his ulterior aim is ever the overthrow of the faith. If they can divert from the faith and inculcate their doctrines their end is achieved.

Men may raise prejudice against sound doctrine by calling it dogma, but they only end by substituting some other doctrines, probably the doctrines of demons. So, you see DOCTRINE DOES MATTER after all.

In the early verses of our chapter the Spirit's warning is against the doctrines of demons, which, if received, altogether turn men from the faith. In verse 7 the warning is against a danger of a somewhat different order, "Profane and old wives' fables." Timothy is urged to stand firm against both errors.

The Apostle's instructions in verse 6 seem to have specially in view the first of these dangers. We are to be kept in remembrance of "these things," and here he alluded not only to what he had just written in verses 4 and 5 but also to the great truth unfolded in chapter iii. 16, and indeed to all his instructions given earlier in the Epistle, for verse 6 of chapter iv. cannot be disconnected from verse 14 of chapter iii. Thus we as well as Timothy may be nourished with the words of the faith and of good doctrine and this will effectually render us proof against the seducing doctrines of the devil. But this must be "attained" or "fully followed up" for it is only as we become fully acquainted with the truth that we can detect error and consequently refuse it.

Godliness is set in contrast with the profane and old wives' fables, from which we gather that they were mainly concerned with the superstitious ideas and customs which have always played so large a part in heathendom and which creep so easily into Christendom. The poor heathen mind is in bondage to endless superstitions connected with the bringing of good fortune or the averting of evil, and all these customs appeal to, and bear far more hardly upon, the womenfolk than the men. Hence the Apostle's term—"old wives' fables." Now godliness brings GOD Himself into the details of one's life, since it is based upon that "trust in the living God" of which verse 10 speaks.

It is instructive though sad to note the great increase in recent years of superstition amongst nominal Christians. The war doubtless gave it a great impetus when hundreds of thousands, if not millions, of charms were made for the protection of soldiers. The cult has spread everywhere and now mascots abound, and more and more people observe customs which are designed to bring "good luck" or avert "bad luck." All this argues the decline of godliness. If God is shut out of the life these stupid abominations creep in.

Our God is the LIVING God. Nothing escapes His notice and He is "the Saviour [or, Preserver] of all men, specially of those that believe." The poor heathen enjoying a wonderful deliverance may attribute his escape to the potency of the charm given to him by the medicine man. The British motorist, a nominal Christian, just escaping a fearful crash may declare that he never comes to any harm so long as he has his black cat mascot on board—he has never known it to fail. They are both wrong though the latter is far more guilty. Both are victims of profane and old wives' fables. The truth is their deliverances came, whether directly or indirectly from the hand of God.

God's preserving mercy is specially active towards those that believe, so a simple trust in Him should mark us. It marked Paul and carried him through his labours and reproaches. We are to exercise ourselves to godliness. This is a mental exercise of far greater profit than mere bodily exercise. That is profitable in some small things whereas godliness is profitable for all things, having promise of life, both now and to eternity.

Here let us recapitulate for a moment. Godliness is, we may say, the main theme of the epistle, and it is enjoined upon us because we are of the house of God. The knowledge of God Himself as He has been revealed in Christ is the secret spring of it, and it very largely consists in that God-consciousness, that bringing of God into all the details of our daily lives,

1 TIMOTHY

which is the result of trust in the living God. All this has come before us, and the question would now naturally arise in our minds as to whether any practical instructions can be given which will help us in exercising ourselves unto godliness according to the instructions given in verse 7?

Verses 12 to 16 supply us with a very ample answer. Timothy was a young man yet he was to be an example to the believers who were to see godliness expressed in him, a godliness which affects us in word, in conversation or conduct, in love, in faith and in purity. To this end he was to give himself with all diligence to reading, to exhortation to teaching. The reading enjoined upon him was, we suppose, that public reading in the presence of believers generally which was so necessary when copies of the Scriptures were few and far between, yet it should impress upon us the importance of reading the Scriptures both privately and publicly. When Paul came Timothy might have the joy of hearing God's Word from the inspired lips of the Apostle; until then he must pay all heed to God's inspired Word in its written form.

The Christian who neglects the study of the Word of God never makes much progress in the things of God nor in the development of Christian character. "Give attendance to reading" should be a watchword with all of us, for only as we are well furnished ourselves can we be of help to others.

Timothy was to exhort and teach others and for this a gift had been deposited in him in a special way. Hence "neglect not the gift that is in thee" is the second word instruction. By reading we take in: by exhortation and teaching we give out. Not all of us have received a special gift but all of us are responsible to give out in one way or another, and we neglect it at the peril of our own spiritual good.

"Meditate upon these things" is the third word that comes before us. By reading our minds become well furnished with truth. By meditation the truth in its force and bearing is brought home to us. Just as the ox not only feeds in the pastures but also lies down to chew the cud so we need to ruminate, to turn things over in our minds, for it is not what we eat that nourishes us but what we digest. If we meditate upon the things of God, getting right into them so that they control us then our profiting, our spiritual advancement, becomes apparent to all.

A fourth word of great importance if we would grow in the ways of godliness is that in verse 16, "Take heed unto thyself and unto the doctrine." First of all we must get the truth itself, which is set forth in the doctrine, clearly before us. Secondly, we must take heed to ourselves in the light of the truth, testing ourselves and our ways by it, altering them as the truth demands. This of course is the crucial matter.

Too often the truth of God has been taken up in a purely theoretical way, when it becomes just a matter of argument, a kind of intellectual battle ground. When however we come face to face with it in practical fashion we

157

at once become aware of discrepancies between it and ourselves and our ways, and serious questions are raised. Now comes the temptation to somewhat alter or pare down the doctrine so that we may leave our ways untouched and the discrepancy largely if not entirely disappears. May God give us all grace to reverse that procedure and rather alter our ways that they may be in conformity with the doctrine. Thus we shall be rightly taking heed to ourselves and to the doctrine as well, and continuing in the truth we shall be saved. The salvation here is from the dangers of which we are expressly warned by the Spirit in the earlier part of the chapter, whether doctrines of demons or profane fables.

Chapter 5

TIMOTHY HAD BEEN entrusted with special responsibilities both as to teaching and as to order in the church. Consequently if he kept right and in a state of happy deliverance from these dangers he would be a minister of deliverance to many others. But then this might bring him into a measure of conflict with some. An elder even might need admonition as verse 1 of chapter v shows us, and Timothy must be careful not to set himself wrong in attempting to set him right. The truth teaches us to render to all our fellow-believers their due, whether men or women, whether old or young.

In verse 3 the question of the treatment of widows comes up and the subject is continued to verse 16. We might be tempted to wonder that so much space is given to the matter did we not remember that it was this very question which first brought the spirit of contention into the church of God, as recorded in Acts vi. 1-7.

The general instruction of the passage is quite plain. Widows 60 years old and upwards without relations to support them were to be "taken into the number," or "put on the list," as receiving their support from the church if they had been marked by godliness and good works. The church is to relieve those who are "widows indeed" but not others. How wise is this ordering!

Other instructions come in by the way. Notice how clearly it is taught that children and descendants (the word is "descendants" rather than "nephews") are responsible for the support of their parents. Thus they shew godliness or piety at home. Let us emphasize this in our minds for it is easily forgotten in these days of "doles" and other forms of public support. The denunciation in verse 8 of the man who avoids or neglects this duty is very severe, showing how serious a sin it is in God's sight. There may be men quite renowned for piety in public who are nevertheless branded as worse than an infidel for lack of this piety at home.

The characteristics of a "widow indeed" as given in verse 5 are worthy of note. The Christian who in the days of her prosperity gave herself to such good works as are enumerated in verse 10, would have recognized that after all it was just God Himself ministering to the afflicted through her hands. He was the Giver and she but the channel. Now the position is reversed but she knows well that she must not look to the channels but to the mighty Source of all. Hence her trust is in God and upon Him she waits in prayer. She too is marked by that trust in the living God which is so large an element in practical godliness.

Contrasted with this is the widow living "in pleasure" or "in habits of self-indulgence." Such an one would be seeing life according to the ideas of the world, but she is here declared to be dead while living—practically dead, that is, to the things of God.

Sometimes worldly-minded believers ask rather plaintively why it is that they do not make spiritual progress or have much spiritual joy? Verse 6 supplies us with an answer. There is nothing more deadening than self-indulgence in pleasure. The pleasure may be life of a worldly sort but it is death spiritually, for the soul is thereby deadened towards God and His things.

The bad effects of idleness come strongly before us in this passage. The younger widows were not to be supported at the expense of the church lest having no very definite occupation they should decline in heart from Christ and come under judgment—not "damnation" which is too strong a word. Their idleness then would assuredly produce a course of tale-bearing and general interference in other people's affairs which is most disastrous to the testimony of God. Idleness in the twentieth century produces exactly the same crop of evil fruit as it did in the first century.

Further instruction as to elders is given in verses 17 to 19. An elder was not necessarily a recognized teacher of the word, though he was to be "apt to teach" (iii. 2). Those who did "labour in the word and doctrine" were to be counted worthy of double honour, and that honour was to be expressed in a practical way as might be needful. If any of them lacked in material things they were to be supplied as the Scripture indicated. The first quotation of verse 18 is from the Old Testament but the second is from the New, Luke x. 7. This is interesting evidence that Luke's gospel was already in circulation and recognized as the inspired Word of God equally with the Old Testament.

Above all, Timothy was to be moved by a care for the glory of God in His house. Those who sinned were to be rebuked publicly so that all the believers might be admonished and sobered thereby, only the greatest possible care was to be taken lest anything like partiality should creep in. Nothing is more common in the world than favouritism, and we all of us so easily form prejudices either for or against our brethren in Christ. Hence this solemn charge laid upon Timothy "before God and the Lord Jesus Christ and the elect angels."

1 TIMOTHY

Connected with the solemn charge of verse 21 against partiality comes the injunction, "Lay hands suddenly on no man."

The laying on of hands is expressive of fellowship and identification, as Acts xiii. 3 shows us. Barnabas and Saul were already prophets and teachers when the Spirit called them to launch forth in the evangelization of the Gentile world. There was therefore no thought of "consecrating" them when their fellow-workers laid hands upon them, but rather of showing full fellowship and identification with their mission.

Timothy was to avoid haste in giving his sanction to any man lest later he should have to discover that he had accredited one who was unworthy, and thereby he might find himself in the unhappy position of having a share in his misdeeds. The believer is to be careful not only as to purity of a personal sort but also as to his associations.

Paul evidently knew how careful Timothy was as to personal purity, hence the instruction of verse 23. This verse has been much quoted in arguments as to the "temperance" question. It shows without a doubt that Scripture does not warrant the propaganda of extreme reformers. It shows however with equal clearness that a really godly Christian, such as Timothy was, kept so clear of wine that he had to be exhorted to take some medicinally, and then he was only told to take "a little."

Verse 24 is connected with the earlier part of verse 22. Many things whether evil or good are not at all open and manifest and we may therefore be easily deceived in our judgments. Ultimately however all will be manifested for nothing can be permanently hid. A solemn thought this!

CHAPTER 6

IN THE APOSTOLIC age, as now, the gospel won many of its triumphs among the poor, hence not a few servants, or slaves, were found in the church. Chapter vi. opens with instructions which show the way of godliness as it applies to them. Slavery is foreign to Christianity yet inasmuch as the rectifying of earthly wrongs was not the Lord's object in His first coming, (See, Luke xii. 14) and is only to be accomplished when He comes again, the will of God for His people now is to accept the conditions which characterize their times, and in them adorn the doctrine and honour His name.

Servants have the lower place, then let them be marked by subjection and the honouring of their masters, and should these themselves be believers far from it being a reason for slighting them or belittling their authority it would only furnish the slave with an additional reason for serving them faithfully. These instructions the Apostle calls "the doctrine which is according to godliness," for they were wholesome words as given by the Lord Himself.

1 TIMOTHY

The present age is marked by a very considerable uprising against authority even in Christian circles. The thing itself is not new for it was in evidence when this epistle was written. There were men teaching things which were in contradiction of "the words of our Lord Jesus Christ," even in the first century; it is not surprising therefore that such abound in these later times. The Apostle writes very plainly about these opponents. He unmasks their true character. They were marked by pride and ignorance. How often these two things go together! The less a man knows of God and of himself the more he imagines he has something to boast in. The true knowledge of God and of himself at once dispels his pride.

Verse 4 also makes plain what is the effect of repudiating the authority of the Lord. Questions and strifes of words come to the fore. This of course is inevitable, since if the Lord's authority is set aside it all becomes a question of opinion; and if so one man's opinion is as good as another, and argumentative and verbal strife may be carried on almost *ad infinitum*, and all kinds of envy and strife flourish.

Men who thus dispute show themselves to have corrupt minds and to be destitute of the truth, and that which underlies their proud thoughts is the idea that personal gain is the real end of godliness—that a man is only godly for what he can get out of it. If that is their idea then of course they would not advocate a slave rendering such service as is enjoined in verse 2, since any gain from that would accrue to his master and not to himself. The truth is that not gain but God is the end of godliness, though as the Apostle so strikingly adds, "godliness with contentment is great gain." To walk as in the presence of the living God with a simple trust in His goodness and with contentment of heart is very great gain of a spiritual sort.

We have to recognize that we are but life tenants of all that we possess. We entered the world with nothing; we go out with nothing. God may indeed give us much for our enjoyment but on the other hand we should be contented with just the necessaries of life—food and raiment. This sets a high standard before us; one that but few of us come up to, though the Apostle himself did. The exhortation of verse 8 is much needed by us all in these days.

On all hands are people who earnestly desire to become rich; the making of money is to them the chief end of life. The Christian may all too easily become infected with this spirit to his great loss. Verse 9 does not speak of those that are rich, as does verse 17, but of those that "will be rich" or "desire to be rich," that is, they set it before them as the object to be pursued. Such become ensnared by many lusts, which in the case of the man of the world plunge him into destruction and ruin. This is so whether they succeed in their aim and amass wealth or whether they do not, for the coveting of money it is that turns men aside from the faith and pierces them through with sorrows, and not the acquisition and misuse of it only. The love of money is declared to be the root of every kind of evil. It is not that every bit of evil in the world can be traced to the love of money, but that the love of money is a root from which on various occasions every description of evil springs.

The appeal to Timothy in verses 11 to 14 sets before us the will of God for the believer, which is wholly apart from and opposed to the idea that gain is godliness with its consequent love of money. Timothy is here addressed as a "man of God." The meaning of this term is evident if we observe its use in Scripture. It signifies a man who stands with God and acts for God in days of emergency when the majority of those who are professedly His people are proving faithless to His cause.

The man of God then, or for the matter of that, all true believers are to flee all these evil things that follow in the train of the love of money and they are to pursue the things which are the fruit of the Spirit. Six lovely features are enumerated which hang together like a cluster of fruit; beginning with righteousness, which ever has to be to the fore in a world of unrighteousness and sin, and ending with meekness, which is the very opposite of what we are by nature, for it concerns our spirit as righteousness concerns our acts.

If we make such things as these our pursuit we shall at once become conscious of opposition. There is plenty of opposition in the pursuit of money for we live in a competitive world. Money-making becomes usually a fight, in some cases a fight of a pretty sordid kind. It is a fight also if we pursue these things that please God, only this time it is a fight of faith, for our opponents now will be the world, the flesh and the devil, and nothing but faith in the living God will prevail against these.

Moreover these excellent things are the working out into expression of that eternal life which is the portion of the believer on the Son of God. The life is ours as is made so abundantly plain in the writings of the Apostle John, yet we are exhorted to lay hold of it, for it is a dependant life, Christ being its Source and Object, and we lay hold of it in laying hold by faith of Him and of all those things which find their centre in Him. The men of the world lay hold of earthly gain, or of as much of it as they can compress into their fists. We are called to eternal life, and are to lay hold of it by going in for all those things in which from a practical standpoint it consists.

Timothy had made a good profession and now he is solemnly charged in the sight of God, who is the Source of all life, and of the Lord Jesus, who was the great Confessor of truth before the highest circles of the world, to walk according to these instructions in an untarnished way until the moment when the servant's responsibility shall cease.

The time is coming when the Lord Jesus Christ shall shine forth in His glory and then the faithful servant shall see the happy fruit of faithfulness and of the good confession rendered. That time is fixed by the blessed and only Potentate whose purposes nothing can frustrate, who dwells in fadeless splendour beyond the reach of mortal eye.

Notice the full and complete way in which Scripture identifies the Lord Jesus and God. In these verses (14-16) it is not easy to discern which of the two is spoken of. It appears however that in this Scripture it is God who is King of kings and Lord of lords, who is going to show forth the Lord Jesus in His glory when the time is come. In Revelation xix. 16 it is without a doubt the Lord Jesus who is King of kings and Lord of lords.

Observe also the force of the words, "who only hath immortality," for there are not wanting those who attempt to press them into service, as supporting the denial of immortality to the soul of man and the teaching of annihilation. Their meaning is of course that God alone has immortality in an essential and unqualified way. If creatures possess it they have it as derived from Him. Did it mean that as to actual fact God only is immortal we should have of course to accept the ultimate extinction of all the saints and even of the holy angels. Read in that way the words mean too much even for the annihilationist.

Having ascribed "honour and power everlasting" to the immortal, invisible God, before whom Timothy was to walk far removed from the spirit and ways of those whose main object was the acquisition of riches, the Apostle turns in verse 17 to give instructions as to those believers who are "rich in this world." His words indicate first of all the dangers attached to the possession of wealth. It has a tendency to generate highmindedness and to divert the possessor from trust in God to trust in money. The worldly man of wealth naturally fancies himself greatly and feels himself secure against the ordinary troubles and struggles of humanity. The wealthy Christian must not imagine that his money entitles him to dominate the church of God and lord it over his fellow-believers.

Secondly Paul shows us the privileges attaching to wealth. It may be used in the service of God, in the help of His people; and thus he who starts by being rich in money may end in being rich in good works, and this is wealth of a more enduring kind. Earthly riches are uncertain, and he who lays it up in store for himself may find his store sadly depleted just when most needed. He who uses his riches in the service of God is laying up in store a good foundation of reward in eternity and meanwhile his trust is in the living God, who after all does not deny us what is good but gives it to us richly for our enjoyment. It is just those who hold and use their possessions as stewards responsible to God that can be trusted to enjoy God's good gifts without misusing them.

We saw that trust in the living God is the very essence of godliness when we were looking at verse 10 of chapter iv. The expression occurs again in verse 17 here. Rich believers are to be godly and to bend their energies not to the laying hold of larger things in this world but to the laying hold of "eternal life," or "that which is really life." The latter is probably the correct reading. Real life is not found in money and the pleasures it procures (See, v. 6.) but in the knowledge and service of God.

The closing charge to Timothy is very striking. To him had been entrusted as a deposit the knowledge and maintenance of the revealed truth of God, as stated more fully in 2 Timothy iii. 14-17. This he was to jealously guard for it would be imperilled, on the one hand by profane and vain babblings—doubtless foolish teachings akin to the "profane and old wives' fables" of iv. 7— and on the other hand by "science falsely so called." These words plainly *infer* that true science exists which is in complete harmony with revelation. They plainly *state* that there was even 2000 years ago a mis-named science which opposed revelation. It was largely composed of the speculations of the philosophers. The mis-named science of today also is composed of partial knowledge based on imperfect or inaccurate observations with a very large admixture of speculation, often of the wildest kind. If that kind of "science" be professed the faith is missed altogether.

As to all this the instructions are very simple. *Avoid* the babblings and AVOID the mis-named science no less than the babblings. We shall need grace from God to do this. Hence the closing words, "Grace be with thee. Amen."

2 TIMOTHY

INTRODUCTION

WE HAVE NO certain knowledge of how many years elapsed between the writing of the 1st and 2nd epistles to Timothy but evidently there had been sufficient time for the development of a big down-grade movement in the church of God. The diverse characters stamped upon the two Epistles make this quite plain. In the first epistle Timothy is instructed as to good order in the church and exhorted to maintain it in the presence of disorders that threatened it. In the second we find that, while there is still disorder, serious defection has developed and that in some quarters even the foundations of the faith are in danger; consequently that which is official is not mentioned and the appeal is to individual faithfulness. This we shall see as we pursue our way through the epistle.

CHAPTER 1

IN HIS OPENING words, presenting his apostleship, Paul strikes a note which is prominent all through this epistle. He is an apostle, not only "by the will of God"—that gave him his authority—but also "according to the promise of life which is in Christ Jesus"—that conferred upon his apostleship an unconquerable character. Nature furnishes us with many illustrations of the extraordinary power of life. Here is a green sapling so tender that an infant could crush it in its tiny fist yet under certain conditions the life that is in it will force it through pavements or cause it to displace great stones weighing hundredweights. Here again is life of a certain order with its distinguishing characteristics. From these characteristics no one can divert it try as they will. Neither training nor cajoling nor whip will make a dog express its pleasure by purring nor a cat do so by wagging its tail. The life of the animal with its innate characteristics will conquer all your efforts.

In nature life is an immense force, but the life in Christ Jesus is unconquerable. The life of nature in all its forms, the life of Adam—which is human life—included, ultimately meets its match and is conquered by DEATH. The life in Christ is beyond the reach of death, for it was as having died and risen again that He became the Fountain-head of life to others. That life was promised before the world began (See, Titus i. 2) and brought to light in the Gospel (See, verse 10 of our chapter). Its fruition will be seen in ages yet to come. Hence it is spoken of as a promise here.

We start the epistle therefore with that which will survive all the failures and defections of believers and all the other ravages of time. How good to be connected with a sheet-anchor which never moves before we face the storms indicated in the epistle. Everything that is "in Christ Jesus" abides to eternity.

Having saluted Timothy the Apostle in verse 3 expresses his prayerful remembrance of him; in verses 4 and 5 he calls to mind the features in him which were to be commended, and then from verse 6 and onwards he exhorts and encourages him in the fear of God.

Both Paul and Timothy came of good stock. The former could speak of serving God from his forefathers with a pure conscience; that is, without defiling his conscience by doing that which he knew to be wrong. He was true up to his light, though, as he confesses elsewhere, once his light was so defective that he was found opposing Christ with conscientious zeal. Timothy was the third generation to be marked by faith. Indeed his faith is called "unfeigned," and faith of a very genuine order is a prime necessity when times of declension and testing set in. Moreover the Apostle can speak of his tears and these indicated that he was a man of deep feeling and of spiritual exercises.

The very remembrance of Timothy's tears filled Paul with joy. How would he feel about us? Would he turn from us sad and disappointed at our feeble faith and general shallowness of conviction and feeling? Depend upon it, unfeigned faith, the maintenance of a pure conscience and the deep spiritual feelings which express themselves in tears are immense assets wherewith to face the difficulties and perils of "the last days."

Timothy possessed in addition a special gift from God, which had been administered to him through Paul, and gift carries with it a responsibility to use it in a proper and adequate way. A person of quiet and retiring mind, as Timothy seems to have been, is sorely tempted to lay up his "pound" in a napkin when confronted by trying circumstances. On the contrary, difficult circumstances are really a trumpet call for the stirring up of any gift that may be possessed, and this is possible for God has given to us His Holy Spirit, and thereby we have a spirit of power and love and a sound mind and not a spirit of fear.

"Power" here does not mean "authority" but rather "might" or "force". We have the force but it needs to be controlled by love, and both force and love must be governed by "a sound mind" or "wise discretion" if the energy that we have by the Holy Spirit is to be rightly employed. We are not therefore to be ashamed of the testimony of our Lord.

There was no danger of Timothy being ashamed of the testimony in earlier days when as recorded in Acts xiv-xix, it was triumphing in spite of bitter opposition. Now however it was in reproach, believers even were growing cold and Paul, the chiefest of its heralds, was in prison with no hope of release. There is nothing more trying than to come into a movement when it is on a rising tide of prosperity and then to see it pass its crest and a heavy ebb tide set in. This is the thing to test one's mettle.

Timothy's mettle was being tested, but the Apostle's call to him was that he should now partake of the afflictions of the Gospel. We are all glad to partake of the blessings of the Gospel, and many of us are glad to have a share in the work of the Gospel so that we may partake of its successes, and finally of the rewards in the coming kingdom for faithful service in it, but to partake of its afflictions is another matter. This is only possible "according to the power of God." Here as in Colossians i. 11, power is connected not with that which is active but with that which is passive—suffering.

Power is in itself a cold impersonal thing. In this passage however the warm personal touch is given to it by verses 9 and 10. The God, whose power it is, is known to us as the Author of both our salvation and our calling. These two things ever go together, for they give us what we may call the negative and positive sides of the matter. We are saved *from* that we may be called *to*. We are delivered *from* the misery and peril into which sin has plunged us in order that we might be designated *to* the place of favour and blessing which is to be ours according to the purpose of God.

What God does in saving and calling is always according to His purpose. It was so when He saved Israel out of Egypt, for He called them to bring them into the land that He had purposed for them. There is a great difference however between Israel's salvation and calling and ours. They were saved in a national way from foes of flesh and blood in this world. We are saved from every spiritual foe and in an individual way. They were called to the Land of Promise with its attendant earthly blessings. We are called into heavenly relationships with their attendant spiritual and heavenly blessings. The kingdom, of which Israel will be the centre-piece was purposed by God "from the foundation of the world" (Matt. xxv. 34), and their land was mapped out for them from the time when "the Most High divided to the nations their inheritance" (Deut. xxxii. 8), that is, from the time of Babel. Our calling, as we are told here, is according to divine purpose which dates back "before the world began."

Moreover the calling which we enjoy as Christians is according to grace as well as purpose. In this too we see a contrast, for Israel brought out of Egypt was put under law, and being thus put on their own responsibility they very soon forfeited their inheritance. Our calling rests upon what God Himself is and does on our behalf, and therefore it can never pass away. Yet once again, both our salvation and our calling were given us "in Christ Jesus," and this could not be said of Israel in the Old Testament. The covenant established with them addressed them as natural men and all stood upon a natural basis, and hence did not stand for long. All that we have is ours not as natural men having our standing in Adam, but as those who are before God in Christ Jesus.

Our holy calling was thus purposed before the world began, and its full blessedness will abide when the world has passed away. As yet we have not entered into its full blessedness, still it has been made manifest by the appearing of our Saviour, and we have a foretaste of it inasmuch as death

has been annulled by His death and resurrection and life and incorruptibility have been brought to light in the Gospel. "Annulled" and not
"abolished" is the right translation. Death most evidently is not yet
abolished, but its power is annulled for those who believe in Jesus. Also
"incorruptibility" is the word and not "immortality." The souls of the
wicked are not subject to death, but we have the larger hope of being
finally placed beyond corruption, where the last breath of it can never
touch us.

Paul had been appointed a herald of this Gospel in the Gentile world and
his diligent labours had brought him into all this suffering and reproach.
Men were beginning to shrug their shoulders and say that his cause was a
lost one. He himself began to see the glint of the executioner's axe as the
termination of the dark tunnel of his imprisonment. How did he feel
about it?

"Nevertheless I am not ashamed" were his words. Of course not! How
could he be? The very Gospel he carried was the glad tidings of life in the
present and a glorious state of incorruptibility to come, consequent upon
the breaking of the power of death. Who is there that really believing and
understanding such tidings as these will be ashamed of them? Moreover
his mission and authority proceeded from One whom he knew and
believed, and this knowledge gave him the persuasion that all was safe in
His hands.

Paul had committed his all to Christ inasmuch as he was a man that had
"hazarded" or "delivered up" his life "for the name of our Lord Jesus
Christ." (Acts xv. 26). He had "suffered the loss of all things" (Phil.iii 8).
He had deposited his reputation and his cause in the hands of his Master,
and he had the full assurance that in the day of Christ he would be fully
vindicated and recompensed. With that blessed assurance in his heart how
could he be ashamed?

All this has been mentioned by the Apostle in order to enforce his
earlier exhortation to Timothy that he should not be ashamed of the
testimony in days when reproach was increasing. In verse 13 he gives him a
second exhortation of great moment. If the adversary cannot intimidate us
into defection from the truth he may nevertheless succeed by filching away
the truth from us.

Now the truth to be of any practical use to us must be stated in words,
and in this the devil may find his opportunity. Timothy had heard the truth
from the lips of Paul to whom it was first revealed. It was a good thing—a
good deposit—entrusted to him and it was to be kept by the indwelling
Holy Spirit, but it only could be preserved intact as he held fast the form,
or outline, of sound words in which Paul had conveyed it to him. There are
plenty of deceivers today who under cover of zeal for the "idea", the
"conception," the "spirit" of the truth advocate extreme latitude as to the
words used. They ridicule verbal accuracy and especially "verbal inspi-

ration;" but this in order to make it very easy for them to abstract from the minds of their dupes the divine idea and substitute for it ideas of their own. We have never heard Paul personally but we have the form of sound words in his inspired epistles.

He can say to us, as well as to Timothy "Hold fast the form of sound words, which thou hast heard of me"—only we have received it not from his living voice but through his pen, which is after all the more reliable way. If held fast "in faith and love which is in Christ Jesus" the truth will be operative in ourselves and effective in others.

Alas! it is very easy to turn away. All in Asia had already done so. The context would indicate that this turning away from Paul was in connection with his inspired unfolding of the truth, to which he had just referred. These Asians were evidently ashamed of Paul and of the testimony. On the other hand there was Onesiphorus who was not ashamed and for whom a bright reward is waiting in "that day."

CHAPTER 2

THE FIRST VERSE of our chapter brings before us a third thing that is needful if the truth of God is to be maintained. A good deposit had been entrusted to Timothy. It had been conveyed to him by Paul in an outline of sound words, and was to be kept by the indwelling Holy Spirit, as verses 13 and 14 of chapter i. have told us. Now to have the truth enshrined in an outline of sound words is good, and yet no such outline can in itself keep the truth alive; for this the Holy Ghost is needed. Apart from Him the sound words do but embalm the truth, as may be seen in some of the orthodox confessions where creed has become altogether divorced from practice. By the indwelling Spirit however the truth may be kept in its living power.

Even so, a third thing is necessary for the truth is not only to be kept but to be propagated: indeed it cannot be effectually kept if it be not propagated—and for this we must be "strong in the grace that is in Christ Jesus." We must be kept in immediate and personal touch with Him that we may be partakers of His grace. The three then are these,

1. The form or outline of truth, which we have in the Holy Scriptures.
2. The indwelling Holy Spirit as life and power.
3. The grace of the risen Christ, as the fruit of communion with Him, strengthening the believer.

Not one of the three can be dispensed with. No two are sufficient without the third.

Thus strengthened Timothy was to diligently teach others, and especially to commit the truth to faithful men who would hand it on to others in their turn. We might almost be tempted to add "faithful men" as a fourth thing to the three already given, but of course a faithful man is one that is strong in the grace of Christ, so he really comes under point number three. We do well to remember all the same that the human element cannot be eliminated from the matter. When faithful men are wanting the grace of Christ remains unappropriated, the indwelling Spirit is grieved, and the light and safeguard of Scripture neglected.

Now anyone who is really identified in this way with the truth—be it an inspired apostle, as Paul, or an apostolic man, like Timothy, or faithful men, or even very ordinary believers, like ourselves—cannot expect to have an easy time of it in this world. Oppositions and tests of all kinds must be expected, and the rest of our chapter is occupied with instructions in view of such things, and we shall find emphasized the characteristics, which found in the believer will enable him to meet them.

First of all comes conflict. This is quite inevitable for we are in the enemy's land and the Christian is a soldier. Two qualities are called for in this connection: we must be prepared for "hardness," that is, we must not complain if we get plenty of hard knocks and suffer many inconveniences in serving the Lord; further we must hold ourselves absolutely at the disposal of the One whom we serve and hence be disentangled from the world. We handle the affairs of this life of course, perhaps we do so very largely, yet we must refuse to be entangled in them.

The Christian also wears the athlete character, he is like those who "strive for masteries." In this connection obedience is stressed. Except he strive lawfully, except he run according to the rules of the contest, he is not crowned even though he comes in first. Do we sufficiently bear this in mind when we serve the Lord? Except we serve according to His instructions and in obedience to His word we cannot expect a full reward.

Further, he is like the husbandman, the farmer. This, man's earliest occupation, is one that entails the maximum amount of real hard physical work. It means downright labour. So it is for the servant of the Lord. He must be prepared for real hard work, yet when the autumn fruits are garnered he has rightly enough the very first claim upon them. We make a great mistake if we favoured British folk in this luxurious twentieth century imagine it is our special privilege to be exceptions to this rule and to be carried to heaven on downy beds of ease.

There is more in these simple illustrations than is apparent at first sight; hence we are bidden in verse 7 to give them a careful consideration, and if we do we may expect to receive understanding from the Lord.

In verse 8 the Apostle reminded Timothy of that which was the very key-note of the gospel which he preached. The verse should read "Remember Jesus Christ of the seed of David raised from the dead." We are to remember Him as the risen One, rather than merely to remember the fact that He is risen, important as that is. Being of the seed of David He has the legal title to God's throne on the earth, and He will in due time bring in all the blessing promised in connection with it, but as risen from the dead far wider regions of blessing are opened up to us. If we keep Him in view as the risen One we shall find it a preservative against innumerable perversions of the truth of the gospel.

Now it was just because Paul himself so firmly maintained the truth of the gospel that he suffered so much trouble culminating in imprisonment. Still even in his captivity he found consolation in three directions. First, the adversaries might bind him, the messenger of the word of God, but the word of God itself they could not bind for that was in the hand of the Holy Spirit who could raise up messengers to carry it as and where He would.

Second, his sufferings were not going to be in vain. They were for the sake of "the elect," i.e., of those who should receive the gospel, that salvation in Christ with eternal glory might be theirs. Paul suffered that the truth of the gospel might be established and propagated. The Lord Jesus suffered in atonement that there might be a gospel to preach. We must never allow any confusion in our thoughts between the sufferings of Christ and those of any of His servants, even the greatest of them.

Third, there was the sure working of the government of God, as expressed in verses 11 to 13. Those who are identified with the death of Christ in this world shall enjoy life together with Him. Those who suffer in His interests shall be identified with Him when He reigns in glory. Those who deny Him will be denied by Him. God's government acts in both directions: there shall be approbation and reward for the faithful believer, such as Paul was, and how great must have been this encouragement for him. Equally there shall be disapprobation and retribution for the unfaithful, and this may be a very serious matter for some of us. There is however just one qualification introduced into the working out of the government of God, and that is that if we "are unfaithful" (that is a better rendering than "believe not") He remains faithful. Hence no act of His government can ever militate against or override His own purpose and grace. His government is necessary for our good and His glory, but His grace is founded upon what He is in Himself and, "He cannot deny Himself." A faint illustration of this is seen in the actions of any right-minded earthly father who disciplines his child but never allows it to abscure the fundamental relationship that exists between them.

In verse 14 Timothy is exhorted to put believers in remembrance of these solemn considerations that thereby they may be delivered from wasting their time over unprofitable matters that only breed contentions, and in this connection Paul appeals to him under the figure of a workman. He was to make it his object to be approved of God, "rightly dividing," or "cutting in a straight line" the word of truth. It takes a skilled carpenter to cut a really straight line, and spiritual skilfulness is needed in dividing up the Word of God so as to set it forth in detail.

When the Scriptures are rightly handled what light and edification is the result! When, on the other hand, they are cut crookedly what confusion is introduced to the subverting of the hearers! Who can estimate the loss that has been suffered by believers in sitting under preaching which has hopelessly mixed up things Jewish and things Christian, confused law with grace, and failed to discern any difference between the work of Christ wrought for us and the work of the Spirit wrought in us? These are alas! but a few mild instances of the havoc that may be made in handling the Word of God.

To Timothy the Apostle proceeded to cite a glaring case which had arisen in these early days. Hymenaeus and Philetus had divided the word of truth so crookedly that they were found propagating the notion that, "the resurrection is past already." In so teaching they tampered with the very foundations of the faith of the gospel and they overthrew the individual faith of any who came under their power. They could not of course overthrow the faith of Christianity for that was a divine foundation, and whatever God founds always stands firm as a rock. Nor could they overthrow anything which God had founded in the hearts of His people. That always remains come what may, and "the Lord knoweth them that are His" even if they became misled under false teaching and hence undistinguishable to others.

The twofold seal of verse 19 is almost certainly an allusion to Numbers xvi. verses 5 and 26, and we shall do well to read and consider that incident at this point as an illustration of the matter before us. The two principles set before us are quite clear and distinct: first, God is sovereign in His mercy and actings, hence He always knows and finally extricates those that are His: second, man is nevertheless responsible, hence every one who takes upon his lips the acknowledgement of the Lord is under the solemn obligation to depart from iniquity. The Christian must never be found in complicity with evil of any kind, from that which is least to that which is greatest.

The case brought before us in these verses was one of great seriousness for it was error as to fundamental truth and also error of an infectious kind, for, says the Apostle, "their word will eat [or, spread] as doth a canker." Instructions are therefore given us as to the course to be pursued by the saint who desires to be faithful to the Lord and His Word. These instructions evidently contemplate the error having spread like a canker to the point when the church is powerless to deal with it as the bad case of moral evil was dealt with at Corinth. (See, 1 Cor. v.; 2 Cor. ii. 4-8). The evidence of other Scriptures, notably of 1 John ii. 18, 19, would show that these early onslaughts of error were repulsed by the church, so that for the moment there may have been no necessity for Timothy to act on the instructions; if so it only emphasizes the goodness of God in seizing the occasion presented by the dangerous situation that arose over this matter to give the instructions so badly needed by us today.

In this connection another figure is used, that of a vessel. Verse 20 is an illustration whereby the apostle makes clear and enforces his instructions. In a large establishment there are many vessels of different qualities, and put to different uses. Only those however that are set apart from dishonourable use are fit for the Master's use. Verse 21 applies this illustration to the case in point. A man must "purge himself from these," i.e., from men such as Hymenaeus and Philetus, and from the false doctrines they teach, if he would be "a vessel unto honour" and fit for the use of the Master.

Let us at this point recapitulate for a moment. Verses 17 and 18 of the second chapter have given us in few words the case of grave doctrinal error which was in question. Verse 19 states in general terms the responsibility that rests abidingly upon all those who name the Name of the Lord. Verse 20 enforces this responsibility by an illustration. Verse 21 applies the general principle of verse 19 to the case in point in a very definite and particular way.

The word in the original which is translated "purge" is a very strong one It means not only to purge or cleanse but to cleanse *out*. The same word is used in 1 Corinthians v. 7, where it is rightly translated, "purge out." The evil was purged *out* by putting the wicked person away *from amongst* themselves, according to verse 13 of that chapter. Here the individual believer—"a man"—is to purge himself *out* from amongst the wicked persons and their teaching; thus he will depart from iniquity and be prepared for all that is good.

These instructions are very important, for experience, no less than Scripture, teaches us how impossible it is to maintain personal holiness and spiritual fitness in association with evil. Righteous Lot may form links with Sodom, God-fearing Jehoshaphat may strike up an alliance with Baal-worshipping Ahab, but both inevitably become lowered and defiled in the process. So it will be for us today. So let us be warned.

We are not however to expect complete isolation because we cut our links with evil for we are to find happy association with those that call on the Lord out of a pure heart, or, "a purged heart," for it is the same word used again only without the prefix signifying "out." In so doing we are to "flee youthful lusts," that is, be very careful as to purity and holiness of a personal sort, for without that all this care as to purity in one's associations would degenerate into mere hypocrisy. We are also to make the pursuit of "righteousness, faith, love, peace" our great concern. This will preserve us from becoming mere separatists in the spirit of, "stand by, for

I am holier than thou!" We shall rather be actively and happily occupied with what is good and of eternal worth.

The four things we are to pursue are intimately connected. Righteousness is that which is right before God, and if we pursue it we shall certainly be marked by obedience to His truth and will. To pursue faith means following after those great spiritual realities made known to us in the Scriptures, for faith serves as the telescope of the soul and brings them into view. To pursue love is to follow that which is the very expression of the divine nature. Peace naturally follows the other three. Any peace apart from them would be no true peace at all.

Verse 23 indicates that, when Timothy or others have carried out the apostolic instructions we have been considering, they still have need to avoid pitfalls which the adversary will place in their way. He will still introduce, if he can, "foolish and unlearned questions" in order to create strife. The literal meaning of the word is not quite "unlearned" but "undisciplined," it indicates, "a mind not subject to God, a man following his own mind and will." There is nothing we ought to fear more than the working of our own minds and wills in the things of God.

The servant of the Lord must avoid strife at all costs. He cannot avoid conflict if he remains true to his Master, but he must not strive, i.e., he must avoid the contentious spirit, he must never forget that though he stands for the Lord he is only a servant, and hence he must be marked by the meekness that befits that position. In reading the earlier part of the chapter we noticed that various figures are used to show the different characters that the believer wears. He is a soldier, an athlete, a husband-man, a workman, a vessel, and now we are reminded that he is a servant, and not only so but a servant of the Lord, and hence he must be careful not to belie the character of the Lord whom he serves.

We might have supposed that anyone obeying the instructions of verses 19-22 would be entirely removed from everybody who would be likely to oppose. Verses 24-26 show that this is not so. The Lord's servant will still come into contact with those who oppose and he must know how to meet them. He must be apt to teach and give himself to instructing his opponents rather than arguing with them. He must be armed with the love that will enable him to meet them in gentleness, patience and meekness; with the faith that will keep the truth clearly and steadily before his own mind and theirs; with the hope that counts on God to grant to them the mercy of repentance and recovery from the snare of Satan.

CHAPTER 3

WITH THE OPENING of chapter iii. the Apostle turns from these instructions, which sprang out of the dangers which were threatening at that moment, to foretell the conditions which should prevail in the last days. The picture that he presents is a very dark one.

In the first verse he gives us the general character of the last days in two words—"perilous times." We shall do well to bear this warning continually in mind inasmuch as there can be but little doubt that we are now in the last days and spiritual perils are thick around us.

In verses 2 to 5 the characteristics of the men of the last days are brought before us. It is a terrible list, rivalling the list given us in Romans i. 28 to 31, when the sins of the ancient heathen world are described. The most fearful thing about the list of our chapter is that all this evil is covered under "a form of godliness," that is, the people who are thus described are Christian as far as their claims and outward appearance go. The real power of Christianity they utterly deny.

"Men shall be lovers of their own selves," this is the first item on the list. The second is, "covetous" or "lovers of money." The list ends. "lovers of pleasures more than lovers of God." Love of self, love of money and love of pleasure are to mark the religious people of the last days, and as for all the evil things mentioned between they indicate the various ways in which the proud, self-sufficient, lawless spirit of fallen man expresses itself—and all this, remember, in people who call themselves followers of the meek and lowly Jesus. If we know anything of the present state of the so-called Christian nations we may well conclude that we have reached the last days.

The attitude of the faithful believer to such is very simple; from such he is enjoined to turn away, rather than go along with them in the hope of reclaiming them. Separation is enjoined for the sixth time in this short passage; the words used being, "shun," "depart," "purge out," "flee." "avoid," and now, "turn away." The present age being one which loves compromise the word, "separation" is naturally not at all popular, still here is that which the word stands for, urged upon us as the commandment of the Lord; and our business is not to reason about it but to obey.

The description of verses 2 to 5 applies generally to the men of the last days. In verse 6 two special classes come into view—first, those who are active deceivers, and second, those who fall an easy prey to their deceits The Apostle's word indicates that there were to be found in his day examples of both these classes. The deceivers, he says, are "of this sort" i.e., of the kind described in verses 2 to 5, and their work is carried on in a semi-private way for they "creep into houses." In the light of this inspired word it is very significant what an amount of house to house propaganda, with considerable success in creeping into houses and beguiling unstable souls, is carried on by the agents of false religious cults, such as Mormons, Seventh-Day Adventists, Jehovah's Witnesses, etc.

2 TIMOTHY

Those deceived are spoken of here as "silly women," doubtless a term of contempt and applicable to that type of person who is always enquiring and yet never reaching any settled convictions, be they man or woman. The reason for their blindness and consequent lack of conviction is their sins and the lusts which bring forth sin. It is a striking fact that this "silly women" class is recruited quite as much from the ranks of the refined and learned as from the rude and illiterate. The rough man of the street generally has pretty definite opinions of some sort; opinions which, right or wrong, he can express with vigour. It is frequently the highly educated who lose themselves in mazes of speculation and finish by accepting some pretentious nonsense which is the very opposite of the truth. Take, for instance, the way in which Christian Science captures its victims almost entirely from the rich and would-be intellectual folk.

We cannot however, shut out from all this the power of Satan, as verses 8 and 9 show us. Jannes and Jambres were evidently leaders of the band of magicians who influenced Pharaoh's court and withstood Moses, working their wonders in league with demons. The deceivers of the last days will be like them, resisting the truth as agents of the devil. God has however, set a limit to their power and ultimately their folly shall be manifest to all. This does not mean that this kind of evil is going to receive an immediate check for, as verse 13 tells us, evil men and seducers are going to wax worse and worse until the end of the age. We are not left in any uncertainty as to what we must expect.

Nor are we left in uncertainty as to our resources in the presence of the evil. They are set before us in our chapter from verse 10 and onwards. Over against the character of the men of the last days the Apostle was inspired to set the character which he bore and which Timothy well knew. What an extraordinary contrast to verses 2 to 5 is presented by verses 10 and 11! Self-love, pride, opposition to and persecution of those that are good, on the one hand; faith, love, patient endurance under persecution, on the other. The one is the full-blown spirit of the world; the other is the spirit of Christ; and it has always been the case that "he that was born after the flesh persecuted him that was born after the Spirit" (Gal. iv. 29). Hence persecution must always be expected by those who "live godly in Christ Jesus," though the form that persecution takes may vary in different countries and in different ages. The type of godliness produced by the law of Moses might excite but little or no opposition whilst godliness "in Christ Jesus" is being hotly resisted.

Paul's "manner of life" was based upon his doctrine; it gave expression to it in practice; hence in verse 10 doctrine comes first. With that doctrine Timothy was well acquainted, and he had but to continue in the truth he had learned from such a source. He also had the inestimable advantage of having known the Holy Scriptures—the Old Testament, of course—from a child. In these two things Timothy's resource lay.

In these two things lies our resource today, only for us the two practically coalesce into one. Timothy had Paul's doctrine from his own lips, ex-expressed in a "form of sound words" (i. 13), exemplified and enforced by his wonderful manner of life. We have his doctrine in his inspired epistles preserved in the New Testament, and no form of sound words is more reliable than that. In the New Testament we have also an inspired account of Paul's wonderful life, and also the other apostolic writings. We have therefore in this respect a little more than Timothy had, and we have the Old Testament equally with him, though alas! we may not be nearly as fully acquainted with it or with Paul's doctrine as he was. For us then the great resource is the Holy Scripture in its entirety.

This being so the Holy Spirit seized the occasion to assure us of the inspiration of all Scripture. Its profitableness for various uses all depends upon this fact. Who can teach or reprove or correct or instruct in what is right, in any perfect and absolute sense, but God? The reason why Scripture can do these things is that it is "inspired of God" or "God-breathed."

The claim here unquestionably is that the Book which we know as the Bible is a God-breathed book. Some of our readers might like to enquire— What about the Revised Version of this passage? Our reply is that the Authorized Version is right here and the Revised* is wrong. In the original, according to Greek idiom, the verb "is" does not appear, being under-stood though not expressed. In English it must appear and the question is as to where it should be? Remarkably enough there are eight other passages in the New Testament of exactly similar construction and every one of them but this the Revisers translated just as the Authorized has translated this. Why make an exception in this case?

Hebrews iv. 13 is one of the eight passages. Had the Revisers followed their rendering of 2 Timothy iii. 16 they would have made it, "All things that are naked are also opened unto the eyes of Him with whom we have to do," which simply reduces the solemn statement to a trivial absurdity; hardly more so however than the rendering they have given us of our passage.

The thing that Timothy needed was to be assured that he had in the Scriptures that which was of God and therefore wholly reliable—something on which he could safely take his stand when confronted with the dangers and seductions to be expected in the last days. This is exactly what we too want, and, God be thanked, we have it in the Bible.

In the Scriptures we have an infallible standard because they are God breathed. By that standard we may test all that is presented to us as truth and detect and expose all the deceits of "evil men and seducers" though

*The R.S.V (1952) text is correct here.

they grow "worse and worse." We have however more than that in them as verses 15 and 17 show us. They can make us wise unto salvation, though it be only a child who is in question. They can equally perfect the man of God and furnish him unto all good works.

In reading verse 15 we must not confine our thoughts of salvation to that which reaches us at conversion. Salvation in that sense is of course included in the statement, but it reaches out to embrace also the daily salvation which we Christians need in a multitude of ways. The whole Scripture—and particularly the Old Testament, which is here primarily in view—abounds with examples which expose before us the snares and pitfalls which beset us, and the workings of our own hearts, and which reveal to us the dealings of God's grace and government. If enlightened by faith in Christ and giving heed to these warnings, we are made wise to salvation from similar snares which exist in our day.

It is one thing to be preserved from danger; it is another to be thoroughly instructed in what is right. The most devoted of God's servants, the man of God, will find in Scripture that which equips him in the completest manner. By it he may be rendered "perfect" or "complete" and be "thoroughly furnished" or "fully fitted" to every good work. These statements make a tremendous claim for Scripture. They clearly infer that within its covers there is guidance in regard to every work that can be called good, and that the man of God, who of all believers most needs light from on high, needs no light outside that which Scripture affords.

We do not overlook the fact that we need the teaching and illumination of the Holy Spirit if we are to profit by the Scripture. That is stated in other passages. Here we have the nature and power of the Scriptures brought before us. We may well rejoice and thank God that the Bible has been preserved to us and that the Spirit of God abides with us for ever.

CHAPTER 4

IN VIEW OF all this Paul solemnly charges Timothy to preach "the word." He carries away his thoughts to the tremendous hour when the Lord Jesus shall appear in glory to judge the living and the dead, so that he should serve and speak in view of that moment, and not succumb to the temptaion to speak so as to please the itching ears of men.

In the four striking verses which open chapter vi the Apostle uses three expressions, all of which are intimately connected with the Scriptures, viz., "the word," "sound doctrine," "the truth." In contrast with them we find "fables," which are desired by those who merely want to hear those things which pander to their lusts. Timothy however was not merely to preach the word but he was to bring it to bear upon the consciences and hearts of his hearers, either for conviction or rebuke or encouragement, and he was to be urgent about it both in season and out of season.

The word "lusts" simply means "desires." The time will come, says the Apostle, when men will insist upon hearing, not what is true but what pleases them, and they will "heap up" to themselves teachers who will give them what they want. That time is now arrived. Many features of the Apostle's doctrine, as recorded in the New Testament are quite repugnant to the "modern mind," therefore, we are told, they must be discarded by all progressive thinkers and preachers, who must learn to harmonize their utterances with the latest fashions in scientific thought and the latest crazes as to popular pleasures. Hence all that advanced modernistic preaching which the Apostle here dismisses in one word—FABLES!

The servant of the Lord, on the other hand, is to keep steadily on with his minstry. He is to "watch" or rather "be sober" in all things: the word used means, "that sober clearness of mind resulting from exemption from false influences—not muddled with the influence of what intoxicates." A very important word this for all of us, for there is nothing that so intoxicates the mind and muddles the perceptions as the false modernistic teaching to which we have just alluded. Further he is to be prepared to suffer, for he cannot expect to be popular, either with the purveyors of fables who stand in the pulpit or with the consumers of fables who sit in the pew. Timothy was to do the work of an evangelist and so fill up the full measure of his ministry.

The Apostle's words here would indicate that to Timothy had been committed a ministry of an all-round character. He was not only gifted to teach and preach the word for the instruction, correction and exhortation of believers, but also to preach the gospel for the conversion of sinners; and he was not to neglect any part of this comprehensive work. Had he reasoned after a human sort he might have concluded that with so much evil threatening inside the church he must concentrate all his energies on inside work in order to meet the situation, and so abandon all effort to reach outsiders. This however was not to be, and we may learn a lesson from it today. It is evidently the will of God that, come what may in the history of the church, the work of evangelization is to go forward. The great Head of the church lives and He is well able to deal in due season with every situation that may arise, however disastrous it may appear to us; and meanwhile an all-round ministry of the truth to both saint and sinner is to be maintained.

Moreover it was to be a special incentive to Timothy that the hour of Paul's "departure" or "release" was just at hand. He knew full well that his martyrdom was imminent, when like a warrior he would leave the field of combat. All the more need then for Timothy to gird up his loins like a man and be fully engaged in the fight. The more difficult the situation, the fewer those who fight the good fight the louder the call to the true-hearted to engage in it. In exactly that way we should view things today.

The earth is filled with fightings as the fruit of sin, and perhaps none have been fiercer and worse than those that have been waged in the arena of "the church." What a tragic misuse of energy there has been all down the ages when brother has drawn the sword against brother over comparatively trivial and oft-times selfish matters, to the great delight and profit of the common foe! Alive to this and tired of it, we must not slip into the opposite error of thinking that there is really nothing worth fighting about. There is such a thing as "a good fight" as verse 7 makes manifest. The Apostle fought a good fight inasmuch as his contentions were for God and His truth and not of any selfish sort, and further he used spiritual and not carnal weapons in his warfare (See, 2 Cor. x. 3-6). If we go to war for ourselves, or if warring for God we use carnal weapons, our fight is not a good fight.

Paul not only fought a good fight but he ran his race to the finish and he kept the faith. Having kept it, he could hand it on intact to those who were to follow him. The faith of Christianity is the great object of the adversary's attack. If he attacks us it is just in order that he may damage the faith. It would almost seem as if the Apostle in these verses had in his mind's eye a relay race. The baton of the faith had been placed in his hands and beating off the attacks of the foe he had raced through to the finish of his section and was now handing it on intact to another, with the assurance that at the day of Christ's appearing the crown of righteousness would be his; and not only awarded to him but also to all others who like him faithfully run their bit of the race with their eye on the goal. The rewards of faithfulness will be seen at the appearing of Christ and that moment will be loved by those who diligently seek His pleasure. To those who seek their own pleasure His appearing will be an unwelcome thought.

It is an inspiring yet a searching thought for each believer who reads these lines, that we are now engaged in running our little section of the great relay race with the responsibility of carrying the baton of the faith and of preserving it and of handing it on intact to future runners, or of handing it over directly to the Lord Himself if He comes within our lifetime.

From verse 9 and onwards the Apostle mentions matters of a personal sort, that concerned himself or his acquaintances. Yet even these personal matters present points of much instruction and interest. Timothy was to endeavour to quickly rejoin Paul at Rome since only Luke was with him. Others had left, some evidently on the Lord's service, such as Crescens, Titus and Tychicus. With Demas the case was different. He had loved the present world and consequently had forsaken Paul, for Paul preached a Gospel that worked deliverance from this present world which it characterized as evil (See, Gal. i. 4). His action in forsaking Paul was therefore only the visible expression of the fact that he had forsaken in heart the real power of the Gospel.

2 TIMOTHY

Demas then stands as a warning beacon, illustrating the fact that backsliding may take place even in one who came under the influence of so great a servant as Paul. In happy contrast we have Mark, who is mentioned in verse 11. In earlier days he had been carried into a position which was beyond his faith and in consequence he had after a while retreated from it, as recorded in Acts xv. 37-39. This act of his was not only to his own hurt but also furnished the cause of the estrangement which came in between such eminent servants of Christ as Paul and Barnabas. Now however we find him fully recovered and reinstated. Paul, the one who had objected to him previously, now declares him to be "profitable to me for the ministry." The case of Mark then is full of encouragement as showing how the backslidden may be recovered.

In Alexander we have an opponent of the Apostle and of the truth, whether an open enemy or a secret we have no means of determining. As to him only one thing is said, "The Lord will reward him according to his works." This seems to be the better attested rendering. Paul just left him in the hands of the Lord, who will deal with him in due season in perfect righteousness. We all may well ask the Lord that we may be preserved from working any kind of evil against His servants or His interests.

Verse 16 shows us that there were others who had not opposed Paul like Alexander, nor definitely forsaken him like Demas, yet they had been guilty of a temporary forsaking, by failing to stand by him in the crisis of his trial. They could not face the stigma entailed by a full identification with this despised prisoner. Still their cowardice only made the faithfulness of the Lord to His servant the more conspicuous and such power was ministered to Paul in that trying hour that instead of summoning every ounce of wit that he possessed and straining every nerve to establish his own innocence, he concentrated upon rendering the fullest and plainest testimony to the Gospel. His trial became the occasion in which "the preaching might be fully known, and that all the Gentiles might hear." Paul eagerly seized the occasion to fully set the Gospel forth before the most august assemblage that then could be found upon earth. There his words stood on record in the official report of the proceedings available for any and every Gentile.

For the moment the Apostle was delivered "out of the mouth of the lion." Just when his case looked hopeless he had been snatched back from the jaws of death by the hand of God, acting it may have been through a sudden whim of the capricious and godless Nero. In verse 18 he looks right away from men altogether. No evil work of man could ultimately prevail against him. Come what may, and martyrdom under Nero did very soon come, he would be carried through in triumph to His heavenly kingdom. The coming kingdom of our Lord Jesus has a heavenly as well as an earthly side, and we as well as Paul are destined to the heavenly.

181

A few more greetings and the Epistle finishes. Verse 20 leads one to think that Paul was released from captivity after his trial since his first voyage to Rome was taken under the circumstances recorded in Acts xxvii and xxviii, when there was no opportunity for his leaving Trophimus at Miletum. The fact that he left him there sick shows that it is not always God's way to heal sick believers directly, as is asserted by some. In just the same way verse 13 shows us that the highest spirituality goes quite consistently with carefulness over quite small and humble details of daily life. This is a thing that we do well to remember.

TITUS

INTRODUCTION

THERE IS A very strong general resemblance between the 1st Epistle to Timothy and the Epistle to Titus; so much so that at first sight we might be misled into thinking that the latter is mainly a repetition of the former. As we examine the Epistle to Titus in more detail we shall soon become conscious that it has features all its own, and that it fills a niche in the scheme of Christian truth which without it would remain empty.

As we remarked when surveying the four personal epistles of Paul, Titus is the epistle of *sobriety* and *soundness*. It is also marked by the strong assertion of *authority*, the authority vested in Paul as an Apostle of the Lord, and in Titus acting as his delegate. The conditions prevailing in Crete, owing to the racial characteristics of the Cretians to which Paul alludes in his first chapter, rendered this strong assertion necessary; but as there is all too much of the Cretian difficulties—if not of the Cretian character—about us and amongst us all today, we shall find the exhortations of this epistle peculiarly healthful to our souls.

CHAPTER 1

PAUL ADDRESSES TITUS in verse 4 but before doing so he points out the characteristic features of his apostleship and service in a series of short and pithy statements. It was "according to the faith of God's elect." Speaking in a general way we may say that the preposition "according to" indicates *character*. What characterized his apostleship was the faith, and also the truth which is "after" or "according to" godliness. There are all too many nowadays claiming to be ministers of Christ who wish nevertheless to minister "according to" the latest conclusions of science, falsely so called, or the latest reasonings of unbelief. Notice that "the faith" spoken of is not the faith of the world nor even the faith of Christendom, but of "God's elect." That unconverted ministers and preachers should deny and even ridicule the faith is very sad but not at all surprising. The faith was never *theirs* though they may have once given an intellectual adherence to it.

Observe too that the truth is said to be characterized by godliness. Here is a very good test which may be applied in either direction. Certain things are urged upon us as being the very truth of God. We may be hardly equal to the task of analyzing them, comparing them with Scripture and demonstrating their falsity, yet we have no difficulty in observing that the practical effect produced by accepting them as truth is the casting off of godliness. That is sufficient. These things are not the truth of God. Or, it may be, a certain course of action is urged upon us which would be quite profitable and seem sensible enough. But it is not according to the truth. Then we may be quite sure it is not godliness and is to be avoided.

Further, as verse 2 tells us, Paul's apostleship was in view of an immense blessing which in its fulness lay in the future. In reading the New Testament we meet pretty frequently with the expression, "eternal life," and if we carefully considered all the passages we should discover that its meaning is not easily exhausted: it carries within it profound depths of blessing.

Nothing is more certain in Scripture than that the believer in Christ *has* eternal life, and has it *now*. This side of things is specially stressed in the writings of the apostle John. We believers already have this life in Christ, and already we are introduced into the relationships, and made participators of the understanding and communion and joys and activities which are proper to that life. Still the fulness of eternal life is not yet arrived, as our verse indicates, and this view of it is in keeping with the first allusion that Scripture makes to it in Psalm cxxxiii. 3. The only other allusion in the Old Testament is in Daniel xii. 2, and in both these passages it refers to the blessing of the bright age which is coming, when the curse will be lifted from off creation and death be the exception rather than the rule as at present. When the earth is flooded with the light of the knowledge of the Lord the blessing of ever-lasting life will be enjoyed.

The Old Testament does not lift our thoughts from the earth as the New Testament does. The verse we are considering shows us that eternal life was in God's thoughts before the world began, and in keeping with that it will abide in all its fulness when this world has ceased to be. We live in hope of it, and our hope is sure because based upon the Word of God, who cannot lie.

If any find difficulty in reconciling John's assurance of the present possession of eternal life with Paul's hope of it in the future, they will do well to remember that we commonly use the word "life" in more senses than one. For instance a man refers to a person critically ill and says, "While there is life there is hope." By "life" he means the vital spark, the vital energy BY which we live. Another man who has been squandering a lot of money in the pursuit of pleasure remarks that he has been "seeing life." He is mistaken of course as to what really constitutes life, but he clearly uses the word as meaning those relationships and enjoyments that go to make up life practically—the life IN which we live.

We have eternal life now as truly and as much as we shall have it, if we are speaking of the former use of the word. But if we think of the latter use we can rejoice that we are going to know it in far fuller measure than we do today. Walking through a greenhouse we espied amongst other tropical plants a cactus which looked like a fairly straight cucumber covered with small spines and stuck upright in a pot. We recognized in it a dwarf specimen of the cactus we had seen by the score in Jamaica standing 20 feet high or perhaps more. The little dwarf was as much alive as the giant cactus. Its life was of precisely the same order. All the difference lay in the environment.

This may illustrate our point, for though we have eternal life the world is an icy place, and the enjoyments proper to that life are found, by the

Holy Spirit given to us, in God's Word and amongst God's people and in God's service, which provide us with a kind of greenhouse in the midst of the cold world. We are in hope however of transplantation into the warm tropical regions to which eternal life belongs. In hope of that the Apostle lived and served, and so do we.

We must notice the word "promised" in verse 2. Eternal life was not merely purposed before the world existed but promised. To whom?— seeing that man as yet did not exist. At any rate we may safely say that when the Lord Jesus became Man to glorify God's name and redeem men it was under the promise that He should become the Fountain Head of eternal life to those given to Him, as is stated in John xvii. 2.

If verse 2 of our chapter looks on into a coming eternity when the promise made in a past eternity shall be fulfilled, verse 3 speaks of the present in which God's word is being manifested through preaching; and the commandment authorizing that preaching has come forth from God *our Saviour*, consequently the result of that preaching when believed is *salvation*. This preaching or proclamation was entrusted in the first place to Paul. It would indeed be well if every one who today has a part in this great work were deeply impressed with its dignity and importance. Woe betide us if we make the preaching a platform for the manifestation of our own cleverness or importance! It is for the manifestation of the Word of God.

With verse 5 the main theme of the epistle begins. Paul had been to Crete and left before he had had time to give the infant churches instructions as to many things. He therefore left Titus behind that he might do it, and also appoint elders with his authority. Verses 6 to 9 follow, giving the characteristics that must be found in such.

These verses are not a mere repetition of what we have in 1 Timothy iii. Conditions in Crete differed from those at Ephesus. There were similar dangers from "unruly and vain talkers and deceivers" in both places, but the natural characteristics of the Cretian race were peculiarly bad, so much so that some prophet of their own, some heathen seer, had been moved to denounce them in strong terms as "always liars, evil wild beasts, lazy gluttons." Such was the old nature of the converted Cretians, and such it remained in them when converted; and alas! it was manifesting itself and hence Titus in verse 13 is instructed to administer to them a sharp rebuke.

A *liar* is evidently no lover of the truth. An evil *wild beast* (for that is what the word used really means) does not love restraint, especially the restraint of good, since insubjection is its very nature. A *lazy glutton* thinks of little save that which ministers to self, and self in its lowest desires. See, then, how completely the apostolic instructions meet this sad condition.

TITUS

Those elder men whom Titus was to appoint as bishops were to be such as held fast the faithful word. They were to be lovers of the truth. Moreover they were to hold it fast as they had been taught; that is, they were to recognize the authority with which it had been originally given and to carefully respect that authority and be subject to it. Hence in addition to being themselves sober men they were to be able to minister sound doctrine with effect. The men branded by the Apostle as deceivers were ready to teach anything if only there were money in it, and this of course would be quite in keeping with the Cretian spirit, for to be able to acquire money easily is a prime necessity for the lazy glutton. On the other hand the bishop is to be a man neither given to wine nor to "filthy lucre," or "base gain." Marked himself then by godly features, the very opposite of those which were natural to the Cretians, he would be well qualified to exercise rule amongst them.

Before proceeding, notice that this scripture assumes that matters in the assembly are to be regulated by God. Had it been just a matter of human preference or choice Paul would have told Titus to stir up the Cretians to develop a church order and to establish church customs as they thought most suited to their island and its ways. He did nothing of the kind, but rather told him to "set in order the things that are wanting" since the divine order has been made known. The fact is that the divine order is extremely simple demanding nothing but lowliness and grace and spirituality—but that really is where the trouble lies, for men naturally love that which is ornate and showy and imposing.

Notice also that the men who were to be ordained as elders, in verse 5, are spoken of as bishops in verse 7. The word in the former verse is *presbuteros* from which we get the words presbyter, Presbyterian. The word in the latter verse is *episcopos* from which we get episcopal, Episcopalian. A presbyter is an elder and an *episcopos* or bishop is an overseer—for that is the simple meaning of the word—and originally they were but different terms for the same man!

Now the bishops were to be men of soberness and sound in the faith, as we have seen, but all believers are to be sound in the faith as verse 13 shows. That is the thing of first importance. If we are right ourselves—pure ourselves—then all things are pure to us for the inward holiness preserves from infection. On the contrary, the defiled and unbelieving defile all they touch.

CHAPTER 2

HENCE IN THE opening verses of chapter ii. the Apostle turns the thoughts of Titus away from the bishops to those whom we may call the rank and file of the church. There were more bishops than one in each of these early assemblies yet not all elder men were bishops. Consequently there were found aged men who could be addressed as a class by themselves, as also aged women, young women and young men. Instructions suitable to their varying conditions are given as to each class. It is striking how the words "sound" and "sober" occur in these verses. Each is found three times, though the words in the original may not be in each case precisely the same. It is worthy of note however that the word, occurring again and again, translated "sound" is one from which we get the word "hygienic" which is so often upon people's lips today. It means *healthful*. Sound doctrine is in very deed doctrine which makes for spiritual health.

In verse 9 he turns to servants. Any kind of service would be like a galling yoke on the neck of one who was an evil wild beast by nature. Yet here were some of these converted. In their old wild beast days they had served under the lash, as a wild beast serves: they answered again and contradicted as much as they dared, they robbed their masters whenever an opportunity offered. Now they are to be obedient to their masters, acting in an acceptable way in all things, shewing all good fidelity, the effect of which would be the adorning of the doctrine of God our Saviour in everything. The doctrine is beautiful in itself, so beautiful, it might be thought, that it is impossible to adorn it further. Yet it may be. When the doctrine of God is exemplified and carried into effect in the beautiful life of a poor slave, who before his conversion was a perfect terror of a man, it is adorned indeed, and made beautiful in the eyes even of careless onlookers.

Now, what can produce such an effect in our lives? What produced it in the lives of some of the degraded Cretians? Nothing but the grace of God. Of that grace and its appearing verse 11 speaks. The law was given by Moses and was made known in the small circle of Israel's race. The grace of God has risen like the sun in the heavens to shine upon all men. Into its shining we have come, for which we shall bless God for ever and ever.

The marginal reading of verse 11, "The grace of God that bringeth salvation to all men, hath appeared," is to be preferred to the text. The point is that now there is salvation for all, and that the grace of God which has brought that world-wide salvation teaches us how to live, while we await the appearing of the glory. The passage is not as clear as it might be in our Authorized Version inasmuch as in verse 13 the words "of the glory" are turned into an adjective, "glorious." There is this striking connection and contrast between the grace which has appeared and the glory which is yet to appear.

The grace of God has shone forth in all its splendour in Christ and His redeeming work. In its scope and bearing it is not confined to Israel, as was the law, but it embraces all; though in its application it is of course limited to all that believe. Hence verse 12 begins, "Teaching us." Not teaching *all* but *us*, who believe. Those who receive this salvation that grace has brought are thereby introduced into the school that grace has instituted.

How often is this great fact overlooked to much harm and loss. Why, there are those who refuse and denounce the fact of the eternal security of the true believer because they think it opens the door to all kinds of loose living! They imagine that if once we were assured of an eternal salvation restraint would be gone; as though the only effective restraint is fear of the whip—the whip of eternal damnation. Grace is far more powerful in its effects than fear, even that fear that was engendered by the law of Moses.

The law, we read, was "weak through the flesh" (Rom. viii. 3) and it failed altogether to restrain its workings. Every true believer is however a subject of the new birth and possesses therefore a new nature. The flesh, the old nature, still remains within him, yet it is a judged and condemned thing and upon it grace lays a restraining hand whilst fostering all that is of the new nature. "Ungodliness and worldly lusts" are the natural expression of the old nature, and grace teaches us to deny all these. The new nature expresses itself in sobriety, righteousness and godliness, and the teaching of grace is that these things should characterize us.

There was of course teaching of a sort under the law, for the Jew had "the form of knowledge and of the truth in the law" (Rom. ii. 20). It consisted in the clear laying down of what was right and what was wrong. The law was like a schoolmaster who impartially hands round a code of rules, very peremptory, very clear and well printed, yet without offering to his scholars the least assistance in putting those rules into effect. Grace teaches in a far more effectual way. There is of course the same clearness about all that it enjoins and the standard set is even higher than that which the law demanded, but there is this in addition, it works IN us. When Paul preached the grace of God to the Thessalonians and they received his message in its true character as the Word of God he was able to say that it "effectually worketh also in you that believe" (1 Thess. ii. 13).

That is the way of grace. It works in us, it subdues us. It not only sets a lesson-book before our eyes but bit by bit produces within us the very things that the lesson-book indicates. This is the case of course where the grace of God is really received. Where it is not really received men may do all kinds of things under cover of it, "turning the grace of our God into lasciviousness" as Jude puts it in his fourth verse. But this is because they are ungodly men and not true Christians.

Grace teaches us to live soberly, that is, "with self-restraint and consideration." It thus puts us each right in regard to ourselves. It teaches us to live righteously, that is, in a way that is right in regard to our fellows. It teaches us to live godly, that is, to give God His right place in our lives. It puts us right in regard to God and man and self, and it sets us in expectation of the appearing of the glory.

Here is a converted Cretian. This wild beast of a man is thoroughly tamed and now plods on serving his master in a sober, righteous and

TITUS

godly way. But suppose he had no prospect! Life to him might then wear a very drab aspect. But grace teaches him to lift up his eyes and look for the approaching glory; the glory being that of "our great God and Saviour Jesus Christ." The glory will be the fruition of all the hopes that grace has awakened. It may well be that by, "the blessed hope" the Apostle indicated the coming of the Lord for His saints, of which he writes to the Thessalonians in his first epistle (iv. 15-17), and if so we have both His coming *for* and His coming *with* His saints set before us as our hope in verse 13.

The One who is soon to appear is the One who gave Himself for us upon the cross, and verse 14 very strikingly states one of the great objects He had before Him in giving Himself. It was in order to redeem us from the "iniquity" or "lawlessness" under which we had fallen, so that being thoroughly cleansed we might be a people for His own special possession and filled with zeal for good works. It is not enough that we should be delivered from the practice of evil; we are to be keen in the pursuit of what is good, and that not only in a theoretical but also a practical way. We are not only to do good works but also to do them with zeal. How strikingly will all this "adorn the doctrine of God our Saviour." Once a liar, an evil wild beast, a lazy glutton: now, redeemed from lawlessness, purified before God, a zealot for good works. What a transformation!

CHAPTER 3

THE FIRST AND second verses of chapter iii. follow up the same theme, giving further details of the godly behaviour that the Gospel inculcates. Obedience and subjection to authorities, and gentleness and meekness unto all men are features very much the opposite of all that the Cretians were by nature. They are also very much the opposite of what we all are, and this the Apostle puts on record in verse 3. "We ourselves" he says in contrast with the "them" of verse 1. What a picture he gives us in this verse of himself and Titus and all the rest of us, if viewed in our natural characteristics: a fearful indictment but true! That, being such, we should hate one another is hardly surprising, but then we were hateful ourselves. Coming after this how wonderful is verse 4!

Hateful were we, every one of us. Though we were each blind to the hateful features in ourselves we were quite alive to what was hateful in other people, hence the world is full of hatred. Now God looks down upon this scene and there breaks upon the world of hatred the light of His kindness and love. That God should love the unlovable is wonderful: that He should love the positively hateful is more wonderful still! Yet such is the case. The words, "love . . . toward man" are the translation of the one Greek word, *philanthropia*. The kindness and philanthropy of our Saviour God have appeared. The word indicates not merely that God loves man as He loves all His creatures but that He has a special affection for man—a specially warm corner in His heart for man, if we may so speak.

189

His philanthropy expressed itself in kindness and mercy, and by His mercy we have been saved.

In Scripture salvation is generally connected with a work accomplished *for* us. This is true whether we consider Old Testament types or New Testament doctrine. We have to stand still and see the salvation of the Lord which is achieved outside of us. The passage before us is however an exception to this general rule, inasmuch as we are said to be saved by a work wrought upon us and *in* us. The work in us is quite as necessary as the work for us. This is very plain if we consider the type of Israel's deliverance from Egypt. By the mighty work of God wrought for them they were saved out of the land of bondage, yet in spite of all the wonders accomplished on their behalf the vast majority of them fell in the wilderness and never reached the land of promise. Why? The answer of Scripture is, "So we see that they could not enter in *because of unbelief*" (Heb. iii.19); that is, they had no faith, no work of God took place within them.

Salvation then, according to verse 5, is not according to our works of righteousness but according to God's mercy, and the means of it are "the washing of regeneration and renewing of the Holy Ghost." In John iii. where the new birth is in question we have the Spirit of God as the Agent or Operator and the "water" as the instrument producing it. Here too we have the Spirit and the water, only the latter is alluded to under the term "washing." But we must note that the word, "regeneration" in our verse is not exactly the equivalent of the new birth. The only other place in the New Testament where the word is used is in Matthew xix. 28, and it indicates the new order of things which is to be established in the day of Christ's glory. We have not got that new order of things yet but we have come under the washing, the cleansing, the moral and spiritual renovation which is in keeping with that day.

This washing is by the Word. It is so stated in Ephesians v. 26, only there it is the repeated and continuous action of the Word which is in question, here it is the once-for-all, never-to-be-repeated action of the Word in our new birth. The Word however is not operative upon us apart from the action of the Holy Spirit who works in renewing power.

This Scripture speaks not only of the Spirit's initial work in us in new birth, and of the renewing which is consequent upon that, but also of the gift of the Spirit. He has been "poured out" on us abundantly. Thus bestowed He energizes the new life that we now have and works a day-by-day renewing within us, which works out a continuous and increasing salvation from the old life in which once we lived. The Spirit has been poured on us through Jesus Christ our Saviour, and as the fruit of His work. He has been poured on us abundantly, and hence it is that we may enjoy that which really is life in abundant measure. We not only have life but have it abundantly, as the Lord himself tells us in John x. 10.

The work *in* us, then, is quite as necessary as the work *for* us. It is equally true that the work *for* us is quite as necessary as the work *in* us, and this is indicated in verse 7. We could not become heirs of God merely by the work of the Spirit in us, for we needed to be justified before God and this is accomplished by the grace that wrought for us in Christ. Washed, renewed and justified it was possible for grace to go further and make us heirs, but all these three things were equally necessary.

We are made heirs, you will notice, according to the hope of eternal life; that is, we share equally with Paul in this wonderful hope, as may be seen by comparing this verse with the second verse of chapter i; though we are none of us apostles as he was.

God saves us in order to make us His heirs and it is striking how He is presented as Saviour in this epistle. It is even more striking how the term Saviour is applied to both God and the Lord Jesus in such a way as to assure us that Jesus is God. In chapter i, it is "God our Saviour" in verse 3, and "Christ our Saviour" in verse 4. In chapter iii., it is "God our Saviour" in verse 4, and "Christ our Saviour" in verse 6. In chapter ii., it is "our great God and Saviour Jesus Christ" in verse 13.

When at the beginning of verse 8 the Apostle says, "This is a faithful saying" it is not easy to determine whether he refers to what he has just written or whether to what immediately follows, but it would appear to be the former. It seems that Titus was to constantly bring before these converted Cretians the way in which they had been washed and renewed and justified and made heirs, in order that they might be stirred up to the maintenance of those good works which were in keeping with such grace, and not only in keeping with grace but also good and profitable to men. How clearly this illustrates what is often said, namely that all suitable conduct flows from an understanding of the place in which we are set. Here again we meet with the fact that the knowledge of grace promotes practical holiness and does not lead to carelessness.

By constantly maintaining and affirming the truth Titus would be enabled to avoid all those foolish questions and contentions about the law which were so common in those days. There is nothing like diligence in what is good to shut out evil. There might of course be a man who carried these questions and strivings to such a point that he became a leader of a faction in the church, a maker of a sect—for this is what the word, "heretic" means. Such an one was to be admonished once and twice, but if then he still remained obdurate he was to be rejected. To make oneself into a leader of a party is a serious sin.

The epistle closes with a few words as to other labourers in the service of the Lord. They were to be supplied with all necessary things, and this leads the Apostle to lay it as an obligation upon all saints to apply themselves to labour of a good kind that they might not only have themselves the necessities of life but have the wherewithal to give and thus be fruitful. The once lazy Cretian is now to be a diligent worker and a helper of others.

PHILEMON

AFTER READING THIS short epistle it would be well to read the last twelve verses of the Epistle to the Colossians, especially noting the various names that are mentioned by Paul. No less than eight of those mentioned in Philemon are found in Colossians, and several of them in a way that throws light upon their history.

Philemon, a much loved friend and fellow-servant of the apostle, evidently lived at Colosse. Apphia would appear to have been his wife, and Archippus his son, who was also a gifted man with a very definite service committed to him from the Lord. Philemon's house was a meeting place for God's people, so that Paul could write of "the church in thy house."

Onesimus, with whom the Epistle is mainly concerned, had formerly been a servant or bond-slave of Philemon, as verse 16 shows. He had wronged his Christian master and then had run away (verses 15, 18). In God's great mercy however the runaway slave had been thrown into contact with Paul at Rome during his imprisonment and through his instrumentality converted (verse 10): converted so soundly that Paul could speak of him not long after as "a faithful and beloved brother" (Col. iv. 9).

Tychicus was at that time leaving Rome for Colosse, bearing Paul's letter to that assembly and the Apostle seized this favourable occasion to send off Onesimus in his company back to his own people, so that again he might meet the master, whom once he had so wronged. It was no light matter for Onesimus to once more stand in the presence of Philemon, even though the grace of God had wrought in his conversion since the time of his wrong-doing, and Paul thoughtfully wrote an explanatory and intercessory letter to Philemon, making Onesimus the bearer of it. That short letter—the Epistle before us—God has seen fit to enshrine, as an inspired production, in His word. It fills its own niche in the scheme of truth, revealed to us in Scripture.

In the first place it shows us how the converted sinner has his feet turned into paths of practical righteousness. When Onesimus wronged his master, Philemon, he was an unconverted man. Now he has become a brother beloved, but this does not relieve him of obligations incurred by his former sin. As regards God that sin was forgiven amongst all his other sins, for he stood "justified from all things" (Acts xiii. 39); but as regards Philemon confession and some kind of restitution was needful. How restitution was made in this case the Epistle shows. Here at once there meets us an important lesson. If we have done some palpable wrong to another, no more effectual proof of our repentance can be given than that of confession and restitution, as far as that may be within our power. It is ever a trying process, but it is practical righteousness, most effective as a testimony and most glorifying to God.

Again, the Epistle endorses and emphasizes courtesy as being a grace that befits Christianity. It is very evident that the Christian is to be marked by an honesty, a candour, a transparency which is the very opposite of that hypocrisy and flattery which so greatly marks the world. Yet he is not to allow candour to degenerate into an unfeeling rudeness. He is to consider and acknowledge the rights of others and express himself with refinement of feeling and courtesy. Notice the happy way in which Paul expresses in verse 7 his approbation of the grace and kindness that characterized Philemon.

Notice too the tactful and delicate way in which he introduces the subject of Onesimus, in verses 8 to 10; beseeching where he might have used apostolic authority and commanded; presenting Onesimus as his spiritual son, given to him during the time of his trial in his captivity—a consideration well calculated to move the heart of Philemon. Divinely given tact and courtesy is also seen in the verses from 13, and onwards. Paul would have liked to retain Onesimus as a helper in his time of trial, but to have done so without consulting Philemon would have been, he felt, an unwarranted liberty. His old master had certain rights which Paul scrupulously observed; acknowledging that for him to have the advantage of Onesimus' help would have been a "benefit" conferred by Philemon. This benefit he would not first appropriate leaving Philemon to learn of it afterwards when he could not do otherwise than acquiesce "of necessity." No: he sends Onesimus back, content to have the benefit, if ever, as the fruit of Philemon's action "willingly."

Perhaps however Onesimus was returning to the place where once he had served sin and to the master whom he had wronged that he might more fully and for ever be at his service—the New Translation renders the end of verse 15, "that thou mightest possess him fully for ever." But in any event all was now to be on a new footing. Notice again the courteous and tactful way in which the Apostle conveyed this fact to Philemon, pointing out that he is now to possess him not as a mere bondman but as a brother beloved. Under these new circumstances Philemon would get service of a far finer quality out of Onesimus, even if it were less in quantity or if he willingly yielded him up to go back to Rome to help the Apostle, or to go elsewhere in the service of Christ.

But apparently Onesimus had wronged Philemon in those earlier days when as yet he was unconverted. His old master had suffered loss through his unfaithful service or defalcations. Knowing or suspecting this, Paul assumes full responsibility for making proper restitution. The damage done is to be put down to Paul's account and he writes with his own hand a promissory note—"I will repay it." But what a master-stroke are the succeeding words, "albeit I do not say to thee how thou owest unto me even thine own self besides"!

So Philemon himself had been converted through Paul; and if he opened in his ledger an account with Paul's name at the head and debited him with the pecuniary loss suffered through Onesimus, he would have to credit him with the value of that devoted service, which had brought to him, through terrific opposition and suffering, life and salvation unto eternal days.

We have but to ponder quietly to feel how irresistible must have been the effect of these words. If Philemon up to this point had been inclined to be righteous overmuch and harsh, what a melting must have supervened. What was his loss after all! How paltry it must all have seemed, even if it ran into thousands in the presence of the mighty debt of love he owed to the Apostle. The effect upon Philemon must have been simply overwhelming.

The Apostle was conscious that it would be so, as verses 20 and 21 disclose. Indeed such was his confidence in Philemon that he expected him to even go beyond what he was enjoining as to his treatment of Onesimus. A wonderful tribute to Philemon this! No wonder Paul addressed him as "our dearly beloved"!

Knowing what fearful damage to the fair name of Christ is wrought amongst God's people in connection with similar episodes we feel as if we could not sufficiently stress this important Epistle. It inculcates:—

As to the *offending* party, a return in all humility to the one offended with confession and an acknowledgement of his rights as to restitution.

As to the *offended* party, the reception of the repentant offender in grace with the fullest possible acknowledgement of all that God has wrought in him; whether it be through conversion as in the case of Onesimus, or through restoration as might be the case with many of ourselves.

As to the *mediating* party, an absence of anything approaching a dictatorial spirit, coupled with ardent love for both the offended and the offender, expressing itself in entreaties marked by courtesy and tact.

We must not leave this epistle without noticing the striking way in which the whole story illustrates what mediatorship means and involves; illustrating really the statement, "There is one God, and one mediator between God and men, the Man, Christ Jesus" (1 Tim. ii. 5). God is the One offended by sin: man, the offender: the Man Christ Jesus, the Mediator.

We can see ourselves depicted in Onesimus and his sad history. We too were "unprofitable." We "wronged" God and consequently were His debtors, owing what we could not pay. We too "departed" from Him, since we feared Him and desired to be as far as possible removed from His presence. Our alienation was the fruit of sin.

Paul's mediation between Philemon and Onesimus illustrates, though only faintly, what Christ has done. Can we not almost hear the blessed Saviour so speaking when upon the cross He charged Himself with our iniquities and took up the judgment we deserved? Shall we not bless Him for ever that in regard to all that was due to us on account of our sins, He said to God, "Put that on Mine account."

There is this difference however, that whereas Paul had to write "I *will* repay it" our risen Saviour does not use the future tense. His word to us in the gospel as the fruit of His death and resurrection is, "I *have* repaid it." He *has been* delivered for our offences and *has been* raised again for our justification. Hence it is that, justified by faith, we *have* peace with God. In this point therefore the illustration falls far short of the reality illustrated.

Our illustration also fails in this, that God needs no such persuasion to the full exercise of grace as was needed in the case of Philemon. He is Himself the Source of grace. He does however need a righteous groundwork whereon to display His grace even as Paul provided Philemon with a righteous reason for grace in assuming all the liabilities of Onesimus. Mediatorship involves the acceptance of such liabilities if it is to be fully and effectively exercised, for only then can grace reign through righteousness.

Praise be to God for the effective mediatorship of our Lord Jesus, the results of which are eternal. As to these our illustration again helps us.

In the first place, Paul's word as to Onesimus is, *"receive* him" (verse 12). He was not to be ignored and much less to be rejected, but to be received. How fully and really has God received us who have believed.

In the second place, the word was, "receive him *for ever."* Formerly the relations between Onesimus and his master were of a sort that could be broken, and in fact were broken by the misconduct of Onesimus. Now there were to be new relations of an order that could not be broken. It is just thus in God's gracious dealings with us. As the fruit of Christ's work we stand before Him in relations that are indefectible and eternal.

In the third place we have Paul making a request of Philemon which might seem utterly beyond his powers to comply with. "If thou count me a partner," he says, "receive him *as myself."* Philemon might well have replied, "With all the good will in the world I simply cannot do it. Receive him, I will. Receive him for ever, I will. But it would be mere hypocrisy to pretend that I can bring myself to the point of receiving him as, my beloved Paul, I would receive you."

That which Philemon could hardly have done, as we venture to think, God has done. Every believer, from Paul himself down to ourselves, and down to the weakest of us and those most recently converted, has no other standing before God than "accepted in the Beloved" (Eph. i. 6). We have been received in all the acceptance and favour of Christ Himself—a thing amazing beyond words, and utterly incredible were it not so stated in the Word of God.

In this the illustration is entirely to the point, as also in regard to the underlying facts which govern the whole. As before remarked, the link between Paul, the mediator, and Onesimus, the offender, was *love*. Between Paul and Philemon, the offended party, it was *partnership*.

As we look up by faith to the glorified Man Christ Jesus, the one Mediator, we adoringly acknowledge that His link with God is that of PARTNERSHIP, for He is God. He is great enough therefore to "lay his hand upon us both" (Job ix. 33). He can lay His hand upon God Himself, being His "fellow" (Zech. xiii. 7). Yet He has laid His hand upon us to our eternal blessing. He has brought us into His own place and relationship, linking us up in the strength of His eternal LOVE.

Yet here again we need to note how the illustration falls short, for God the Father loves, equally with Christ the Son. The Father's love and the love of Christ are sweetly intertwined. We rightly sing:—

> *"Father, Thy sovereign love has sought*
> *Captives to sin, gone far from Thee.*
> *The work which Thine own Son has wrought,*
> *Has brought us back in peace and free."*

www.ingramcontent.com/pod-product-compliance
Lightning Source LLC
Chambersburg PA
CBHW031839090426
42741CB00005B/292